Drawn from Life

Drawn from Life

AN AUTOBIOGRAPHY

John Skeaping

COLLINS
St James's Place, London
1977

William Collins Sons & Co Ltd
London · Glasgow · Sydney · Auckland
Toronto · Johannesburg

First published 1977
© John Skeaping 1977
ISBN 0 00 216028 5
Set in Monotype Bembo
Made and Printed in Great Britain by
William Collins Sons & Co Ltd Glasgow

Contents

Illustrations

Acknowledgements

I had been writing my autobiography on and off for the past ten years, when I finally abandoned it because I had too many other things to do. I should never have taken it up again had I not been urged to do so by some of my friends who insisted that my life story was odd enough to merit publication.

Laura Warner volunteered to co-ordinate, catalogue and edit the material I had so far written and under her direction a team was formed. My wife Maggie, knowing my story better than anyone else, reminded me of important omissions and got me down to writing again. Sue Adderley deciphered the sheets of my hand-writing as they were handed to her for typing. Both Lady Huxley and Marion Hart were able to remind me of many incidents of long ago. I had, of course, always consulted my sister, Mary, about anything to do with our childhood.

My thanks are due to all these people but most of all to Laura Warner, who not only guided the story to a conclusion but found the publishers, and to Maggie, who kept a watchful eye on the whole operation. I did write the book however.

Foreword

When buying a race horse the first thing you want to know is, 'How is he bred?' Nevertheless the fact that a horse may have an illustrious pedigree is no guarantee that he will win races.

I give you my pedigree now at the end of my career, too late for you to forecast what might happen but none the less interesting to a student of human form who would like to know why I ran my life in the manner which I have done.

If one ever hears people talking about their relations they all sound excruciating, and it makes one wonder where all the nice people can come from. Mine were a mixed bag. My grandfather was a wood carver and a cabinet maker *par excellence*. He was very popular, and a drunk. His days ended, so the story goes, when in a condition slightly more than usual the worse for drink, he cut off his thumb with a gouge. He stuck it back on with the glue-pot and twisted some shavings round it, but the operation was unsuccessful.

Grandfather was a bit of a mystery man. As you will see from the photographs of my father he looks very Jewish, although the male line hails from the land of the Vikings. He once told me that as a child he had been out walking with Grandfather in the street when they were approached by a Jewish woman with a 'peeler' in tow. The woman pointed to my grandfather and said: 'That is my husband who has deserted me,' and then turning to my father, 'and that is my son'. The 'peeler', who happened to know Grandfather well – perhaps they were drinking pals –

supported him when he denied ever having seen the woman in his life, and vouching for the respectability of the gentleman assured her that there must have been some mistake.

My grandfather was as far as I know the first man to realize the advantages of mass-produced furniture. What he did was to rough out enough pieces himself to keep six men occupied finishing them off. He employed a little boy to come in the early morning and at night to sweep up the workshop. This lad was from the poorest quarter of Liverpool and my grandmother used to make up sandwiches for him to take to school as he never had enough to eat. He was known as 'Sam Jim'.

Sam Jim kept his eyes open and grasped what Grandfather was after: the mass-production of furniture. His full name was Samuel James Waring. He became Lord Waring, the king of the furniture world, while my grandfather died a poor man and is buried somewhere under the foundations of Liverpool Cathedral, which was built on the site of the old churchyard.

Grandfather had a large family of registered children. Child mortality was very high in those days, and of the survivors I knew Uncles John and Joe, and Aunts Jessie, Nelly, Aggie and Lily. Uncle John was headmaster of St Helen's Art School. Aunt Lily, also an artist, was married to an Alsatian painter called Bernard Kaufmann; I believe a descendant of Angelica Kaufmann, the first woman RA. Aunt Nelly was a very talented pianist. She married a brilliant man of science, Dr W. B. Davidson, the coal-tar by-product expert and head of British Dyes. Aunt Jessie, a beautiful blonde (both Nelly and Lily looked like Spanish gypsies) was married to Max Kaufmann, the brother of Bernard. He ran a big laundry in Liverpool.

There was an Aunt Maggie, whom I never knew but only heard about. She apparently was confined to a nut-house. It was my wont when boasting with other children, 'My father is a policeman', etc., to add that my Aunt Maggie was a raving lunatic and jumped about in a padded cell brandishing a carving-knife. I won, as none of the other children had such a distinguished relation.

My favourite of all was Captain Joseph William Skeaping, extra-master in the Merchant Marine. In the days when I knew him he was with the Amazon Steamship Company, but he had spent his life under canvas in the big windjammers. When he retired he took over the management of the laundry in Liverpool and lived at Castletown in the Isle of Man. He bought himself a fourteen-foot dinghy, which he sometimes sailed across to Liverpool and back again at the end of the week, so great was his attachment to the sea.

I don't think John Hislop, a well-known authority on horse-breeding, could have contrived a better pedigree if he had wanted to produce me. I carve wood, love my booze and women – Grandfather. I am an artist – Aunt Lily and Father – and an amateur musician – Aunt Nelly and Mother. My favourite hobby of late is sailing – Uncle Joe. My love for horses is quite unaccountable unless, as they say in the horse-breeding world, the 'teaser' may have intervened. And don't forget Aunt Maggie with her leaps in the padded cell!

If this isn't line breeding, I'd like to know what is.

I

Childhood

I was the third child of a family of four, my brother Kenneth
and myself, and my two sisters, Sally and Mary. One of my
earliest memories was of Mother quoting the old jingle:

> 'Monday's child is fair of face,
> Tuesday's child is full of grace,
> Wednesday's child is full of woe,
> Thursday's child has far to go,
> Friday's child is loving and giving,
> Saturday's child works hard for its living,
> And a child that's born on the Sabbath day
> Is fair and wise and good and gay.'

I was born on the Sabbath day, 9 June 1901 in South Woodford,
Essex.

I can remember everything quite clearly from the age of three years old. I can even go further back than that, to being wheeled out in the perambulator, the bump as the pram was pushed over the curb, and the acrobatics I used to perform. My star turn was to loop-the-loop by walking around the shade, pivoted on my belt.

However, what remains clearest in my mind are my earliest journeys like the time I went to a tea-party at my Uncle Will's in Woolwich. I was three, and Mother had bought me a pair of shiny brown boots especially for the occasion, they were the first boots I had ever owned. As I walked with Father along Malmesbury Road to Woodford Station the squeak of them echoed loudly off the creosoted fence along the garden walls. We made the trip across from Essex to the Kent side of the Thames on the old paddle-steamer, and that was the greatest fun, but my elation rapidly subsided when I saw the strange faces of my cousins sitting at the tea-table. I buried my head in my lace collar and refused to eat, drink or speak. It was my first experience of being away from home and at last, when Dad said, 'We're going home now, Jack,' it was like the sun coming out again after a thunder storm.

Later Father took me to London. I must have been five years old then. We travelled in a carriage divided into compartments by a series of low barriers, so that if I stood up I could see right to the far end. Occasionally a busker would get in at a station, sing or play the concertina, pass the hat around, and move on to another carriage at the next stop. These men would buy a penny railway ticket in the morning and travel the trains like this all day, never getting out at a station until the day's work was finished.

We arrived at Liverpool Street Station at ten in the morning. As the train pulled in thousands of sparrows flew up into the iron girders of the roof and then descended again to pick over the piles of horse dung along the cab ranks. The horses in the ranks, which were feeding from nosebags, would repeatedly throw up their heads in an effort to shake out the oats from the bottom of the bag, scattering bits on the ground. This action made the bells ring that were attached to their collars; like a dinner gong it brought hordes of sparrows down from the roof who gobbled up the scattered oats. Each of the thirty or so horses carried a ring of bells of different notes and the carillon-like sound echoed through the station building. This sequence was repeated again and again, for all horses when not working had nosebags on to keep them quiet and contented, in the same way as all babies used to have dummies stuffed in their mouths.

From the station we took a cab, as it was too far for me to walk to Roberson's Art Shop at 99 Long Acre, where Father bought his materials. We made the journey in a fourwheeler, a 'growler'; only the rich city gents took hansoms. You could see them sitting inside with their top hats, puffing away at their cigars. That was something else I shall always remember, the smell of cigar smoke in the London streets, which oddly enough blended excellently with the smell of horse dung. This might well be explained by the quality of many of the cheaper cigars that were available at that time. Father, when he was in the money, used to treat himself to a 'twopenny Darvel Bay' – otherwise he stuck to his old Churchwarden clay pipe. When he had only the stump of a cigar left he would stick it in the pipe and finish it off.

We must have been in the money then, for at Roberson's he bought canvas for his paintings instead of the usual linoleum. That was generally a sign that he had a commission on hand. Afterwards, when the shopping was over we went to Jo Lyon's teashop for a cup of coffee.

Joseph Lyon, the man who started up these teashops, was an artist himself. In his day there had been nothing between the expensive restaurants and the dirty low-down coffee-houses like Lockhart's, with sawdust-covered floors, spittoons dotted around, and for heating, a fuming coke stove burning in the middle of the room. Jo Lyon had a friend called Wilkinson, who owned a marble-yard in the Pentonville Road, and they got

B

together and built a café. The floors, the walls and the tables were all made of marble, so that at the end of each day the proprietor could just hose down the whole place and sweep all the filth out into the gutter. The idea caught on quickly, and it was not long before these cafés sprang up all over London. Lockhart's and the old-time coffee-houses began to disappear. They were very inexpensive of course, as is well expressed in the line from a contemporary music-hall song by Harry Lauder:

'I took her out to Lockhart's and ordered wine;
Bang went sixpence of my four and nine.'

Although Lockhart's in Covent Garden was still going then, Father would never have taken me there. I didn't see the inside of it until a few years later. Instead we sat at a marble table in the wholesome atmosphere of Joseph Lyon's café, after which we returned by growler to the station, Father leaning back satisfied, puffing on a Darvel Bay.

Everything of course was horse-drawn; cabs, carriages, fire-engines, buses, trams. The tradesmen's carts were the ones I liked best, each one distinctive in style and instantly recognizable – the butchers' carts standing high on their varnished wheels, drawn by excellent shiny-coated trotting ponies, with the butcher

himself in his striped apron and straw hat perched on top of his box; the milkmen's floats with their white metal and brass churns, polished and shining in the sunlight; the bakers' carts with their hooded tops and the gorgeous smells that emanated from within. And the different types of private vehicle all had a character of their own. The grand carriages in the park would have Dalmatians running underneath the back wheels, while greyhounds walked under the slow-moving gypsy caravans.

Almost as common as the ringing of church bells in Italian villages was the sound of the blacksmith's anvil. If you wanted to find out where his shop was, all you had to do was to stop and listen for a minute or two and you would hear this beautiful, rhythmic, bell-like sound. I was a frequent visitor. It was fascinating to watch the men at work. When the blacksmith had a thick piece of metal to beat out he would be aided by a couple of strikers, working in unison. The skill of these men in making tires for cart-wheels was phenomenal. They could take a long bar of iron and beat it into a perfect circle so that, on completion, the two ends would meet up and the tire fit exactly on to the wooden frame of the wheel.

It was a horse world. There were familiar signs on the hills: going up – 'Please give your horse its head'; and going down – 'See that you have a properly adjusted skid-pan'. The skid pan, a steel disc which was pushed under the rim of the back wheel as a brake, would sometimes, with the friction of the grit road on the steel, become red-hot and set the wheel on fire. When this happened the driver would piss on the wheel to put the fire out. There was no danger of his being prosecuted for indecency, as he was protected by a special law allowing a carter to piss on the off-side back wheel of his vehicle where and when he chose. This was very necessary even under normal circumstances, because a carter could never leave his horses unattended – except when he saw the sign: 'Good Pull-In for Car-men'. He knew then that it was safe to pull his cart off the road and put nosebags on his horses while he went in to get some grub and a pint for himself.

Gone with the other amenities of horse life are the two societies dedicated to the protection of the horse's interests: The Anti-Bearing Rein Society and The Metropolitan Cattle Trough and Drinking Fountain Association. Our Dumb Friends' League, happily still in existence, used to provide beautiful Clydesdale horses smartly turned out in black leather harness studded with brasses, their tails and manes plaited with straw and interwoven with cornflowers. They were stationed at the bottom of all steep hills to give a helping hand to heavily-laden vans. At the bottom of Shoot-Up Hill I would wait for a van to come along. Eventually one would roll up which was big and heavy enough to warrant the assistance of this splendid beast. He would be hitched to the centre-pole in front, and on the word from his driver would set his magnificent, rippling, shining muscles into action. Quite often heavy loads ascending Shoot-Up Hill could not go straight up but had to make a zigzag course in order to lessen the incline. Once the trace-horse was given the order to do this by his handler he would continue the operation on his own, crossing from curb to curb until he reached the summit, where he would be unhitched. Then he would be led slowly down again to the bottom, with steam rising from his powerful body like a boiling kettle on an iron stove.

There are many people I knew quite well at that time whose faces and appearance have gone completely from my mind, even the girls for whom I had a passion; but not so these trace-horses, which I can still see vividly in my mind's eye, remembering every detail of their harness and turn-out. Writing about it now, I am reliving every one of those joyful moments, just as though it was happening before my eyes and ears. This was the background which formed my life, and particularly the liking and understanding of horses which has never left me. Much as I appreciate the benefits bestowed by progress on humanity I would gladly relinquish them all to return to the grace, silence and beauty of the days of my childhood.

There is no doubt that at this time human suffering amongst

the poor was very great, but this was something of which I was unaware. We ourselves were by no means rich; the most my father ever earned was £250 a year, but we never seemed to want for anything. All our clothes were made by Aunt Liz, and having been taught by Mother, I would mend boots for all the family. Mother was responsible for cutting our hair. When it grew too long she would lop it in a random way with a pair of scissors, an operation I hated almost as much as having the dirt scrubbed from behind my ears. The result of these combined family efforts on our appearance was pretty appalling. We children looked like urchins who had raided a dressing-up drawer; but maybe that had its charms. For my parents there was no saving grace. My mother was the original frump. She would wear anything that would stay on her, insisting that the object of clothing was to keep one warm and regarding any form of display – which to her meant any attempt at fashion or prettiness – as immoral. Thinking about it now, I don't think I have ever seen anyone so appallingly dressed as she was, with the exception perhaps of my father. His clothing, however, had a little more style, supplied by the permanent addition to his costume of a Turkish fez and a pair of carpet-slippers. Otherwise his clothes were in the mainstream of family tradition, useful, shapeless and above all unbelievably shabby. Father's reply to tramps who came to the door asking for old clothes, would be, 'I'm sorry, I can't help you. I've got them all on.' In winter Father was more tramp-like than ever, wrapping newspaper round his body to keep warm (woolly pullovers didn't exist in those days) and putting his clothes on over the top. Whenever he moved he crackled, as if in some strange way affected by the frost. It used to embarrass me terribly in front of strangers, who could never completely conceal their curiosity as to where the noise was coming from.

However it must have achieved its purpose, for Father was never ill. He didn't believe in illness at all. If ever I asked him what someone had died of, he would always shrug his shoulders and say: 'Shortness of breath'. He had once in his life conquered sickness in the most remarkable way, and it seemed that ever since it had acknowledged itself beaten and left him alone. While working as a young man for Sir Robert Jones, the father of orthopaedic surgery, he had become seriously ill, and Sir Robert had called in some of the leading specialists of the day to examine him. They diagnosed an incurable growth in his intestines, which, they said, would bring about his death within six months. Father asked them whether returning to work would reduce his chances of surviving for this length of time. They replied that it would make no difference one way or the other, whereupon Father sat up in bed and said: 'Give me my clothes. I'm getting up now and going back to work, and you can all take your leave.' He got up from his death-bed and lived without another day's illness to the age of ninety-one when he died, seated in front of the fire, with his clay pipe in his mouth.

Whether it was pure will-power that cured him God alone knows. He was certainly a rare character, an almost impossible mixture of optimism and fatalism. When things were going badly he loved to look on the darkest side. His favourite sport was to twist the proverbs which traditionally offer consolation, ruthlessly eliminating from them all cheering alternatives. 'Never one door closes but another door shuts,' he used to say, or 'It's an ill wind that blows the last straw off the camel's back.' Over the years he had developed a kind of armoury of these perverse maxims, and he employed them continually, greeting with irrepressible pleasure any situation which provided him with an opening for quoting one of them.

It is true that things were often bad and money scarce but our lack of money was balanced by a total absence of false pride, which made us ready to make open and unembarrassed use of any scraps that came our way. 'Status' was a concept my mother was unaware existed and had she known of it she would undoubtedly have deplored it most strongly. Respectability she understood and valued, though I think the margins she set to it were wider in some places than the neighbours would have liked.

We none of us ever took into account that they might be shocked by some of our goings on. Looking back on it now I see that they most certainly were. We had a Victorian two-wheeled perambulator with an old tin bath attached to it, with which Father and we kids would sally forth into the streets and lanes collecting horse dung for the garden. It was the greatest fun to go out and bring home a big load. If any of the tradesmen's horses did us the good turn of performing outside the house that was better still, and we rushed out at once with a dustpan and brush.

There was never any feeling of skimping about the house; somehow there was plenty of everything – plenty of food, good food at that, and always the barrel of assorted broken biscuits from Huntley and Palmer's standing in the corner of the kitchen. Costing one halfpenny a pound, they provided an inexhaustible lucky dip for us kids. My mother must have been a good housekeeper, if an unconventional one, and we were certainly brought up to be useful. I could cook, crochet, mend boots and later on even shoe a horse, and do innumerable things which children today are never taught.

All the same I dread to think what the result of our upbringing might have been had not all of us turned to the arts, for to this day I cannot do the most simple arithmetic beyond the multiplication tables. The reason is that I was never sent to school. None of us was. My father was against it on principle, having no use at all for what was known as 'general education' which, as he saw it, was just a multitude of smatterings of different subjects, all of them forgotten within six months of leaving school. Having then wasted the ten most valuable years of one's life, one had to start learning properly almost from scratch. I think he would have appreciated Bernard Shaw's remark about education, likening it to 'casting artificial pearls before real swine.' He had himself a great respect for the innate ability of children. He realized that their outstanding qualities were the powers of imitation and imagination and believed it to be of primary importance that these be developed and encouraged. This meant in practical terms that the basic essential of education was a training in the arts; and this is what we as children received, to the exclusion of all else.

These ideas were wholeheartedly shared by my mother. She added to them her own brand of perfectionism, impressing on all of us the immorality of achievement other than by ability in one's profession. The idea of dressing up for an interview, for instance, or trying to make an impression on someone who could be useful to us, was utterly repulsive to her. This uncompromising attitude gave to our education a seriousness of purpose which it might, in the natural course of things, have lacked.

Once a week Father would take us to London to the galleries and museums, or Mother would get tickets for concerts, the theatre or the ballet. In this way we were introduced to the work of many of the great artists, both past and present. Ballet, not yet recognized as a great art, was usually put on in the variety theatres, being regarded as a kind of sophisticated music-hall turn.

Of all the things we saw, dancing made the greatest impression on us. I remember queuing with Mother for a performance by Madame Adeline Genet, the great Danish dancer of the period, and getting into the gallery for sixpence each. I shall also never forget the Diaghilev Ballet when it first came to England and the fantastic acclaim it received. I must have been only ten at the time, but it has remained for me ever since the height of perfection in the art of the dance.

In our new and more spacious house in Bexley Heath, Kent, we had plenty of time to digest what we had seen and we had the space to put our ideas into practice. The whole day was taken up with painting, modelling, music, dancing and writing stories. We were allowed to improvise as much as we liked.

I learned to paint mostly by observation, watching Father and seeing how he did it, while sitting for him. I would get plenty of opportunity to do this as he was always painting us in one guise or another. We hated it – it was a really irksome chore, endlessly being told to do this or that, and worse still to keep on doing it. 'Keep your head up', 'Turn your head more to the left', 'Lower your chin just a bit', 'Keep still, I won't be long now'. I don't know for how long I sat at a stretch, but it seemed as though I was keeping still for hours on end. However, Father would sometimes return the favour, standing in if I needed a model for one of my stablemen or carters – the only human elements in my pictures, which were of horses to the point of obsession. (I had, in fact, become a horse, at least in my imagination. When I painted them I was a horse painting self-portraits.)

My Father was a very competent artist, but conservative in his views. He had been a student in Paris in the 1880s when the Impressionists were young and struggling, and he did not think much of what they did, considering it incompetent and out-landish. His idea was to paint every conceivable detail with minute accuracy so that it looked exactly life-like. In truth he did not know the meaning of art and the great painters he did admire, such as Vermeer, Velasquez, Holbein, Van Dyck, he admired for their great technical achievement. However, this attitude of his was helpful when he came to teach me to draw and paint, for he spoke only of technical matters and not of artistic ideas or ideals. He never suggested to me that I should learn from him, and never approached me to offer criticism while I was working unless I asked him a question on some technical problem, which happened rarely. Besides, my paintings were all of horses, about which he knew little, having no interest in them.

Father could not afford to buy drawing paper and materials for us. We made our own charcoal and drew on the walls all over the house, as high up as we could reach. There were obvious economic advantages to this system, the wall surface seemed almost in-exhaustible and even when it was covered we could brush off the charcoal and start all over again. Later on he bought us some Plasticine for modelling which we would roll out on the dining-room table and flatten with a hammer. It would be an under-statement to say that neither of my parents was house-proud. The house was there to shelter us and provide us all with a workshop.

It was clean but by any ordinary standards chaotic. We had no carpets on the floor, and apart from a busted sofa and a couple of armchairs in the same condition, all the furniture was of plain unvarnished wood.

Mrs Price, the woman who lived next door to us in Woodford, was the exact opposite of Mother. She was house-proud to an extreme degree. When the wooden floors were scrubbed at home, as they quite often were by Mother, helped by all of us, the verb applied was to 'Mrs Price' the house. (In fact this term is still in use in my family to describe any meticulous cleaning or polishing activities.) She had an only child, Will, who was a frequent visitor to our house. As soon as he entered the place he would jump on to the sofa or the armchairs and bounce up and down wildly for ten minutes before he could even speak. It was a liberation, a demonstration of the freedom non-existent in his own home. This behaviour was accepted by my parents with their usual tolerance, nor was it regarded as being in any way odd by us children.

But although the armchairs were jumped on, the dining-room table covered in dents and nearly all the furniture damaged in some way, the piano remained sacred. We would never have dared to play it with dirty hands or even stand a glass on it. Music, too, and books were exempted from the general rough treatment. We were taught from an early age how to turn pages from the top right-hand corner and not from the lower binding edge. In this way we did acquire some sense of respect for the right things in life, although I sometimes think it might have been profitably extended to include a few other articles besides pianos and books.

The piano was Mother's domain. She taught us all to play. She was in fact a professional teacher of some stature and the leading exponent of the new tonic sol-fa system of piano teaching known as the Curwen method. Of the four of us it was Kenneth who inherited Mother's aptitude for music, but when he took it up seriously his instrument was not the piano, but the violin. This came about in a strange way. Father had painted a portrait of a violinist who was unable to pay for it when it was finished. Instead he offered to teach any one of us to play the violin. Ken accepted. Up to that time he had been a dedicated modeller, showing a far greater interest in sculpture than I did, but once started on the violin, he gave up modelling almost entirely and devoted himself to music, with so much success that at the age of ten he was hailed as a child prodigy.

I remember going to hear him play at the Blackheath Concert Hall, accompanied on the piano by my mother. Both of them were dressed in clothes made by my Aunt Liz. Ken wore a black velvet suit with a lace collar, Lord Fauntleroy style, and Mother a wasp-waisted dress with a train about two yards long dragging out behind her. Their performance was received with thunderous applause, and the critics in the press were immensely flattering. But all of this went right over my mother's and my brother's heads. They had no interest in worldly success, to the point of folly. Ken was eventually to become Professor of the Violin at the Royal College of Music and played with some of the top British orchestras. He is now an authority on ancient music and musical instruments.

I was nine when we took up ballet dancing – Sally, Mary and I, since Ken was by now too involved in his music. We used to go to Sismondi's once a week. After two years of these lessons I became impatient. I found my activities were too restricted. I wasn't allowed to ride a bicycle, I couldn't play football, in fact I was stopped from doing all the outdoor things I really enjoyed. So I gave it up. There was another reason which was perhaps equally compelling, and that was the behaviour of the other boys in the class, who were all older than me. There seemed to be something wrong with them. Obviously they were queer, but at the time I was ignorant of such things and I found their passes incomprehensible and unnerving. Mary and Sally, who were spared their attentions, and had in any case more natural enthusiasm for the art, kept up with the classes after I left. Ballet was to become Mary's life. At quite an early age she toured with Anna

Pavlova, eventually becoming a world authority on ballet dancing. She became ballet mistress to the Sadler's Wells Company and worked in the same capacity with the Swedish Opera Company for eleven years, reviving the now famous Drottningholm Theatre. She was made a Dame of the Order of Vasa, for her service to the country. Mary has been of inestimable help to me in later years in the study of rhythm and movement which I have applied to my work as an *animalier*. Sally wrote fantastic stories, inspired by Hans Andersen and Grimm, illustrating them herself.

Ken was a voracious reader and a mine of information on most subjects. Having started reading at the age of four he never stopped until he had read every book in the house, which was a great many since Father had at one time worked as an illustrator for George Newnes, the publisher, and the house was crammed with their publications – quite apart from the considerable collection he had made on his own account. But even this did not satisfy Ken's craving. I still have a vivid recollection of him sitting at meals in a most uncomfortable position with his head screwed round at an odd angle in order to read some article in the newspaper that served as a tablecloth, and Mother saying, 'Ken dear, your food is getting cold . . .'

As children we got on marvellously well together. We never quarrelled, and were always interested in each other's activities. And then so many things were going on around us. We would run to the window countless times a day to see what was happening outside. A German band would arrive, or perhaps a Russian with a huge muzzled performing-bear on a chain, or there would be a barrel-organ playing that made all the dogs in the district howl – dogs seem to be so accustomed to musical sounds nowadays that they howl no longer. Then there were the street criers; the muffin man who came round at tea-time with a tray of muffins on his head covered in a green baize cloth, ringing a hand bell and crying, 'Muffins and crumpets, all hot!', and the lavender seller with her pretty song, 'Who will buy my sweet lavender, makes your drawers smell very nice'. As girls' panties were known as drawers, I took it to mean just that.

There were the cockney wits who ran street stalls in the market square on Saturday mornings. They were tremendous showmen. In order to gather a crowd they would perform conjuring tricks with their wares, keeping up an astonishing flow of patter the while. The master of this art was the owner of a kind of travelling department store, selling everything from pins and pairs of sheets to purgatives and pos. He would take his pos and spin them into the air to a great height, crying out, 'Large size breakfast cups, small size shaving bowls, don't let the baby do it on the floor'. When the turn of the purgative came, he would recite his patter which always produced roars of laughter from the more bawdy members of the audience. He reeled it off at great speed as follows: 'I don't come here to be laughed at, chaffed at, spat at, thrown stones at. I come here to sell my pills. My pills are it, they make you shit. Run, come, cock your bum. Shit through the eye of a needle without splashing the sides. If they don't pass through you in twenty-four hours you're a corpse.'

There was an unfortunate man in the same market who ran a patent medicine stall. Cough cures were one of his specialities. He would hold up a packet and wheeze out, 'Cures coughs, colds, and difficulty in breathing', whereupon his rival at the next stall would invariably shout, 'Why don't you take it yourself?' He fared no better with his corn plasters (although there was no direct evidence that his toes too were guilty of resisting treatment). He would start out patiently on his demonstration, 'Take the plaster between the finger and thumb, heat it by the light of a candle or gas, place on the corn; take the plaster between the finger and thumb . . .' and before he could finish, his speech was drowned by a chorus: 'And the toe comes off!'

Something which is definitely associated in my mind with these pantomime characters, and which like them has sadly disappeared, was the Crayford Chartered Fair. This was an annual event of tremendous importance in our lives. The most exciting aspect of it, from my point of view, was the roundabouts with their gorgeously painted wooden horses bounding up and down to the music, which was projected with considerable force from a steam-operated organ. This was covered, like all the other paraphernalia, in flamboyant gypsy decoration. I saved up my weekly pennies for months in order to ride at will on these horses with their real leather reins, steel stirrups and bits. They were my first experience of sitting astride a horse of any kind.

There was one recurring disappointment on these occasions, and that was Father's refusal to allow me to go on the helter-skelter. Every year his ban increased my frustration, until I became determined to ride on the mat at all costs, and gave him the slip. On the way down I somehow tore the seat of my trousers. The large gypsy woman who stood at the bottom of the ramp to catch us as we came down, grasping the situation immediately, said, 'Come along, dearie, I'll sew you up so as no one can see.' She took me round to the back of the caravans where she laid me face downwards across her broad lap and was as good as her word. That night when I tried to get undressed I found to my dismay that my trousers, underpants, vest and shirt had all been sewn together. It was impossible to get out of them without assistance from Mother. The inevitable questions were asked, and of course it came out that I had been on the mat. I was on the mat for the second time!

Another yearly event to look forward to was the Christmas visit to the aunts at their house in Clarendon Road, Lewisham. Mother's spinster sisters Emma and Liz were kindness itself. Aunt Liz used to make the most wonderful Turkish delight and coconut ice, and if we hung up our stockings on the brass balls of the bed rail at night we would find them in the morning stuffed with goodies of all kinds. The house was a museum of Victoriana. Everything was draped in lace curtains or dripping with beads. They had a large four-poster bed with a feather mattress at least a yard deep, into which these two large women sank like cement bags in a canal. We too slept in feather beds when we were there, a luxury I disliked very much indeed for the reason that it was almost impossible to get out of them as one could get no purchase on anything. It was like sleeping on a cloud.

Aunts Emma and Liz, unlike Mother, who never laced herself up, did their best to keep pace with the fashion. They were both very stout women with gigantic fronts which were, as a result, pushed together in a large heaving mass which bulged over the tops of their blouses. I shall never forget being clasped to their bosoms when they kissed me; the frightening feeling that I would be suffocated like the Princes in the Tower who, I had heard, were stifled with a pillow. I hated being kissed by anyone, but in their case the ordeal presented grave risks.

It may be my imagination, but I am sure the seasons in those days were more distinctly marked. The weather changed more decisively; we had snow in winter, winds in March, April showers, hot summers, autumn mists. Of course when one is four years old, a year is a quarter of one's life, and as the fraction diminishes the seasons merge into a blur. But perhaps they were more memorable then because they were more important. People's lives were regulated by them in a way that they no longer are today. For us children every season brought with it a definite succession of happenings. Spring for me meant following the plough horses in the fields and hearing the birds singing; summer, jumping out of bed as soon as it was light and being able to stay out all day; autumn, walking through the forest at Epping or round the lake at Higham's Park, the smell of bonfires in the air, kicking up the piles of dead leaves as one went along; winter and Christmas, the indoor season, log fires, Santa Claus and pantomimes and the braziers glowing in the High Street where men roasted chestnuts and baked potatoes, inviting you as you passed to 'Warm your hands and fill your belly for a halfpenny'.

There was the yearly cycle of tramps and vagabonds who turned up at the house, each at his own time, regular as clockwork – 'Dreamy Daniels', 'Weary Willy' and 'Tired Tim', as we called them, were our most regular visitors. 'Dreamy Daniels' was the one I got to know best. Sitting on the grass behind the house one day, eating a hunk of bread and cheese that Mother had given him, he told me how he had spent his whole life walking the length and breadth of England, Scotland and Wales, coming south as the weather got colder, and had never, to his recollection, spent one single night under a house roof. He would tell me of the virtues of different trees as shelter, being able to calculate just how long it would take the rain to come through each one, and would hold forth on the effect of snow on agriculture. He revealed a wealth of botanical knowledge besides, including a large menu of edible plants and fruits not known to be good outside the world of the vagabonds.

'Two Thumbs', a gypsy who used to come to the door selling clothes-pegs and props (she really did have two thumbs on one hand, and carried her basket in the crook of them), was another mine of information. She happened to call one day when we all had whooping cough, and strongly recommended to Mother the following remedy: 'Get a little mouse and cook it with some herbs, which I will give you. Give this to the children to drink. They will be cured immediately.' Perhaps the treatment we were receiving was almost as primitive, for we all had necklaces of tarred rope, which at that time was believed to be a cure. This advice must have been given to Mother by Dr Berdilly, who called on his daily round of visits in a fine carriage and wearing a top hat. On this particular occasion I was kept out of the nursery while he examined my sisters, so I went and got his top hat off the hall table and peed in it. I do not remember the outcome of the incident, but I am sure it was not very popular with Dr Berdilly, who was proud of his appearance. His horse had better manners than I, for it had been trained never to leave droppings outside a client's house or to relieve itself in any other way.

Although there were many visitors to the house of one kind and another, invited guests were few. My parents had no social life, they couldn't afford to entertain, and the house was not designed for hospitality, being run exclusively as a kind of children's nursery. There was one great friend of my father's who used to visit us, a man called T. B. Foreman. Among his many talents was shorthand, which he taught to us, assuring us that it would come in useful one day. The only other visitors to the house that I remember were the amateur musicians who used to come and make up a party for a musical evening. They were Mr and Mrs Carter, who played the violin and sang, and Mr Martin, a bank clerk, who played the piano. Little remains of Mr Martin in my memory, but the Carters I remember on account of their hairstyles. Mr Carter wore his ostentatiously long, while Mrs Carter's was piled mountainously on top of her head.

I shall never forget a particular musical evening when they were all present. The first performer was Carter. As he played he closed his eyes and threw his head around as much as the fiddle under his chin would allow, the sweat flowing from his forehead. Martin followed, playing the piano with great vigour. He banged so heavily on the keys that various framed photographs slid off the mantelpiece, and I was seriously afraid the instrument would break up at any moment. He too flung his head about,

although his movements were severely restricted by a stiff collar at least four inches high. I could not take my eyes off him, as I was convinced his head would be cut off and I didn't want to miss the fun. My disappointment on this score was more than made up for by an occurrence of a less fatal though far more interesting nature. The last item on the programme was '*Il Bacio*', sung by Mrs Carter. The piercing soprano notes escaped as by a miracle from the tight lacing which encased her body, pushing her large bosom right up to her throat. The miracle, however, ceased with the song, and as the last notes died on her lips she fell in a faint on the piano, knocking over a small table holding a vase of flowers, though providentially missing the oil lamp which would have set the house on fire.

The dramatic scene which ensued was enjoyed to the full by one at least of the spectators, as Mrs Carter was released from her lacing and people rushed about the house fetching water and smelling salts. Smelling salts were an indispensable household item in those days – women were always fainting on account of tight lacing, especially when they were pregnant. How on earth they ever gave birth to any children that were not deformed is beyond me. I had long been intrigued to know what went on under this mysterious corseting, and taking up an advantageous position behind Mother, I seized the opportunity to gratify my curiosity.

But the Carters' visits could not be relied on to be always so entertaining. The ones we really looked forward to were those of our Uncle Joe. He came only rarely as he lived in Manoas, but when he did come he would always bring some treasure for us kids; a parrot in a cage, a sack of Brazil nuts, native spears, bows and arrows or colourful Indian feathers. He was a small man, shrunk by the weather but tough and strong, and in his trading days had earned among his crews the reputation of a man of iron. His methods were inspired, if harsh. He was famous for treating men who went sick with paraffin oil from the lamps (a remedy which proved singularly effective in that it secured prevention as well as cure). Tales of his exploits were legendary. One of our favourites was when he told how he dealt with the giant negro, who, seated on the quay, rashly thought to make fun of his ears. Uncle Joe had ears very much like a chimpanzee's, and over the years had lost his sense of humour on the subject. So, when asked by the negro if he could wag them, he picked the man up by his own, saying, 'No, but I can certainly wag yours', and flung him into the dock.

It was these stories that we adored, and he told them as only sailors can. His greatest nautical achievement, a long story which we got him to repeat again and again, was when he had been asked by the Amazon Steam Navigation Company to explore the possibilities of a natural harbour, known to exist somewhere along the coast of South America.

Setting out from Liverpool in his clipper, he became becalmed some way off the South American coast. There was no wind and fog limited visibility to one hundred yards or so. In these conditions he drifted helplessly for days. Then a slight breeze sprang up but the fog didn't lift. He sailed on slowly towards the coast and when he guessed that he must be somewhere in the vicinity he got one of the crew to fire a gun at frequent intervals, hoping to get an echo off the cliffs. Receiving the first echo he was able to determine how far he was away, and he steered on a course parallel to the coast line, continuing to fire the gun. Getting echoes, and then a gap where there was none, then echoes again, he concluded that here was the entrance to the harbour. Returning he sailed into this gap, finally getting echoes on both port and starboard sides of his ship. He dropped anchor. Two days later, when the fog had lifted, he found that he was right in the harbour, having sailed through an opening in the cliffs no more than four hundred yards wide! I believe the history of this expedition is recorded at Lloyds.

Not all his stories were so exciting, but they were all, without exception, charming and full of fascinating and colourful details – like the Chinese cook being discovered in the galley brushing white of egg on a cake with the tip of his pigtail. But then the world that Uncle Joe inhabited was fabulous, certainly by today's standards. He was, to us children anyway, the Ancient Mariner personified.

It is not really surprising, considering the surroundings in which we were brought up, that we all became artists of one kind or another. Our own unbridled imaginations, encouraged by our understanding parents and the grace and beauty of everyday life, made it inevitable that we should find some form of artistic outlet.

I realize now how thoroughly exceptional my parents were, although at the time it did not occur to any of us that there was anything unusual in what they did. They sacrificed their whole lives for us – their sole interest was in the well-being, happiness and success of their children. It was an extraordinary case where two married people shared exactly the same ideals. They set themselves out to construct a simple, primitive family framework outside the context of the world in which they were living, at the same time retaining the best of civilization. To a remarkable extent they succeeded.

There was a great deal in their ideas. There is no doubt at all in my mind that art flourishes much more under primitive conditions than those of the modern world, where every encouragement is given to mediocrity. The natural qualities of children are doomed to be crushed in an educational machine which unashamedly professes to aim at an 'ordinary level'. If my parents sinned at all, it was in contravening Degas's rule: 'Art should never be encouraged'. But then I myself knew from the age of four exactly what I wanted to do, so all Degas could have accused them of doing was taking a horse to water.

II

Learning my Trade

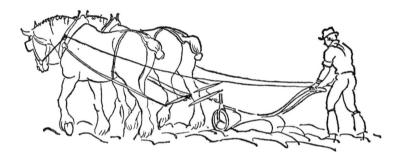

As time went on our individuality developed in a remarkable way, something which could never have happened had we been sent to a conventional school. My sister Mary was of a studious character, whilst Sally was a romantic. Brother Kenneth was a stay-at-home bookworm, this in vast contrast to myself, I becoming a wild, adventurous, inquisitive person, not prepared to accept anything as it was presented to me. This characteristic had begun to manifest itself at quite an early age when I used to wonder what I should see if fat Aunt Liz were to remove her stays.

Although life at home was heaven, I wanted to see what was on the other side of the fence and at the age of thirteen persuaded my father to let me go to Blackheath School of Art. This was my first adventure into the wide open spaces. I was by far the youngest student there but well up to the standard of those ten years my senior.

It was at Blackheath that I discovered the joys of modelling and sculpture and soon I was doing nothing but model under the able tuition of Frederic Halnon. Halnon had been assistant to Alfred Druary RA, whose sculpture of Sir Joshua Reynolds stands today in the Royal Academy courtyard.

The great sense of security which I had acquired from my upbringing was suddenly shattered when war was declared on 14 August 1914. I just couldn't believe such a thing could happen to disrupt the blissful world in which I had been living. I was in despair and could not work.

I remember one day climbing my favourite birch tree in the garden and hearing the clip clop of horses' shoes on the cobbled stones as they drew the heavy guns of the Garrison Artillery along the High Street on their way to embark at Dover for France. Many of the beautiful local farm horses that I knew so well by name and sight had been requisitioned by the army to draw these guns. They were going to face an agonizing death, dying in the mud with no one able to care for them. Never again were they to return to the fields nor to the care of the ploughman who loved them dearly.

This was a black day for me. I gave little thought to the men, as I felt that the war was a man-made thing. If I did think about man at all, it was to hate him for taking away my beloved horses. There was nothing for it but to throw myself into my work and try not to think about the horrors of war. This I did and after a year at Blackheath, on Halnon's advice, I moved on to Goldsmiths' College where the facilities were much better.

On arrival, I found that I was the only day student in the sculpture school. All the young men over eighteen years of age had been called up for military service. I had two very large studios to myself and did as I liked quite undisturbed. I went to the Zoo every Wednesday to draw and model and I was now beginning to take an interest in other animals, particularly lions and tigers.

Whilst walking in the College playing fields one day, I found a dead cat which I took back into the school to dissect so that I could make some anatomical studies. First of all I skinned it, then made a plaster cast. Just when I had finished, I heard someone coming. I hastily wrapped the carcass in newspaper and stuffed it behind the radiator in the life-room. I intended to dispose of the body by throwing it into the central heating furnace when no one was around, but other things occupied my mind and I completely forgot about it.

A week or so later, Mr Halnon and the students who came to evening life classes complained of an awful smell which could not be explained. Being there all day and every day, I had got progressively used to it and had not noticed that anything was wrong, nor did I connect it with the cat. Eventually the sanitary inspector was called in and it was decided to inspect the drains. The sinks were dismantled and the floor boards taken up. As I watched these drastic operations I heard the men say that if they couldn't find anything there, they would have to dismantle the radiators – radiators! Then I remembered what I had done with my cat. I stayed late that night and recovered the body, now in an advanced state of putrefaction, and threw it from the third-floor window into the yard below.

I was working well and producing some very good animal models. Absorbed in my work, I had put the tragedy of the war horses out of my mind.

I had been just a year at Goldsmiths' when suddenly another tragedy struck us all down. My beloved sister Sally died of peritonitis at the age of seventeen. She was really my first love. The whole family was completely knocked over by it, and it took us all some years to recover.

It was in 1915 that she died. She knew that she was dying and told me so as I stood beside her bed holding her hand until the horse-drawn ambulance arrived at one o'clock in the morning to take her nineteen miles to Guy's Hospital, and during a zeppelin raid at that. Mother returned the next day, a pallid ghost of herself, and couldn't bring herself to utter the words: 'Sally is dead.' She had no need to speak for it was plain from her very appearance that the greatest disaster of all had befallen us.

It was obvious to everyone that the war was likely to last some years and that England was in a precarious situation. German submarines were sinking many of the merchant ships bringing much-needed food. Everyone had to turn to. All bits of waste and park land were dug up and made into allotments to grow vegetables.

I went to work on Sheldon's farm during the three months' summer holidays. I could drive horses and soon learned to plough, eventually being given two horses of my own to look after. Once a week I would drive my team nineteen miles to the London Borough Market with a load of strawberries or vegetables. Starting out at ten o'clock at night I would strap myself to the box seat and the two Clydesdales, Gipsy and Sharper, would trot all the way to London whilst I slept. They had done this journey many times and knew the way. Anything the horses could pass through, the cart would pass, as they were wider than the cart itself.

I would be awakened by the horses pulling up in the market and by the clatter of arriving carts, the cries of the porters and the stentorian voices of the auctioneers. I would then unharness the horses, tie one to the other and hang a paraffin lantern on the collar of the lead horse. They would find their own way to the stables a few hundred yards away where I should tie them up and feed them.

Breakfast at Lockhart's cost me sixpence. It consisted of a cup of tea, freshly made for each customer, a rasher of bacon, two fried eggs and two thick slices of bread and butter. The way to order this was to ask for a 'small special, a rasher, two fried and two thick'.

The horses walked back to the farm as there was no hurry to get home. I can so well remember the clank of their shoes on the cobbled stones of the Old Kent Road. They were a good even pair and both pulled their weight.

A family group at Woodford about 1905.
From left to right: Sally, mother, Kenneth, myself, father, Mary.

above: Aged 14, learning my trade at Goldsmiths' College.
below: The relief panel submitted for the preliminary exam for the Prix de Rome.

right: The relief panel, size 5 ft by 3 ft, with which I won the Prix de Rome.

above: With Barbara Hepworth shortly after our marriage. Tom Monnington is on the left and his wife on the right.

left: My marble bust of Barbara Hepworth. A self-portrait bust in the background.

One talked a good deal to these farm horses and they understood a strange language, which must have been of ancient origin, as the words in no way resembled those of any currently known. This language was of vital importance as subtle control was needed when ploughing or breaking between rows of strawberry plants. If the horse was walking slightly to one side of the row, which made it difficult to prevent the implement from tearing out the plants, it was necessary to bring him back into the centre. Perhaps it was only a matter of two inches which could not be done by pulling on the reins. To move slightly to the left the order was 'cobertherwee' or 'leurwee', and to the right 'geeware'. I am spelling these words phonetically as I have never seen them written down. They would, of course, vary from county to county.

Although I could drive I had never ridden a horse apart from the farm horses when I used to take them to the blacksmith's to be shod. I was longing to try and the first opportunity came whilst I was on holiday at Birchington, a rather smart seaside resort. One morning I paid a visit to a grand livery stable to hire a horse. As far as I can recollect my attire was not exactly conventional; the groom who was to accompany me gave me some very dirty looks and was obviously not believing all that I told him of my vast experience as a horseman. I was given a racey-looking mount which I boarded, and accompanied by the groom, an ex-bombardier rough rider, I set off.

It didn't take the groom two seconds to see that my experience was somewhat less than limited. He offered me a continual stream of advice. 'Keep your chin up, Sir.' 'Keep your heels down, Sir.' 'Don't lean so far forward, Sir.' As he became more and more exasperated with me he dropped the 'Sir' saying, 'Keep your arse on the saddle an' don't pull his bloody head off!'

Reaching open country, we turned into a field covered by large heaps of dung ready for spreading. Once off the road and feeling the soft turf under his feet, my charger took off at a split-arse pace. My horse was much faster than that of the groom and was also aided by the lighter weight he was carrying, the groom at around eleven stone and I at about eight. I was nicely weighted to beat the groom as far as you could see a white cow, which I promptly proceeded to do.

I was soon out of ear-shot of the torrent of abuse. Flying across the country I imagined, like Walter Mitty, that I was Fred Archer riding the race of his life. The faster the horse went, the more exciting the adventure became. Successfully jumping a dung hill I managed to remain with my horse on landing. Although completely out of control I was not only wildly excited but full of confidence. Ahead of me loomed a stiff hedge. I could neither stop the horse nor turn him. We continued straight at it and as he sailed over the top we parted company in a very undignified manner.

The groom's only concern now was to catch the horse, probably hoping that I had broken my neck, and he paid no further attention to me. I made my way home, avoiding the stables, thereby escaping payment of the half guinea for this memorable outing.

Undaunted, I was determined to take the next opportunity to ride that presented itself. I didn't have to wait long. I made the acquaintance at Sunday School of the church verger, oddly enough named Church, who was an ex-jump jockey. He had two horses in training, one of which was an entry for the Grand National. I offered him my services as an exercise boy, which to my pleasure and surprise he accepted, explaining that at that moment he was unable to ride himself owing to an accident.

The following Saturday morning, I turned up at the stables. Church himself wasn't there as he was keeping a rendezvous at the Red Lion. He was a drunk and with beer at twopence a pint, the pubs open all day and skilful manipulation of the church collection plate he could afford to drink from first thing in the morning until last thing at night.

I waited in the stable yard for quite some time before a weedy youth appeared from the hay loft. When I explained why I

had come he replied that Church had given him no instructions and that he wasn't accepting any responsibility. If I was to ride a horse it would be the one he indicated, which to my dismay was the meaner-looking of the two. He handed me the tack, saying, 'Saddle it yourself.'

I soon realized why this lad was having nothing to do with the operation, for this horse seemed to have more back legs than an octopus has tentacles, most of which were in the air and flashing in my direction. It was fully fifteen minutes before I saw anything of this ferocious beast other than his back view. Eventually by bribing the horse with oats I managed to get to the port side and saddle up. This done I led him out, mounted with some difficulty and put to sea.

The way to the gallops was down the High Street. Immediately opposite the stables was Hide's Draper's Shop, surrounded by women staring through the large plate glass windows. Leaving the yard at some considerable speed the horse mounted the pavement, scattering terrified shoppers in all directions. Hanging on for dear life, the horse bucking and fighting for his head, I was greeted by a cockney flower seller who yelled out, 'Let go of 'is bloody 'ead!' This I did. The horse whipped round immediately,

returning to the stables, where I quickly dismounted and, putting the horse in his box, went home to change my underpants.

*

Unlike my brother and sister, who had remained closely tied to the family and home, I had gone out into the world and met other people apart from my immediate relations. I had a great friend and constant companion named Douglas Jenkins whom I had met playing marbles in the street. He came from a totally different background to my own. Until then I had made no approach to the ordinary run of social life, least of all to girls. Douglas made me inquisitive to learn about these matters, as he would relate to me the joys of sexual intercourse which he had experienced when screwing the family maid. Previously the only information I had received on such matters was from my mother, who had instilled into me the deepest fear of putting girls in the family way and had implied that, apart from mothers, sisters and respectable married people, all women were whores, probably suffering from syphilis.

Torn between these conflicting counsels, I gingerly started to make the acquaintance of girls, unknown to my mother of course. My first girl friend was Susie Mitchell, a short, good-looking girl with red hair and the biggest breasts I have ever seen in my life – they stuck out like Rolls-Royce headlights in reverse. I only went out with her after dark as I was embarrassed by boys staring at her and the wolf-whistling which accompanied their remarks such as 'Cor! Look at those tits!!' This association broke up when she asked me to take her dancing. In the first place I had never been to a dance; in the second, it would have been difficult to get close enough to her to control her movements; and in the third, of course, it meant appearance in public.

By now I was getting more interested in the subject of sex relationships. Mother had a pupil to whom she was teaching the piano. She was also a red head but a real beauty, with perfect vital statistics, eighteen years old and a nymphomaniac into the bargain. I started going for long bicycle rides with her into the country. When requiring a rest we would find a convenient hay stack and sit down to talk. She informed me that she had eight regular lovers including the local bank manager and that she would be happy to accommodate me in ninth position if I so wished.

With this girl I could talk freely and I learned a great deal from her. It was she who took the lead all the time and I made rapid progress in this new 'do it yourself' art, up to but not including the final act, as mother's early warnings kept looming up in my mind. Although my parents still had great influence over me I now began to realize that they were no ordinary people. They were both eccentric and unworldly to a degree, at times even embarrassing, as they in no way fitted into contemporary society.

*

Nothing diverted me, however, from my artistic ambitions. I left Goldsmiths' College as life classes only took place there in the evening. Starting work at eight o'clock in the morning I was tired by seven o'clock when evening classes began. I moved on to the Central Schools where we had models all day and every day. Alfred Turner, RA was the teacher of modelling, whilst Richard Garbe taught stone carving. We had excellent models; one in particular whom I remember was a negro student of Economics who posed in the life classes so as to raise money for his education. His name was Jomo Kenyatta. All I wanted from the teachers was technical information. For artistic inspiration I paid frequent visits to the British Museum to study the antiques – Greek, Etruscan, Roman etc.

I had little or no use for contemporary sculpture. Like most artists I was only interested in what I was doing and at that time had only contempt for such sculptors as Frank Dobson, Modigliani, Lipchitz and Zadkine, all of whom had international reputations. I liked some of Epstein's portrait heads but most of his work struck me as being crude. In truth, due to my teaching I mistook ingenuity and craftsmanship for art. After working at the Central Schools for two years I was very proficient technically in all branches of sculpture and felt that I could learn no more from my teachers.

I applied for entry into the prestigious Academy Schools where there were opportunities to win valuable prizes and no fees to pay. I was amongst the few fortunate applicants. The School was limited to about sixty students and many more than that applied for entry each year. The School buildings had not been altered since they were built in the late eighteenth century by order of Sir Joshua Reynolds, first President of the Royal Academy. The painting school where J. M. W. Turner used to teach still possessed the original furnishings, likewise the life-drawing room where I was taught drawing by Sir John Sargent whilst he was visiting master. The atmosphere was ideal and gave students the feeling that they were following in the footsteps of the great. In the two years I was there I won every prize that was open to sculpture students, culminating in the Royal Academy Gold Medal and Travelling Scholarship. For this competition the set subject was a relief panel, five feet by three feet, to be modelled in clay and cast in plaster. The subject was Diana and Endymion. I first of all read Keats's poem to get some inspiration and then worked for three months, using a professional male model for Endymion and a fifteen-year-old girl for Diana. I knew that the prize would be awarded for the most competent piece of modelling. Aware that I had no rivals in this field I worked free from worry with every confidence that I would win. I exhibited this relief panel in the Royal Academy Summer Exhibition. All I had to do now was to await the great annual ceremony of prize night. This, like the school building, was unchanged since the days of its inauguration.

The prize-giving was in the evening and the awards were announced by the Secretary and presented by the President. Evening dress was obligatory. Of course, this was something that I had never possessed, so it meant going around and borrowing the necessary rig-out. I managed to borrow tails which were somewhat out of date, the tails being excessively long and the trousers very baggy. To this lot, I added a black ready-to-wear bow tie, not knowing that it should have been white.

It was traditional that the winner of the Gold Medal should stand a dinner to the runners-up, so four of us went to a restaurant in Soho to wine and dine before the prize-giving.

Needless to say we had had a drink or two before going to dinner, and as none of us were accustomed to drink, we were doing quite nicely, thank you! For some reason, unknown to me, I was hailed by clients every time I went through the restaurant to the 'gents'. I could not understand why people should think I was a waiter. When I mentioned the fact to my companions, one of them told me, with some embarrassment, that it was because I should have been wearing a white tie with tails – only waiters wore black ties with such outfits. I felt awful, but it was too late to do anything about it as all the shops were long since shut.

In those days one could eat cheaply and well in these Soho restaurants. There was no cover-charge or any nonsense like that. You ordered whatever you liked off the menu, paid for it, and that was that. *Hors d'oeuvres* were sixpence and were brought to the table on a large *table roulante* and left so that one could help oneself. There were a great number of assorted dishes; rollmops, sardines, pilchards, raw ham, anchovies, liver sausage and the usual variety of vegetables. Bread was provided free of charge. We ordered *hors d'oeuvres* and between the four of us ate the lot, including all the bread. We then asked for the bill, which came to two shillings. This, with a sixpence tip to the waiter, gave the four of us dinner for half a crown.

I can well remember how displeased the management was and I can also remember the proprietor addressing us in Italian, which fortunately I was unable to understand. We got out of the restaurant as fast as we could and into a pub for a last drink, before presenting ourselves before the President and Council of the Royal Academy.

One of the party who, like myself, was unused to drink of an alcoholic nature, had consumed a large whisky which knocked him right out and he fell unconscious to the sawdust-covered floor of the public bar. Unfortunately he was a hefty chap and difficult to carry along. This we tried to do, however, having no money to pay for a taxi, and Soho to the Royal Academy proved quite a long haul.

The fact that we survivors were the worse for drink didn't make our task any easier. We went a back way round which took us down Savile Row, at that time of the evening quite deserted. Someone had the bright idea of lifting up one of the many area grilles and depositing our unconscious friend there until after the show, when we would come back and fetch him. A splendid notion, quickly and efficiently executed.

Off we set for the final two or three hundred yards, singing away and I playing the mouth-organ. We were a bit late getting there, and as we were to be the principal recipients of the prizes, we found everyone waiting for us. All members of the Academy Schools were present including some hundred-odd students, the President, Sir Aston Webb, Charles Lamb, the secretary, Sir

George Frampton and other Knights of the paintbrush.

We quickly took our seats at the back and the proceedings started. What form they took I have no idea for within a minute of settling into my chair, I fell sound asleep, whilst Charles Lamb was waffling on about something or other. I was woken up by my neighbour shaking me violently and saying, 'They are calling your name, you've got to go up'. I gathered myself together and made my somewhat zigzag course up the aisle to the platform, struggling the while to stow away my mouth-organ into my trousers' pocket. This would have been a difficult operation at the best of times as the pocket seemed to be situated rather far back, and owing to the length of the trousers was also too low down for convenience.

Arriving on the platform, a last violent effort to stuff the mouth-organ into my pocket ripped open all my fly-buttons and my trousers came down just as the President was offering his hand for me to shake. Pandemonium broke out as everyone in the place burst into roars of uncontrolled laughter, which took longer to subside than it took me to adjust my clothing.

At the end of the proceedings I had recovered somewhat from all these shocks, comforted by the fact that I had collected three other prizes besides the Gold Medal.

Afterwards we went to an all-night café to sleep things off and sober up a bit before returning to our respective homes. Fortunately, whilst reminiscing about the whole evening we remembered our poor friend who was imprisoned down under the grille. We dashed off and found him there sound asleep. When we woke him up he had recovered sufficiently to be able to walk, and he returned to the café with us and finished sleeping off his drunken stupor.

Next day I returned home with my twenty-four carat gold medal in my pocket and displayed it before the family. Mother said: 'Give it to me and I will put it away in my jewel case for safety.' This she did. However, I knew where the jewel case was kept and also that it didn't have a lock on it. Some two or three days later I took it to the bullion market where it was duly weighed and I was given £35 for it, which was a great deal of money in those days. Poor Mother was broken-hearted when she heard what I had done. I suppose it was a pity, but things like medals, trophies and certificates have never really meant much to me and never will.

III

Italy

Three months after receiving the Gold Medal I set out for Rome. It was the first time I had been out of the British Isles. It was a strange feeling to look back from the ferry and see the white cliffs of Dover slowly fading away in the distance. I felt lonely for the first time in my life. But the excitement of not knowing what lay ahead kept me buoyed up, along with the great expectations which were a permanent feature of my character.

Taking a stroll up to the forepeak of the ship I saw a young man sitting on a bollard playing a mouth organ and we soon got into conversation. He was obviously a seasoned traveller and a man of the world, just the kind of person I was hoping to meet, and I was delighted to make his acquaintance. He asked me where I was bound, and when I told him Rome, he said that he was also going there. He told me that he was a Maltese sailor and was stopping in Rome on his way home to Malta, where he planned to spend a few weeks' leave before joining his next ship. He asked me if I spoke Italian. I said no, and explained that it was my first trip away from home, at which he declared that he would be glad to look after me. This offer was comforting and I was glad to take advantage of it.

On arrival in Paris he took me to a restaurant somewhere near the Gare de Lyon, where he was greeted with extravagant demonstrations of affection by the proprietor, a burly Sicilian, who rattled away to him in Italian. He seemed to have friends everywhere. I was given my first taste of Italian food, which I found excellent, and it was all paid for, which I found better still.

The train for Rome was due to leave at about ten o'clock that night. It was January and very cold but we hired pillows and blankets and my friend assured me that we were in for a really comfortable night in a compartment all to ourselves. I was puzzled as to how we were going to achieve this, but he merely said, 'Leave it to me'. His method was simple and effective. We arrived ahead of time at the station and installed ourselves in an empty carriage, where he stood at the window grimacing, accompanied when necessary by strange growling noises, at anyone who threatened to approach. Since the journey to Rome took two days it was just as well to be comfortable and be able to put one's feet up.

In no time at all we were on the friendliest of terms and were exchanging intimate details of our lives and aspirations. My Uncle Tom had given me twenty gold sovereigns for winning the scholarship and these I had in my pocket in a little leather bag. I out with them, needless to say, halfway between Paris and Modane, and my friend's face lit up with glee. He begged me to sell him one, so that he could make a ring out of it for his sister and offered me twice its value in other coinage, but I insisted on making him a present of it in return for all his kindness. He was patently delighted and I could see I had made a friend for life.

At Modane, on the French-Italian border, the train had a two-hour wait, and we went into the little town for lunch. It was the first time I had seen snow-covered mountains, the air was crystal clear, and a strange silence prevailed as we walked along, our footsteps muffled in the carpet of deep snow. There was a delicious smell of coffee and French cigarettes in the air. The restaurant was typical of those days: a lovely wood-fire burning in a stove in the middle of the dining-room, and a sawdust-covered floor, serving the dual purpose of absorbing the dust and keeping one's feet warm in the winter. After an excellent meal, we rejoined the train which took us through a long mountain tunnel, bursting out at the other end into the most magnificent mountain scenery. I stood in the corridor with my face glued to the window, staring in wonderment at this majestic sight until it became too dark to see anything but the few little lights shining up in the mountain villages.

The panorama of wonderful scenery accompanied us right down through Tuscany to the Campagna Romana. In the afternoon at about three o'clock, two days after leaving Paris, the train approached the outskirts of Rome. We started to gather our things together and prepare for arrival. My friend drew a knife from his pocket and proceeded to remove the letters SNCF from his blanket and pillow, after which he handed the knife to me, intimating that I should do the same. This behaviour astonished me, and I was reluctant to follow suit. I said that I had no use for a pillow and blanket, but he simply reacted by taking them himself, removing the initials and packing the lot into his luggage. He informed me by way of explanation, that all the blankets at his home in Malta were the kind donation of the different railway companies which he patronized from time to time. I was relieved of some considerable anxiety when we got beyond the barrier.

My friend, on hearing that I had made no arrangements to stay anywhere in particular, offered to take me to the house of some friends of his who lived in the district of San Lorenzo near the railway station. We walked to the house, which was only four hundred yards away, and climbed up a flight of marble stairs to the fourth floor, where he tapped on a door. A woman's eyes appeared at a little grilled slot and peered at us, but at the sight of my friend the door was quickly opened and in we went. The eyes belonged to a small woman who was introduced to me as Signora Vicardi. A long conversation ensued, all in Italian, accompanied by the usual profusion of gestures and facial expressions which are inseparable from the Italian language, making it so easy for the foreigner to understand. I could tell from this pantomime that my friend had been giving an account of how he met me on the boat whilst playing his mouth-organ, of our journey down and my kindness in giving him a gold coin, but mixed up in this there was also a lot of excited conversation the content of which was quite beyond me. This did not worry me at all at the time and I dismissed it from my mind as being of no importance. My anxiety was to find a place to live and I was glad of my friend's help.

After an hour or so my friend departed and I was left to my own devices. These were pretty inadequate. For the first week or two I couldn't understand a word of what was said to me and felt like a deaf-mute, completely isolated from the rest of the world. Sheer necessity forced me to learn Italian quickly. I went every evening to the Berlitz School and after three months began to speak quite fluently. As I never heard a word of English spoken, opportunities for practice were unlimited.

I spent my days tramping the city from end to end. I visited all the churches, monuments and museums, returning to the latter again and again, until I got to know every item. I made drawings, and kept a diary in which I recorded my experiences and discoveries. Three nights a week, after my sessions at the Berlitz School, I would take myself off to the Costanzi Opera House, where I could get into the gallery for two lire, or stand behind the stalls for one. The disadvantage of this position was that it exposed you to the wafts of garlic exhaled by your neighbours, who were packed in around you so closely that there was no possibility of escape. On one occasion I was unlucky enough to find myself in front of a man who was actually chewing the stuff throughout the performance. All evening I concentrated on timing my inhalations and exhalations to coincide with his, but every now and then I would get out of pace, owing to his yawning or some other such irregularity and I would receive the full blast of his breath, which would have felled me had I not been too tightly packed in to fall.

For the first few months I had to depend almost entirely on my own companionship. Then one day, in the gardens opposite the railway station, I saw a strange long-haired figure sitting on a seat drawing on a small pad. I went over and spoke to him. He was a Hungarian student named Eudre Kunitzer. From what I saw that first day in the park, he was obviously a beautiful draughtsman and, as I soon discovered, an excellent musician, philosopher and poet. He was, in fact, the first intellectual I had ever met.

We became immediate friends and from then on were together all the time. I used to advance him small sums out of my scholarship money when he hadn't enough cash to buy food, which happened frequently as he was practically penniless and had no regular source of income. In return he confided to me his life story, which was one of real drama. Some eight years before – he was now twenty-nine – he had contracted a venereal disease from a girl with whom he had been in love and, being ashamed and nervous, he had postponed treatment for too long. In consequence he suffered a great deal from the after-effects. He was, on the whole, a melancholic and depressed character. I had never encountered anyone like him, and I began to realize that there were many people in this world who were not as happy or as lucky as I was. My upbringing had kept me remarkably naïve and unworldly and meeting with such a man as Kunitzer was a shock to me. I was to learn much from him.

We used to walk prodigious distances together to visit places outside Rome. On one occasion we went all the way to Ostia Mare and back, leaving Rome at six in the morning and getting back at two o'clock the following morning. The total distance was fifty-six miles. We stopped only once, to see the Roman mosaics which were the object of our visit, and to bathe our blistered feet in the sea.

Shortly after this Kunitzer took himself off for a while, and I was left once again on my own. I fell back into my old habits, spending my days sight-seeing and my nights at the Opera. One night, dining in a restaurant in San Lorenzo before going to *Il Tabarro* at the Costanzi, I was accosted as I waited for my bill by a strange man, who came over and sat himself at my table. 'Aren't you the Englishman who lives with the Vicardis?' he asked. I said that I was. He wanted to know if I was doing anything that night, and I told him that I was going to the Opera. 'Do you want to do a job?' was his next question. Having no idea what he was getting at I volunteered: 'Yes, what kind of a job?' 'A piece of cake', he replied – or words to that effect. 'You're going to the Opera anyway so it's no skin off your nose. It's like this. There's a woman going to the Opera tonight, an American, with a wonderful three-rope string of fine pearls round her neck. She's wearing a white lace dress, gold shoes and a tiara. Be in the hall just before she comes out, and go up to her and say in English: "Aren't you Mrs So-and-So?", or some such remark, to make her stop. When you discover that it's a case of mistaken identity, you can apologize and go on your way. I'll take care of the rest, and will meet you back here afterwards.' I managed to conceal my astonishment and control my nerves just enough to get out the words 'OK' and leave, not for the Opera House as I had originally intended, but straight back home to tell my landlady what had happened.

The moment I got back I threw open the door and called out to Signora Vicardi, who was in the kitchen by herself having coffee. She was surprised to see me back so soon, and said, 'I thought you were going to the Opera?' Her surprise at my premature return was nothing to the expression of consternation that appeared on her face when I told her my story. I expected this reaction but not the reason for it. 'Sit down', she said, then continued: 'Tell me, who are you and what are you?' 'I'm an art student, you know that', I said. 'Yes', she replied, 'I know you say that, but what do you really do? You do no work, you are out all day and half the night saying you are going to the Opera or some such place. Where do you go, what do you do when you go out at nights? You never work and you always have plenty of money.' I repeated that I was an art student on a travelling scholarship and that was why I had come to Italy and why I had money without having to work for it. She stared hard at me for a little while without saying anything. Then she ventured cautiously, 'How well do you know the Maltese who brought you here in the first place?' I answered that I hardly knew him at all, and related how I had come to meet him on the boat and had travelled with him to Rome. I didn't even know his name, and had never seen him before or since.

She then told me that he had brought me to the house under false pretences, saying that I was an old and trusted friend of his who was in the same racket as the rest of them – namely a thief. Her son, she explained, was a guard on the Paris-Rome express and their apartment was a clearing-house for goods stolen on the railways. Had it not been for the Maltese's introduction I would never have been allowed to stay there. All the same, seeing that I was happy there and they liked having me, she said that I could stay, on condition that I kept my trap shut.

Although she assured me that there was nothing for me to worry about I never felt completely secure from then on. I was grateful for their kindness, remembering how she had looked after me when I was ill, doing all my washing and countless other little services, but all the time I was looking for an excuse to get away. In the end I hit on the idea of going to Naples.

When I told Signora Vicardi this plan she became very distressed and did all she could to persuade me against it. She said that Naples was a dangerous place to visit and that I would be much wiser to stay where I was. This was good advice as at this time the Fascist revolution was brewing up all over Italy, and even in the streets of San Lorenzo there were frequent gun battles between the Communists and the Fascists. Fortunately most of the gunmen were such bad shots that the greatest damage done was broken bedroom windows. But Naples was still the 'hot spot' of Italy, where apart from the casualties inflicted during the gun battles, the city averaged two assassinations per day. However, I was determined to get away and left the next day.

On checking in my bags at Naples railway station I went straight into the town to sniff out the situation and to buy myself a firearm of some sort – the Signora's warning had made some impression on me. I did not have to go far before I came to a gun shop. I asked the proprietor if it was necessary to have a licence to purchase a revolver. 'Of course it is', he said. 'You may not even carry a penknife with a blade of more than half an inch in length'. Meanwhile he produced a tray of pistols and put them down on the counter in front of me. 'Pick what you want', he said. I selected a small Belgian five-chamber revolver, bought twelve rounds of ammunition, loaded the gun and made to put it in my pocket. 'Put it in your raincoat pocket', the gunsmith advised me, 'then if you are frisked they are less likely to find it.' I obeyed, and set off back to the station to claim my bags.

As was usual at railway stations, there was a fellow lounging up against the counter wearing a peaked cap with the word *Albergo* written on it in gold letters. As I pulled my bags over the counter and dumped them on the ground, the luggage labels must have been clearly visible giving away my nationality, for he wasted no time in addressing me in English, with a strong American accent: 'Do you want a room, cheap, very clean, overlooking the bay – very nice, very pretty ?' As I hadn't booked anything I said I would go with him.

We took a horse-drawn cab and drove a couple of miles right

up the hill to the outskirts of the town. There was certainly a grand view of the bay from up there. Stopping the cab at an isolated house, the porter took my bags and carried them up to the top floor. The house seemed to be oddly deserted: there was nobody about at all. He opened a door and showed me into a very large room, every detail of which I can remember to this day. It had large red tiles on the floor, a wash-stand with an enamel bowl and jug, an iron bedstead, a small side-table with a candle-stick on it, and a chair. I asked him the price of the room, and was astonished when he said five lire. My suspicions were imme-diately aroused as one could not get the smallest of rooms for under seventeen lire at that time.

Without waiting for my approval he went out of the room saying, 'I'll just go down and let them know that you are here'. I heard his footsteps going down the stairs. By this time I was beginning to feel a little panicky, again remembering Signora Vicardi's warnings. I did something which I had never done before – I turned back the bedclothes to see if there were bugs in the bed. There were no bugs, but, to my horror, I saw a large red patch of blood.

All kinds of possible explanations sprang to mind. Had some woman had a baby in the bed? Or had someone been murdered in it? In either case, why hadn't the bedclothes been changed? Whilst all these ideas ran through my head I heard someone coming up the stairs. I put my hand in my pocket and gripped my pistol. As my guide walked in I pointed it at him. Without taking my hand out of my pocket, I told him to pick up my bags and carry them until I told him to put them down.

Walking behind him with my hand on my gun I made him carry the bags right back into the centre of town. Then I told him to put them down and scram. He was gone in a flash.

Immediately I was assailed by doubts. Had I done something really stupid? Had he gone off to inform the police? I had taken no chances up at the house, and didn't feel like starting to take them now. I went straight back to the station and booked myself on the midnight train to Rome.

It was five o'clock in the morning when I arrived back at the Vicardis' house, and I was forced to spend the next two hours sleeping on the cold marble staircase, having no wish to wake anyone at that hour. I felt ashamed of the whole escapade, having ignored the express advice of the Signora.

Eventually I plucked up enough courage to knock on the door, which was answered by the Signora herself. She looked astonished to see me, although she said that she wasn't surprised in the least. 'Come in', she said, 'and tell me what has happened.' Over a welcome cup of coffee and a strong reviver, I told her the whole story. All she could do was to repeat: 'What did I tell you? What did I tell you? But no, you wouldn't listen to me.'

The following week an article appeared in the national papers reporting the arrest of a gang of assassins in connection with seven murders which had taken place in Naples. The scene was the very house on the hill to which I had been taken by my pseudo-porter. The eighth victim was, no doubt, intended to have been myself. The others were all Americans. The government had recently cancelled all Italian passports in an attempt to prevent members of the Mafia escaping to America, and consequently American and British passports were fetching one thousand pounds apiece on the black market.

This news really shocked me and in order to get right away from the activities of the clearing-house I decided to leave for Siena as soon as possible.

Shortly before leaving Rome I was to witness yet more violence, though this time of a hilarious character. The Italians had just taken up football, and there was to be a match in the Campagna Romana. I decided to go to see what football *all' Italiano* was like.

There was a big crowd – some two thousand people – at the ground, a large open space in the Campagna. Its surface would have left something to be desired even without assistance from the recent thunderstorms. It was clear from the start of the game that progress was to be slow. Whenever a player fell in the mud, the referee blew his whistle and stopped the game. The man's second would then rush out on to the pitch with a sponge and towel and clean him up. Owing to the tripping and rather boisterous charging that went on, the game was held up in this manner at least once every five minutes.

At the beginning of the second half, the referee gave a foul against one of the players. Whilst a furious argument raged in the centre of the field, the ball rolled out towards touch. An infuriated spectator, whose team was apparently losing, whipped out his stiletto and dealt the ball a blow which deflated it like a flat tyre. Since it was probably the only representative of its kind in the whole of Italy, chaos ensued. The last I saw of the game was the culprit disappearing into the distance, chased by both teams and two thousand spectators.

By comparison with Rome and Naples, Siena was a haven of peace. I found a nice room in the Via Sallustio Bandini and spent a really happy time wandering about the city. The only traffic consisted of wagons drawn by beautiful pairs of white oxen, their wide-spread horns reaching from one wall to the other in the narrow medieval streets. At midday I would sit in a café in the Piazza del Campo. While the melodious bells rang out the *Angelus* I would watch the clouds of pigeons rise in the square and fly up to the towers, frightened by the sudden noise.

I had only been in Siena two or three days when a grey-haired Irishman and his wife arrived. They were charming people. Together we would visit the museums of Siena and go to places like San Gimignano and Volterra. Then we would sit in the cafés by the hour talking of this and that. I was sorry when they left. It was not until some time afterwards that I discovered that my friend was W. B. Yeats, the famous Irish poet.

From Siena I moved on to Florence. Of course I already knew Florentine art through reproductions but the reality transcended my wildest hopes. I had only been there a day or two when I began to regret the long time I had spent in Rome. This town contained so much more that was of interest to me. In Rome most of the sculptures were, of course, Roman. This period has never particularly interested me except for its remarkable portrait busts, which are for me its only original contribution to the history of the art of sculpture. Florence offered instead Michelangelo, Donatello, Mino da Fiesole, Giacopo della Quercia. This was the graceful period of sculpture that I really admired. I spent hours and hours looking at these works, until I could see them in every detail in my imagination. It was here that I had my first real meeting with Michelangelo. But although I was attracted by the powerful movement and vitality he got into all his works and impressed by his prodigious technical skill, it was the works of Donatello and his school that really won my admiration. I thought them better than anything I had ever seen. They came to represent for me the height of sculptural achievement. The Uffizi Gallery was a paradise for me with its wonderful paintings of the Florentine School and, more wonderful still, its library of original drawings of the great masters. Students could handle and copy these at their leisure.

Quite apart from the aesthetic delights of the museums, the streets were full of beautiful girls strolling about at that graceful sexy pace which characterizes the Florentine women. The men, too, were very handsome. To me they looked exactly like the early portraits of Renaissance noblemen.

There were some English tea rooms in Florence, frequented by the 'smart set,' where I used to go several afternoons a week. Here were beautiful girls in abundance. There was one in particular for whom I developed a great passion, but she was always accompanied by her mother. We made eyes at one another, but I was too shy to press the matter further. In any case I didn't know how to approach such a situation – a weakness not shared by my Italian counterparts. But I had little desire to follow their example. In fact their over-sexed behaviour disgusted me, and I wondered how the women stood for it, especially when I saw them pinching the bottoms of passing girls or making lewd comments about their figures as they followed them down the streets.

On one occasion in a café, whilst in the middle of an earnest discussion on Italian literature with an elderly professor, a very attractive girl passed by. Without finishing his sentence, the professor got up from his chair and followed the girl down the road, exactly as a dog would follow a bitch in season. He got the usual rebuff and returned to his seat, saying: 'Where had we got to? . . . Ah, yes, I remember, Torquato Tasso . . .', and the conversation went on as though nothing had happened.

Florence was at that time the resort of a clique of European intellectuals, centering round such people as Berenson, Aldous Huxley and Norman Douglas. Douglas, an excellent writer and a bawdy wit withal, was 'queen bee' in the hive of queers who hung around this group. It was the first time in my life that I had met such people and I found them most entertaining, quite unlike the scout masters, parsons and old-fashioned buggers calling themselves confirmed bachelors who had constituted my only previous experience of this breed – the kind who squeezed one's youthful arm in a public lavatory saying, 'What big muscles you have', and then proceeded to offer one sweets.

There was an American woman living in Florence who possessed more money than sense and was quite prepared to dispense with a great deal of the former commodity in order to get in with the 'smart set'. She had an attractive daughter in her early twenties whom it was her ambition to see married to an Italian nobleman. To this end she decided to give a large and showy dinner at which her daughter might have the opportunity of meeting some suitable *Conte*. She asked Norman Douglas to help draw up the guest list, knowing that he was well acquainted with the cream of society.

Douglas undertook to make all the arrangements for the party, having been given an entirely free hand. He ordered everything to be in pink, from the table linen to the flowers, the food to the wines. They were to drink pink champagne and all the ladies were to wear pink dresses. It was to be the top social event of the season.

Finally the great day arrived, all arrangements having been made and the seating meticulously worked out. As the guests trickled in it became evident that every one of the men, without exception, was a screaming queer, hand-picked in every sense of the word by Douglas, who had scoured Rome as well as Florence to find the most exaggerated examples of the fraternity. It is easy to imagine the course this party took, and the result needs no description by me. Seated on his hostess's right, Douglas's sense of fun was rampant. Questioned by her as to the significance of the title of his latest book, *The Centaur*, which was much in the news at the time, he replied: 'Madame, a senator is half a pig and half a goat'.

It was shortly after this wild party that Kunitzer turned up in Florence. I found a great change in him. He had become desperately melancholic and talked only of the futility of everything, saying that nothing existed other than in the imagination and that we had no proof of anything.

He was thin and weak from under-nourishment, but refused to accept any help at all from me. Instead he sold his overcoat to buy me a book on Indian sculpture. He would sit in my attic room, doing nothing, eating nothing, and rarely uttering a word. One day he gathered together his books and the few drawings he had with him, removed his name from the books and signed the drawings. Then he handed them to me saying, 'Keep these and my memory in your imagination.' That night he went to sleep in the chair from which he had hardly moved for the past three weeks, and I found him dead in it the next morning.

He had neither passport nor papers, which made it impossible for me to contact his family, not knowing who they were, where they lived, or indeed if they were still alive. I told my landlady, who informed the police. A doctor arrived and pronounced him dead from starvation and pneumonia. His body was removed to the morgue. I had certain papers to fill up, and that was that.

I tried to apply Kunitzer's own philosophy to this tragic event – that it had not really happened, and existed only in my imagination – but I was too much of a realist to be able to see it in this way. Profoundly shaken, I decided to abandon my travels and return to England.

IV

Prix de Rome and Marriage

When I arrived in England I found I had some difficulty in speaking English again, so great had been my total absorption in things Italian. Ordinary people had not yet started travelling abroad and it was still considered a big adventure to do so. I was something of a curiosity to my friends who all wanted to see and hear of my experiences. I had plenty of these to tell, and was always being asked out to dinner to entertain the guests with them.

I had changed quite a lot in many ways, even in my appearance. I was sunburned and wearing Italian clothes, a large Borsalino hat and co-respondent shoes. This also attracted the local girls, who had never seen anything quite like me, and I wasted no time in finding myself a girl friend, having been starved of female company for so long. I selected a very suitable character, a half-French, half-American girl who was a nurse at the local lunatic asylum. It was fun while it lasted but once the novelty had worn off I realized that all I wanted to do was to get back to work.

I engaged a famous Italian male model from whom I did an over life-sized figure of a walking man. I worked at it ten hours a day for a year and a half, but halfway through I ran out of money. I mentioned my predicament to Alfred Turner, RA and shortly afterwards received a visit from him as he wanted to see the figure. He was very impressed with it and said: 'Finish it, and send it to the Academy Summer Exhibition and you will have a good chance of being elected an associate.' 'How was I to finish it without money?' I asked him. 'Leave that to me,' he replied. Two weeks later I received an anonymous cheque for four hundred pounds. I'd never had so much money in my life. Then I did something really stupid. Dissatisfied with this work when it was finished, I destroyed it, causing great offence to the members of the Academy from whom this money had come.

I decided to enter for the *Prix de Rome* Scholarship. In those days it was a very stiff examination divided into two parts, a preliminary and the final following six months later. Passing the preliminary exam I then got my first teaching job at Armstrong College, Newcastle upon Tyne, whilst I awaited the final. It was there that I met John Grierson who was assistant registrar at the college. John and I became friendly. An intellectual and an advanced thinker, he opened my eyes to the real meaning of art. It was the first time I had met someone who was a scholar and I learned a great deal from my contact with him.

Through Grierson I was invited to give a lecture on sculpture to the Literary and Philosophical Society of Newcastle upon Tyne. I had never, of course, given a lecture before and needed all of the four months before it was to be delivered to write and prepare my talk which was to be of an hour's duration. Three days before the lecture Grierson asked me how long my talk was to be. I said, 'One hour.' He then asked me if I had timed myself reading the paper; if not, I should do so in front of a mirror. The object of this exercise was to try to look at the audience and keep my head up as much as possible.

This I did, and found that the paper I had spent four months preparing only took me ten minutes to read. I tried desperately to add to it and lengthen it, but without much success. I was in a real dilemma and scared stiff when the time came to give my talk.

I got up on the platform and Grierson introduced me to the learned audience. Being frantically nervous, I spoke in a feeble voice that was scarcely audible to those in the front row, let alone those in the back. I also read at great speed, and was told afterwards by Grierson that no one heard a word of this first part of my lecture.

Having come to the end of the paper in about eight minutes flat, a divine inspiration came to me. I went on ad-libbing about my early life, and in fact said anything that came into my head, most of which was complete fantasy. Encouraged by my spellbound audience, who were by now giving me their undivided attention, I went on and on and easily kept going for an hour. I would have kept on even longer, had I not caught sight of a cousin of mine sitting in the audience with his mouth wide open and his eyes sticking out like onions, for he knew that much of what I was saying was untrue, a figment of my wildest imagination. I stopped dead as though shot by a gun, brought the lecture to an abrupt close, and ran from the hall as fast as I could, leaving the astonished audience to their applause.

It took me a great deal of time to recover any sort of calm, but aided by kindly and experienced advice from Grierson, I eventually forgot the whole experience and went on my confident way.

Back in London again, the final test for the *Prix de Rome* was about to start. This took place at the Royal College of Art during the summer vacation. On entering the room, each competitor was closeted in a separate cubicle. One was handed a paper with the title of the subject, in this case a relief panel to go over a hospital doorway. No one was allowed to leave until they had completed and submitted a sketch design which had to be adhered to absolutely. We were allowed two months to complete the final work.

I had only done about a week's work when I started to have violent stomach pains which continued throughout the whole time I was working. The moment the competition was finished, I went straight into Guy's Hospital and had an operation for appendicitis and suspected duodenal ulcer. The results were not too satisfactory, and I never really recovered properly, but managed to learn to live with an almost perpetual gut-ache.

I won the scholarship. Barbara Hepworth was the runner-up of the three others in the final. The scholarship was for three years in Rome at the British School.

When I had recovered sufficiently from the operation I went out to Rome. The first person I contacted there was Giovanni Ardini, a *marmista* – that is a professional marble carver – whom I had known before when first I went to Rome on the RA Traveller. I went to work with Ardini to learn marble carving, quite a separate technique from soft stone carving at which I was fairly competent. Ardini was regularly employed working for Mestrovitch, the Serbian sculptor. It was the common practice at that time for sculptors to model their works in clay, cast them in plaster, and then hand them over to a *marmista* to copy in marble. Mestrovitch, although a good wood carver, could not carve in stone or marble, likewise Rodin. All the works in marble that exist by these two renowned sculptors were carved by *marmistas*, the artists doing nothing to the marble itself.

The modelling style of both these artists was really not suited to translation into marble. The natural rough surface of the original models made this impossible and the results look like sucked sugar almonds which have been spat out. I worked with Ardini for six months, helping with the roughing out of some of Mestrovitch's bigger works which he was engaged in copying. At the end of this period, Barbara Hepworth, who had been awarded a travelling scholarship by the County Council of the

West Riding of Yorkshire, came out to Italy. She first of all went
to Florence and then came down to Rome to see me.

*

During the competition for the Rome scholarship I had been too
absorbed in my work to take any particular notice of Barbara.
She was just another competitor. But now, relaxed in the sunshine
of Italy, I saw her through different eyes. She was only twenty-two
years old and good looking. She had a most unusual head; her
forehead projecting further out at the hair line than at its base;
brown eyes with the upper lids scarcely visible, like those of
orientals; a silken fair skin and a good nose and mouth. I remember
how struck I was with her appearance when I met her at the
station. She was wearing a long coat with an astrakhan collar
and cuffs and a black pill-box hat with a tassel hanging from the
crown similar to the one worn by Mussolini at that time. She
attracted a good deal of attention from the young Romans as
we walked through the streets visiting museums and historic
monuments. I was proud to be seen with her, in fact I spent as
much time looking at her as I did at the museum pieces. I took
in every detail of her qualities and defects; of the latter she had
only two and both were flat, her chest and her feet. Later on I
took her to Siena, my favourite Italian city. I knew she would
enjoy it as she was more interested in primitive sculpture and
painting than in the classic periods, which were my own interest
up until that time. There was the wonderful gallery of paintings
of the Sienese School, which we both found very stimulating.

Travelling together to such heavenly places as Siena, San
Gimignano and Volterra, it was inevitable that we should fall
deeply in love with each other. Both being prudish at that time,
particularly Barbara, I never got to 'first base' as they say in
baseball, but it was really hard for us to part when Barbara had
to return to Florence and I to Rome.

It so happened that an architect friend of mine called Bertram
Carter was staying in Rome when I got back, and all I could talk
to him about was my love for Barbara. Bertram said to me, 'If

that is the way it is, why don't you marry her?' What a wonderful idea, it had never occurred to me. I wasted no time in writing to Barbara to ask her if she would marry me. I got a return-of-post reply saying, 'Yes.'

I set off for Florence, as soon as I could get away, to arrange our marriage. Consular marriages were for some reason no longer possible, and we would have to get married by Italian law. This presented many complications, not the least being that as I was under twenty-five I had to obtain my father's permission. Since I had not said a word to my family about Barbara, this was not going to be easy to obtain. I did all the legal business myself as I spoke fluent Italian. This, however, took two or three months and many bribes to civil servants, whose wages were always twelve months in arrears. They would do absolutely nothing unless bribed to do so. All completed, and the wedding day fixed, I made the awful discovery that my father would have to be present to sign the register. An English journalist whom I knew, called Eric Whelpton, readily stood in as my father and we were married on 25 May 1925, in the Palazzo Vecchio.

Both Barbara and I were virgins. The condition was not unusual for young women at that time but it was quite rare for men not to have had some pre-marital experiences. How different to the present day where quite a large percentage of girls go to the altar pregnant. Sometimes this can be quite an economy as the champagne does for both the wedding and the christening parties.

Whilst I think the need for freedom is very much overstated today, to get married without previous experience can be risky. The partners may find out later on, to their distress, that they are temperamentally and sexually totally unsuited to one another.

We lived for three months in the lovely little apartment which Barbara had been occupying in the Costa San Giorgio, near the Ponte Vecchio. Barbara had a strong influence on me. She was a great admirer of Henry Moore and all things modern. I started to change the style of my own work. Perhaps I was jealous of her admiration for Moore and felt that she really didn't think much of my work.

That summer we returned to England. Having forewarned my parents that I had married Barbara, I was wondering what their reaction might be. I showed them photographs of some of my recent works done under the influence of Barbara. Father, being an academic artist himself, was obviously not best pleased, especially when Barbara started going round my studio pulling out all of my old things and condemning them as rubbish and I destroying them. There were signs of considerable hostility towards Barbara on the part of my family. We went up to Yorkshire to meet her parents where I was well received but not too happy. I found her father pompous and her mother stupid. I had never expected Barbara to have come from this very middle-class background.

The holiday over, we were both glad to return to Rome and get down to work. We bought a lot of tropical birds, pigeons and a monkey. I taught Barbara to carve marble. She could not learn from Ardini as she did not speak a word of Italian and never learned to do so during the whole time we were in Italy. She had a natural skill and turned out some beautiful things. One carving of two pigeons, now in Manchester City Art Gallery, is quite superb. I did, at this time, have considerable influence upon her and she stopped copying Henry Moore for the time being, developing a style of her own. She also did some lovely wood carvings, a craft I had also taught her, having learned from a wood carver myself whilst I was teaching at Armstrong College.

We were blissfully happy and the future looked bright for us both in every way. Confining ourselves to carving, I carved a portrait direct in marble of Barbara, which was the best work I had done to date. This carving has disappeared, despite the many advertisements I have put in the papers and enquiries I have made everywhere.

There were frequent visitors to our studio who came to admire our work. Among them was Eddie Marsh who bought a drawing from me and was later to become quite an important person in my life. There were also less happy characters such as Alfred Gilbert, the sculptor of the Eros statue in Piccadilly. He came to see me as a down-and-out drunk, begging for a job, even for a crust of bread. I was shocked to see what had become of this man whose work I had so much admired. Looking at this gross and flabby figure clothed in rags, his face and hands swollen with drink, it was difficult to conceive that he was the creator of that graceful figure known throughout the world.

We had been in Rome for two years when my insides started to give me real trouble. My scholarship time had not finished but being a sick man suffering from a duodenal ulcer, I thought it wise to return to England for treatment. Italian hospitals left much to be desired and had hardly changed from the time when they were built to accommodate the hundreds of people dying of the new plague, syphilis, which had been introduced into Europe by Columbus's returning sailors. Over the main entrance of all these ancient buildings was the inscription: '*Ospedale degli incurabili*'. True in those days and true today, I thought!

It was a sad day when we had to pack up and return to England in early 1927. I gave Pipi the monkey to an old lady who had a beautiful garden where he could enjoy himself and we took the birds back with us to England.

V

Bloomsbury

We took a studio in Chalk Farm, next door to Nevinson's, where I spent the first month confined to bed, while what little money we had saved disappeared in doctors' fees. However, we managed to keep going as we received a commission from a wealthy friend of Barbara's father, who asked us to do portrait heads of his two children.

The moment I recovered, things began to pick up. Leo Walmsley, the writer, offered to let us his basement flat with studio attached, and we moved in there. I built a huge aviary, the length of the studio wall, to house the birds we had brought back from Italy – a colourful collection of budgerigars, weavers, waxbills, and Nyasaland love-birds. Now settled into our spacious new workshop, Barbara and I got down to carving in earnest.

Life was delightful – the only commodity we lacked was money. In those early days I was prepared to take on anything to raise it. One of the first things I did was the model for the prancing horse which is the trademark of Aveling and Porter of Rochester, the manufacturers of steam-rollers. For this I was paid the noble sum of £18. My next job was for Wedgwood, who commissioned a series of ten animal figures from me for the ridiculous fee of £10 each and no royalties. I was too unbusiness-like to concern myself with such matters in those days. The royalties would, as it turned out, have been worth a fortune, for the figures sold in thousands all over the world, and were reproduced mercilessly by Wedgwood until the moulds were so worn out that the animals were scarcely recognizable. But I was content, for with the £100 I got for the animals and the £18 for the prancing horse, we had enough capital laid by to enable us to concentrate on our own work with a view to mounting an exhibition, which was held at the Bruton Galleries in Bruton Mews a year after our return.

My own work at this time consisted mainly of carvings of animals and birds in Cornish Serpentine, some of which were, I think, very good, though it is difficult for me to judge now as they have all long since disappeared, as is the way with nearly all my work. Along with these I exhibited animal drawings, engravings and dry point etchings – antelopes, leopards and tigers, mostly, drawn at the zoo, where I would go once a week as in my early days at Goldsmiths'. Barbara also exhibited drawings and stone carvings, though her subjects were predominantly human figures.

The exhibition was a sell-out, but more than that it brought considerable recognition. We had made a mark in the established art world: some of my dry point etchings had even been bought by the British Museum and the Victoria and Albert. This was indeed encouraging.

One of the visitors to the show was Richard Bedford, head of the Sculpture Department at the Victoria and Albert Museum. He was himself an enthusiastic carver of hard stone, having learnt marble carving from the masons who worked in the museum, and was anxious to help young carvers of talent. Barbara and I belonged to the small group of 'direct carvers', a movement pioneered in England by Henry Moore, whose aim was to return to the old tradition of carving directly in the material without recourse to the intermediary of the clay model: i.e., our ideas were to be conceived in stone and cut directly out of the block. There is a lot of sound sense in this principle. It is obviously best to think in the material in which one is going to work, for the processes by which one arrives at the final object in a particular medium differ radically from those used in any other. With clay you are working in a soft material which you're building up from nothing; with stone in a hard material, cutting down to the object. Bedford was himself passionately interested in these ideas, and a great admirer of the work of Gaudier Brzeska and Modigliani, two of their earliest exponents. He took Barbara and myself under his wing, along with other members of the group, including Henry Moore, Morris Lambert and Alan Durst, and exerted himself with great generosity – never sufficiently repaid – to put us on the map. It was he who introduced us to the wealthy collectors of the time: George Eumorphopolis, one of my first patrons, who bought from me the marble bust I carved of Barbara in Rome, Sir Michael Sadler and Sir George Hill, amongst others.

Meanwhile in the wake of artistic recognition came social acceptability. In this sphere I, for one, was on shaky ground. My first experiences were not calculated to increase my confidence. Sir George Hill had introduced me to Captain Spencer Churchill, who had a large collection of valuable works of art. He also became a patron of mine, and bought several of my small bronzes and drawings. One day he invited me to stay with him at Blockley

Park, where his collection was housed, in order that I might see them *in situ*.

This promised to be a somewhat hair-raising experience, as Churchill was an arch-snob, and my own upbringing could not have been less conducive to coping with life in high circles. I really did not know what was or was not done in the homes of the landed gentry, and Blockley was about the worst school I could have chosen for elementary training in these matters. However, I was not going to admit this even to myself, and I put on a brave front – an attitude which was bound to lead to disaster.

Churchill was an expert fly fisherman and used to lecture on tying flies and other refinements of the sport. One morning after breakfast he asked me if I would like to fish in the lake on the estate, which was stocked with rainbow trout. I readily accepted this invitation, thinking of a bent pin and a tin of worms, but when Churchill produced a fly rod and a box of flies I realized that I was taking on something of which I had no knowledge or experience. However, I managed to think of a face-saver, which was to say to Churchill that, knowing he was a great expert, I would very much like to see how he tied the fly on the cast, and what kind of knot he used. The only knot I knew was a 'granny'.

Obviously flattered, he did as I had asked, and duly equipped I sallied forth across the park, where his famous herd of shorthorn cattle were grazing. Once down by the lakeside I started to survey the situation, and noticed that about thirty feet out from the bank there were plenty of large fish rising to the hatch of flies which were coming out on this lovely sunny morning. With a terrific swish of the rod I tried to cast the fly in their direction. It wobbled out in an untidy manner and settled with a splash some six feet in front of me. I made more violent efforts to get my line to go further out, failing to observe that an inquisitive cow was standing not far behind me absorbed in watching my wild and inexplicable movements. One particularly strenuous effort succeeded in foul-hooking the cow and she went off at a canter, the line streaming out behind her until finally the cast broke.

Not dismayed, at least not as much as I should have been, I got another cast out of the box. My memory served me well and I managed to tie on the fly in the way Churchill had shown me. But by now my thrashing of the water had driven all the fish from the area, so I decided to move off to a smaller pond which looked more promising, teeming as it was with fish, who were congregated by the bank in such vast numbers as to look almost like a race crowd. They were not so big as the ones in the other lake, indeed they were quite small, but they seemed less timid and were much closer to the bank.

It seemed unnecessary to make any energetic casts, so I settled for the simple method of dipping the fly on the surface of the water and waiting. I didn't have to wait long, for almost before the fly touched the water about twenty fish jumped out at the

hook. One of them managed to secure the bait, and removing it from the hook I proceeded in a like manner until I had caught about ten of them and laid them out beside me on the grass. As I removed the last fish something made me turn my head. Standing behind me was a man in a green tweed suit and knee breeches, with a very red face, who said to me: 'What do you think you are doing here?' I explained that I was a guest at the house and had been given the Captain's permission to fish, at which he inquired in an icy tone, 'In the hatchery?'

My confusion and embarrassment could not be overstated. Little did I know that this was only the beginning of the Churchill saga, which was to end some months later in real disaster.

Churchill bred Labrador dogs, and he was expecting a litter from a bitch who had been mated by his many-time champion stud dog. He offered to give me one of the puppies when they were three months old if I would come down to collect it. Gratified by his offer I accepted, although I had no use for such an animal and nowhere to house it. I suggested to a farmer friend of mine that he keep it on his farm and train it as a gun dog, and when the time came to fetch the puppy we went down together to Blockley in his car.

We arrived at the house and rang the bell, and the door was opened by a liveried footman who asked for our names and then disappeared upstairs. On his return he drew me aside and said: 'The Captain would like to know who your friend is, Sir.' I told him that he was a farmer who had come with me to collect the puppy. The footman disappeared again and returned this time with the message: 'Captain Churchill says will you go upstairs to his study, and your farmer friend can come with me to the servants' hall where he will have his lunch.' I was mortified, particularly as 'my farmer friend' was an ex-public school boy and far more of a gent than I was. Seeing that my relationship with Churchill was already fairly compromised I faced the situation head on and stated that if my friend was to eat in the servants' hall I would be forced to join him there. Would the footman please deliver this message to the Captain with my respects. The reply came immediately that we were both to go up to his study.

Churchill himself was no less embarrassed when he realized the gaffe he had made in suggesting that this boy be sent to the kitchen. He put himself out to rectify the situation but his efforts were of little avail, as the embarrassment to all three of us had by now reached unmanageable proportions. After a lunch which nearly choked us, despite the excellence of the food, he asked as a parting gesture of goodwill if we would like to see round his collection, which was a very fine one indeed, boasting several Rembrandts, some early Greek bronzes and a set of rare Chinese porcelain reputedly priceless. I believe that his collection fetched over £4m. when sold at auction after his death.

The gallery was beautifully kept. The highly polished parquet floor was scattered with magnificent Chinese rugs interspersed at intervals along the walls with frail Chinese tables displaying the most exquisite Ming vases. Churchill had recently imported from America a special lamp which threw a strong light on to a picture without causing reflection off the glass. He was very proud of this lamp, the only example of its kind in England, and as he went from picture to picture he plugged it in, trailing the flex on the floor behind him.

I had by this time recovered some of my composure, but my friend had not. Moving forward to take a closer look at a picture he slipped on the polished floor and caught his legs in the cable of the lamp, which was wrenched from Churchill's hand and smashed to the ground. Meanwhile, in an attempt to save himself, he made a wild grab in space, and fastening on a small table standing near at hand, on which a particularly beautiful Ming vase was displayed, he brought it down with a crash. The vase exploded on the ground into a thousand pieces.

Out of the corner of my eye I caught a last glimpse of Churchill standing like a white marble statue, completely immobilized by the shock. There was nothing for it. My friend gathered himself up off the floor, and we both shot out of the gallery at high speed, making for the kennels. Before news of the disaster could spread we had claimed the puppy and departed at all the thirty miles an hour of which my friend's car was capable.

It was some forty years before I saw Churchill again, which is not altogether surprising. We met in St James's shortly before his death; he must have been about eighty years old. His memory had apparently failed, or perhaps he had reached the age when few things seem important, for he was obviously pleased to see me and enquired why I had not been to visit him for so many years.

Luckily, our position in the artistic world was unaffected by cataclysms of this kind – artists are, thank God, expected to behave badly. Within a couple of years of our return to England our reputation as leaders of the modern movement in sculpture was assured. Bedford worked continuously on our behalf. Indeed, it was largely due to his efforts that recognition came to the movement as early as it did, for there was still a good deal of academic opposition.

In the spring of 1928 we held a second joint exhibition, this time at Tooth's Gallery in Bond Street. The second show, like the first, was a sell-out. Finding ourselves in the money for the first time, we moved to a better studio on Primrose Hill Road, close to Henry Moore's.

As near neighbours we began to see a great deal of each other. Harry had married a Russian girl, Irena, a student at the Royal College, and the four of us would often hire a model for an evening's drawing in our studio. In the summer we rented a cottage together at Happisburgh in Norfolk along with my old friend Douglas Jenkins and his wife. It was always a pleasure to be with Moore, for he was not only a remarkable draughtsman but a very nice chap indeed.

Barbara and I were now members of 'The London Group' and the newly formed 'Seven and Five' – a group of seven painters and five sculptors, all of them direct carvers, one of whom was of course Moore. Most of the distinguished younger artists of the day belonged to either one or the other of these societies. It was at this point in our careers that Herbert Read began to take an interest in us. Formerly head of the Ceramics Department at the Victoria and Albert Museum, he had left the museum wanting, like Bedford, to take a more active part in the art scene, and was busily making a name for himself as an art critic and essayist. He began, as Bedford had done, to back the younger set of up-and-coming artists, giving them write-ups in his book on contemporary art, *Art Now*. He did have a certain amount of taste, as well as sense, for he hitched his wagon to such sure winners as Barbara, Harry and Ben Nicholson. For my part I distrusted him – his style of writing struck me as a specious use of pseudo-intellectual jargon. Admittedly I was prejudiced against him from the start simply in his role as a critic, for I have always felt strongly that the more one talks about Art, the further away from it one gets. I go along in this with J. M. W. Turner, whose only known comment on the subject was: 'Art is a rum go.' But more than that, I felt instinctively that this man was dictating to us what to do. It didn't worry the others, but it grated increasingly on me.

The relationship between Read, fast establishing a position for himself as the foremost art critic of the day, and his young protégés tipped by him to be the foremost artists of the future, had all the elements of a back-scratching operation. As my dis-satisfaction grew I began to notice features of the modern movement, which at the height of my enthusiasm I had accepted without question, but which now seemed arbitrary and alien. I realized that I had been led by my involvement with it into doing what I thought a work of sculpture *ought* to be like, never mind what I felt. For instance, because Barbara carved her figures with great hefty legs and Harry carved his with great hefty legs, I carved mine with great hefty legs. It occurred to me now that I didn't like fat models, that I preferred women with graceful, slim figures. I wanted to break out of the charmed circle, to get back to what it was that *I* wanted. Naturally it was splendid to be taken up by the critics and hailed as a member of the great modern movement – it was very good for sales – but in the end I rebelled against it. Breaking off all my previous connections I resigned from both 'The London Group' and the 'Seven and Five'.

Since my return from Italy I had met up again with Eddie Marsh, Private Secretary to Winston Churchill, who had bought one of my first animal drawings when I was on the travelling scholarship in Rome. He came to my first exhibition at the Bruton

Galleries where he bought some more works of mine – a couple of my small sculptures of birds and some drawings. Eddie was a great collector of art and artists, and we soon became friends. He would invite me to the parties he gave in his apartment at the Inner Temple which was covered from floor to ceiling with paintings – even the lavatory door was covered back and front – all of them by contemporary artists whom he had patronized when they were young: Paul and John Nash, Edward Wadsworth, Stanley Spencer, Christopher Wood, Lett Haynes, Cedric Morris. Many of the artists would be present in person, on show alongside their pictures. I found the company of these people far more congenial than that of my old associates. Eddie's friends were less serious; more gay, in every sense of the word. Being himself a queer, his parties were a natural focus for all the famous 'queens' of the day. It was at his apartment that I met many of the great theatrical personalities – Ivor Novello, Ernest Thesiger, John Gielgud, Noel Coward, all of them, as can be expected, most entertaining.

He also introduced me to James Agate, the *Sunday Times* theatre critic, a notorious character and bosom friend of 'Bella of Barnet'. Agate bred hackney ponies, of which his friend 'Bella' was considered the great judge at the time. This interest constituted the sole basis of my friendship with the two. 'Bella' led a turbulent existence, being almost always in trouble on account of his practice of approaching young guardsmen in public conveniences with evil intent. I rarely saw him without either a black eye or a large piece of sticking plaster adhering to his face, covering up some injury inflicted by the straight left of an unco-operative grenadier.

Agate's villainies were more of a professional nature. One night I was dining with him at his house, when towards the end of the meal he suddenly remembered: 'Oh dear, I should be at a first night tonight – eat up and we will go.' We finished the meal and left, arriving at the theatre at the beginning of the second act. I did not have time to find out what the play was about, for after five minutes Agate was complaining, 'This is boring. Come on, we'll go to the Club.' The next day a scathing review appeared condemning the play in its entirety. The incident did little to temper my inherent suspicion of people of this calling.

Cedric introduced me to Lady Ottoline Morrell, and it was at her Thursday afternoon tea parties that I met the intellectual élite of the day, people I should never otherwise have had the chance of knowing: the Sitwells, the Stracheys, Leonard and Virginia Woolf, Rebecca West, Bertrand Russell and many other distinguished people.

Ottoline Morrell loved people. They were her dominant interest in life. She took a great interest and delight in helping her guests with their emotional problems, which were legion in such a heterogeneous community of artists, writers, poets, philosophers and men of letters. She would always make a point of inviting three or four young people of talent who were trying to make their way in the world, to give them the opportunity of meeting men and women of distinction and importance. She had a genius for bringing these people together on an equal footing, whatever their social background may have been.

In appearance Ottoline was an imposing figure, tall and elegant, with a long intelligent face. I never remember seeing her without a flamboyant hat on her head. Her dresses, made to her personal specifications by her maid, were long and always of beautiful materials, often flounced at the bottom – at any rate giving a great impression of abundance. She was totally unself-conscious, and carried off the most extraordinary garments with tremendous style, even in the street, quite unmindful of the rude remarks passed by navvies working at the roadside. There was something regal about her, noticeable particularly in the way she moved slowly and gracefully towards each guest as he or she arrived –and like the Queen she never forgot anyone's name, who they were, or what they did.

At her parties Ottoline was undeniably the central figure, commanding rather than demanding constant attention. This was no mean achievement, for there was considerable competition from some of her guests. Of the rival personalities, Edith Sitwell probably came nearest to vying with Ottoline for attention. Her appearance was certainly out of the ordinary. Like Ottoline she was tall. She had an equine head and skin like an Italian ivory carving of the sixteenth century, a smooth, yellowish white, and no eyebrows. Her hats were large and drooping at the borders, and her long dresses, of the sackcloth and ashes type, hung down to the ground in heavy Grecian folds. She always seemed to be motionless, like a statue. In fact I cannot remember ever seeing her move, though she certainly possessed what we call in sculpture 'static movement'.

Whenever Edith spoke you could be sure that her words were chosen with the greatest care to give full impact, be it poetic or malicious, to what she had to say. She could when she wanted produce a razor-edged tongue, and I would not have liked to incur her displeasure. Talking with her one day about intellectualism in art, one of my pet hates, I mentioned the name of Herbert Read. 'That crashing bore', she said, and went on, 'Sachy and I went to dinner with him some weeks ago, passing a long and tiresome evening. Finally, I said to Herbert, "We really must be going now, our last bus goes at 12.30 and we daren't miss it", whereupon Herbert looked at his watch and said: "But Edith, it's only 9.15".'

Edith Sitwell became a patroness of mine in a small way. She had a passion for amber jewellery, and commissioned me to carve amber medallions to hang round her neck. I had never made jewellery before and enjoyed the experience. The work involved was very intricate. I carved compact animal forms curled up in different positions in the style of Chinese jade carvings. She was delighted with them and they became one of her favourite adornments.

Through Edith I got to know Osbert Sitwell, who also became a patron of mine. I quite often went to dine with him at his home in Chelsea, but although I saw a lot of him and his sister I never really became close friends with them. They were intellectuals, and being completely unintellectual myself I could never master their dialectic. Conversation was on a rarefied plane, far above my head. There was no small talk. It was either tricky intellectual stuff, or gossip of an intensely caustic nature; so that at the same time as being highly flattered to be accepted by them I was never at ease in their company.

On the other hand there is no doubt that my further education, such as it was, was partly due to my association with the 'Bloomsburyites'. They were always kind to me and never gave me any feeling of inferiority. Resentment of the exclusivity of Bloomsbury by outsiders was really quite unjustified. It is true that they cultivated an intellectual jargon which was at times obscure to the uninitiated, but what I found so stimulating was their love of cultural things and the interchange of views, which was of real value.

My own *milieu* was on the wilder fringes of Bloomsbury. I felt more at home amongst those who frequented its two annexes, the Fitzroy Tavern in Charlotte Street and the Café Royal. You could walk into either of these establishments on any night and be surprised if there was anybody there whom you did not know. Here you could expect to find the active artists, Cedric Morris, Lett Haynes, Augustus John and countless others. Absinthe was not illegal in those days, and it was a favourite tipple of the more serious drinking community at the Café Royal. Conversation was easy, lewd and loud, effectively drowning the music drummed out by the small orchestra which played every night. The atmosphere was decidedly thick, and one could hardly see the Toulouse-Lautrecian figure of the woman band-leader for the dense cloud of tobacco smoke. It was great fun.

But the real hard-core drinkers, the 'pissy-arsed drunks', as they were known, were to be found at the Fitzroy Tavern, where they gathered with the object of getting pissed in congenial company. One lady patron refused to cut short her drinking time even to go to the 'ladies'' and used to remain stubbornly, if precariously, balanced on her stool throughout the evening, wetting herself when she could no longer hold her alcohol. (I won't say water, she never drank it). Liz, as she was called – further than that I dare not go – was always alloted the same stool, which after some years of this treatment smelt extraordinarily like the small cat house at the zoo.

Another patron of the Fitzroy was Jimmy Grant, an excellent painter and self-confessed alcoholic. One day a stranger came into the pub and was introduced to him. 'This is Mr Grant', he was told. 'Oh!' exclaimed the stranger in delight, 'Duncan Grant?' 'No,' replied Jimmy, 'Drunken Grant'.

The world of fringe-Bloomsbury was schizophrenic, elegant and scholarly on the one side and rough, often sordid on the other. Between the two there was never a dull moment. It was characterized more than anything else by its fantastic parties, usually set around some theme. I remember particularly one party where those attending were to be dressed either from the waist up or from the waist down. These people were accustomed to nudity and made their decisions as to which of the two alternatives they adopted purely on the basis of individual pride in different parts of their anatomy. Some of the more self-confident in this respect removed all their clothing during the evening in order that nothing should escape the eye of the admiring beholders. I went timidly, stripped to the waist – as far as exhibitionism went I was not in the running. My main role was to play the accordion for dancing. I played well in those days and was in constant demand.

The stars of these *soirées* were Billy Chappell and Freddie Ashton, both of them excellent dancers with a natural theatrical flair. They used to dance together, improvising steps as they went along. It was a form of dancing entirely their own, spontaneous and gay, which made these events really go with a bang. Billy Chappell's costumes alone were calculated to steal the scene; fabulous outfits rivalling the Bakst designs for the Diaghilev Ballet.

The twenties were the great era of parties, and they were certainly not the prerogative of the artistic world. 'High Society' competed in lavish entertainment on a grander scale, often inviting several token artists in order to put them on show – in the same spirit as the gents of Georgian England would arrange visits to lunatic asylums in order to have a good laugh at the maniacs' antics. Occasionally this would bounce back at them. I once attended a very grand party, given by the elegant, perfumed Lord Alington and his mother. Her guests were all out of Debrett, while young Alington's friends were from the studio and the theatre. These two factions were drawn up on different sides of the room, when at a lull in the proceedings, Tallulah Bankhead, the gorgeous red-headed film-star, suddenly got up and moved across the room to where Lady Cunard was sitting. Grabbing hold of Lady Cunard's dress, a skimpy affair held up on the shoulders by two tiny straps, she ripped it down to her waist, remarking in a loud gin-voice as she did so: 'I always wanted to see your tits'. Pandemonium broke out and the Bankhead was wafted away, screaming with laughter.

The great attraction of this world was the infinite variety of people and entertainment which it offered. According to your inclination you could have your wine sweet or dry, your company 'BM' (Bloody Manly) or homosexual, your parties 'camp', cultural, or extraordinarily grand, like the party given by Audrey Debenham where we ate swan in aspic by special permission of the Royal Household.

'Bloomsbury' in all its manifestations was vital, lively and stimulating; never in any real sense vicious. I myself had been brought up in a sheltered way, but none of these people's *avant-garde* ways shocked me simply because they were so nice. I was at ease with them, and when you're at ease you don't question. Basically there was little to disapprove of. There were drunks in abundance but the only cases of doping that I knew of were the Dean-Pauls, Nappa and his sister Brenda, a raging beauty, who were both heroin addicts. But they shocked everyone, even the most outrageous members of this society.

My introduction to this *milieu* represented an important stage in my life and development, and I felt it would always continue to exist. I never thought it was the product of a mood or a mode, something that would disappear. It was a part of English artistic and cultural life, and to me it was a solid structure. It is tragic to see that so many of the painters acclaimed at that time as outstanding are completely unknown or unrecognized today, their works fetching tiny prices whenever they come up in the sale rooms.

Looking back on it now I realize that it was a kind of golden age we were living through, and golden ages are in the nature of things doomed to pass.

VI

Everything goes wrong

After four years of marriage to Barbara our temperamental differences began to manifest themselves more and more and we were making less effort to compromise or adjust our differences of outlook. I was gregarious and Barbara reclusive. Barbara never entered into the frivolities and gaieties of Bloomsbury. Determined to get to the top of her profession, she only associated with people whom she thought might be useful to her in further-ing her ambitious ends. She had no time for many of my friends. Barbara was very un-sexy and I was just the opposite.

As the first flush of love wore off, I began to realize that we were drifting apart. Becoming restless I looked for diversions outside. Learning to ride really well was something I had always wanted to do and I signed on for a riding course with the King's Battery of the Royal Horse Artillery, in St John's Wood. These courses were primarily designed for people taking up civil posts in outlandish places in the empire, where it was essential to be able to ride. There were one or two others like myself who were taking advantage of these facilities to receive really first-class riding instruction very cheaply.

Amongst this small group of people there was an attractive and sexy-looking character called Eileen Friedlander who was an accomplished horsewoman. A highly sophisticated person, she knew most of the moves on the board and one of these she directed at me. Realizing that my instruction was not likely to be strictly confined to horses, I avoided this young lady like the plague, for I knew quite well that if I got caught in her net I would be a 'goner' and my marriage would collapse like a pack of cards.

Fearing this, I approached Barbara directly, saying that a marriage without children was like bricks without mortar, one push and the whole thing would topple over. We ought to have a child to cement our crumbling relationship. She agreed and in due course became pregnant.

Our life showed signs of returning to its former happiness. We got the evening drawing sessions going, with Henry Moore joining in again. When work was done we would open a bottle of wine and play shove-halfpenny at which Henry was expert. Henry was a good bond between us for we both had the greatest admiration for his talent and he was also great fun. He and I used to fish in my tiny garden pond for the goldfish I had installed. This was an inexhaustible pleasure as they would readily take the worms we dangled in the water. They were always put back again ready for the next angling session.

I continued my riding, now feeling fortified against the onslaught of the sex image. Under the rigorous instruction of the Bombardier rough rider I started to become a really good horse-man and this in itself gave me a lot of satisfaction.

We had another happy summer holiday in Norfolk. Henry, Barbara and I used to pick up large iron-stone pebbles on the beach which were ideal for carving and polished up like bronze. I rode and fished on the broads. Henry accompanied me on one of my fishing trips but he couldn't leave sculpture alone for long and took with him a piece of iron-stone and a rasp. Sitting at one end of the boat he filed away continuously, occasionally hauling in his line to see if he had got anything on the end.

Returning to London I really thought that we had overcome our estrangement and I went happily on my way, working and riding. I started to get a few rides in small races at country meetings which meant my being away from home quite often. Barbara followed her own way of life and, despite being pregnant, worked just as hard as ever.

There was, however, still a basic difference in our characters, and as time went on she showed a marked indifference towards myself and my way of life. I had a riding accident which kept me in bed for a week and in consequence I couldn't look after or feed the wire-haired terrier that I had bought as a puppy some months before. Whilst in bed I overheard Barbara talking on the telephone in the next room. She was speaking to a vet and was asking him if he would put my dog to sleep if she brought him round. I shot out of bed as fast as I could and in a violent temper told Barbara in no mean terms what I thought about her, not taking into account, of course, that her strange behaviour may well have been due to her condition, and that she felt unable to cope with the dog. We were back at square one again. Although very distressed I tried to keep the peace. This was indeed difficult, particularly when I found out that Barbara had slept with a mutual friend of ours.

I didn't tax her with this until some time after Paul was born in August 1929 since there was still a slender hope that the advent of a child might bring us closer together. This hope was short-lived. Barbara got a nurse for the child more or less to take him off her hands so that she could get on with her work. She was determined that nothing should interfere with her sculpture and her progress towards her final goal, the top. In desperation I challenged her about her affair with our mutual friend. She readily admitted that my accusations were justified.

From then on I made no further efforts at reconciliation and went my own way, putting in more and more time at the riding school. I no longer tried to resist the onslaught of Eileen which I now found to be a welcome diversion. Our riding school was invited to go down to Tidworth for a weekend's cross-country riding with another battery. They asked three men and three girls and Eileen arranged with the battery Sergeant Major that I was to be paired off with her.

That weekend was an eye-opener, or more correctly a 'fly' opener, for me. We were on the back of the beast during the day and before you could say 'Freud' we were in bed at night; as Shakespeare says – 'Making the beast with two backs'.

The weekend over, neither of us returned to London but went on in my car to a hotel in Essex where we spent the rest of the week. I cannot remember what excuse I gave to Barbara, if I said anything at all, nor even if she commented on my absence. I no longer cared. Spending more and more time with Eileen, I realized that sooner or later I was bound to be found out.

Tense as the situation was, it had its comic moments. Eileen's father was the rails bookmaker for Ladbroke's, and with the Grand National coming up we counted on having the house to ourselves for a few days. We consulted with the Irish maid, who was a great ally of ours, and concerted plans. His departure was planned for seven o'clock on the evening before the big race. At ten past seven I was around at the house, where Eileen was waiting to let me in. Delighted with the success of our venture so far, we celebrated Dad's departure with some drinks, and then moved upstairs to Eileen's bedroom, where she had a gramophone. She had a big collection of jazz and dance records, and on a drunken inspiration we stripped off to execute some exotic dances to 'La Comparsita'.

So engrossed were we in this performance that we did not hear the front door open. By the time we came to our senses someone was stumbling up the stairs screaming out 'Eileen!' The voice was horribly familiar – it was her father. In a flash I grabbed my clothes and jumped out of the window, landing in a rose bush. It was very cold. Wildly, without really knowing what I was doing, I rushed into St John's Wood Park with my clothes under my arm. When I got to the gate, a taxi was going past. I hailed it, waving my clothes in the air to attract attention. The driver, completely unmoved, drew up and asked, 'Where to, Sir?' Comforted by his tone, which seemed to suggest this was quite a common occurrence in that part of London, I jumped in, muttering that I did not mind where to, but could he keep driving until I got my clothes on.

One afternoon when Barbara was out, a couple of weeks later, Eileen and I met in my studio for a return match. God knows, we should have learnt from the disastrous end of the last performance not to repeat it, but we could not resist doing so. It must have been intensely enjoyable. This time we were a little more on our guard, and we did hear the front door open. Eileen grabbed what garments were in reach, ran into the garden and jumped over the fence which divided our garden from the grounds of a Dominican monastery. She landed by a bench where a monk was sitting reading his breviary. The monk, reacting to the intrusion with enviable calm, bid her good afternoon and politely continued his reading aloud while she got dressed. When a decent interval had elapsed, he looked up from his book and asked if he could help her in any way, to which she replied, 'Yes, where's the way out?' This information received, they parted company.

While this example of self-possession was going on over the monastery wall, inside the house I was in real trouble. There was no doubt as to what had been going on and my sins were exposed to the harsh light of reality. To see them like that in black and white, predominantly in black, shocked me as much as anyone. Our child, Paul, was now about a year old, and I was determined to make a valiant effort to free myself from the clutches of Eileen. As a move towards reconciliation I suggested to Barbara that we take a holiday together in Happisburgh, with the Moores and the Jenkins. I thought we should return there with the same friends, as the place held happy memories for us. She agreed to the idea, but I don't think that in her heart of hearts she could bring herself to forget the last infamous episode with Eileen. Her attitude was understandable but I hoped it would pass. Putting on an optimistic front in spite of it, I quit Eileen, which I found extremely difficult to do. Nevertheless, do it I must, if I was not to go back on my promise to make a genuine effort to save our marriage.

For some reason I went to Happisburgh a week later than the others and on arrival found that Ben Nicholson was there, and that Barbara's attentions were firmly focused on him. I could make no impression on her at all. She had clearly set her heart on Ben, and there was nothing I could do about it. After three days I left and returned to London to take up again with Eileen.

It was impossible to return to the studio, so I found myself without anywhere to live or work. Eventually I rented a cottage at Good Easter, in Essex, which I shared with Eileen and her grandmother. The grandmother was a graceful and charming lady, and I got on with her extremely well. Although she disapproved of our living together, she tolerated it in the hope that we would eventually get married, which, of course, was now my intention.

Life at Good Easter was heavenly, but it was a fool's paradise. The only money that I had coming in was from my teaching job at the Central School, and living with a two-handed spender, as Eileen turned out to be, I started to accumulate debts. Eileen, I discovered, had an extraordinary attitude to money. She was very generous indeed with it, when it belonged to other people. For instance, for my birthday she bought me a beautiful and most expensive-looking gold watch. A week later the bill arrived, addressed to me. It was as expensive as it looked.

My financial difficulties were rendered incurable by the fact that I still had no place to work, and could produce nothing which would bring me in any money. Meanwhile I was steadily acquiring possessions I couldn't afford: a horse, some dogs, a car. I had been living like this for about a year when, on returning from London one weekend, her grandmother, in a state of great distress, told me that Eileen was not there. She had gone off with an alcoholic ex-RAF type whom she had met the week before. This was shattering news to me as I really had every intention of marrying her. I was mortified. They say that love is blind, but when it is as intense as mine, it does not have to be blind. I knew what kind of a character she was, but I had not been able to extricate myself. I also knew deep down that if I did marry her the results would be disastrous. As it was, in the short time we were together I had spent all my money and my life had, in every practical sense, gone to pieces. Now, when things were at their worst, she had left me.

Granny, seeing her plan for Eileen's salvation cracking at the seams, begged me to stay. She assured me that Eileen would come back, and that together we could reform her. I was at my wit's end, but I knew that there was one thing I needed and wanted, and that was to be free of the whole affair. I told Granny that I was finished and was going to end it for good. I took my sporting gun and went out into the orchard at the back. I don't know why I took the gun; it was a kind of symbol of destruction. There was nothing I wanted to shoot. I did not want to shoot the mare Jenny – that would have been a terrible thing – I did not want to shoot the dogs. What I really wanted to shoot was the girl, or the spirit of the girl. That was an impossible target. Instead I did an awful thing, which has haunted me ever since. As I stood in the orchard, a dove was cooing up in the big elm tree making that most delightful sound which has always had some special evocative power for me. I pointed the gun and shot it dead. I remember how awful I felt as I saw it falling limp and fluttering, through the branches. I felt that I had hit a target, and that the target was within my own soul, and that what I had done was to kill the last decent feelings I had left.

I returned to London in a low state of morale and broke. My first thought was to go and stay with my parents until I could improve my situation. In a state of profound depression I dragged myself out to Chalk Farm. When I arrived I found that my parents had already heard Barbara's side of the story and would have nothing to do with me. Although Barbara's version was loaded against me, I had to admit the justice of their harsh view. Their own standards of morality were exceptionally high, and I had by any reckoning fallen well below what they expected of me.

Barred from my parents' home I found myself without anywhere to live, my total wealth amounting to £2. A stonemason friend of mine, Tom Gumbrell, allowed me to sleep on a busted camp bed in his office. I lived by cadging, dropping in casually on people at meal times. It was only now, as the floodwaters receded, that I realized the magnitude of the disaster. I had lost everything which I had built up from childhood.

The prospect of living on £2 was unbearably bleak. It was also impossible. I realized that I must get some money from somewhere. The only means I could think of was the well-tried one of borrowing. I had some friends living at Manor Park, and I made up my mind to go out there and tap them for a loan. I set out in the evening when I had finished work and took a bus that took me to Finsbury Park. That was the end of the line. While I was waiting for another bus that would take me on to Manor Park, a group of bookmakers carrying umbrellas and the other tools of their trade joined me at the stop. They were chatting away about dog racing, and in particular were discussing a dog which they said was an absolute certainty that night, that nobody knew about it, and that it would be a skinner for the book. I didn't catch the dog's name, and the more I listened to their conversation the more valuable this piece of information seemed to be. I was becoming increasingly anxious, being a betting man, when a bus drew up and the bookies boarded it.

Just before they got on I heard someone say the name 'Oxford Down'. I followed them on to the bus, and keeping my ears skinned heard them buy tickets for Harringay. At Harringay I got off, and entered the track. The entrance fee was sixpence, and it was sixpence more for the programme. I had just enough loose change to cover this without breaking into my £2. I quickly looked at the race-card. Sure enough there in the fourth race was a dog called Oxford Down. This was reassuring – my information was evidently genuine. Patiently and against all my natural instincts I kept my money in my pocket until the fourth race, but when the time came and I saw the prices put up on all the other dogs except Oxford Down I began to despair. It seemed that my dog was going to be odds-on favourite, and I wouldn't have a chance in hell of winning any money by putting £2 on it. I stood with my eyes glued to the board, and when at last Oxford Down was put up at 16-1 I banged in at once with my £2. It disappeared off the board almost immediately.

The race was run and my dog won it by as many lengths as there were odds against. £32 was a lot of money in those days, and I was able to cancel the Manor Park expedition. The episode is worth mentioning because it reminds me that there were moments of light relief even in this period of intense gloom. Also it was my first experience of greyhound racing. It gave me a taste for the sport which has remained with me ever since.

Whilst still with Eileen I had given Barbara all the evidence for divorce, making myself the guilty party. Although now living with Ben she refused to do anything about it. I went to see her one day to try to persuade her to start divorce proceedings for the sake of us all. Now pregnant by Ben, she still refused to act, despite the fact that Ben was far more suited to her than ever I could have been. This was inexplicable to me.

I went back to my parents, told them my side of the story and was once again re-united with them. At the same time I instituted divorce proceedings against Barbara, pleading the discretion of the court. This posed problems. Barbara's living with Ben was public knowledge, but there was another co-respondent in the case whose name I did not want to mention as to do so would have seriously jeopardized his career. He was not an artist; if he had been it wouldn't have mattered so much.

The whole suit was fraught with difficulties, not the least of them being that my solicitor, Sir Walter Frampton, my counsel and the judge were all Catholics and of course divorce was against their religious principles. Frampton told me that by law this man's name would have to come out. I said if that were the case I would not proceed. 'Leave it to me,' he said. Being a brilliant KC he made the most eloquent speech on my behalf without ever mentioning this man's name and my divorce was granted.

Thus ended a saga of destruction and self-inflicted wounds which were to have a profound effect on the course of my life for many years afterwards. I had annihilated myself almost completely and was left with nothing save for one or two staunch and loyal friends who stuck by me.

VII

Morwenna

It would be incorrect to state that I started life again with a 'clean slate', more accurate to say I had to start from scratch.

Cedric Morris came to my rescue and invited me to come to live with him and Lett Haynes, at 'The Pound', a lovely house on the borders of Essex and Suffolk in the Constable country. He had also rescued my mare Jenny after the break-up with Eileen. I spent my time between 'The Pound' and London where I was still teaching at the Central School of Art or working up at Tom Gumbrell's yard. Then I got the idea of taking some private pupils to supplement my income and arranged with Tom to start a work-shop school up at his place.

The first two to arrive were Elizabeth Spurr and Lalla Churchill. They were quickly followed by Valetta Swan, Marion Stansfield and Marion Hart, an American divorcée. Then came 'Mooie' Lucas, so named because she bred Jersey cows, and the last two to come were Mrs Leonard Woolley, wife of the famous archaeologist, and Agatha Christie. I cannot think why Agatha came, unless it was that she knew my story and thought I might be good raw material for a 'whodunnit'. I can well remember her as a tall, handsome and forceful person but I cannot remember for the life of me what she did whilst she was with me. Of this group, Elizabeth Spurr was by far the most talented, and as nice as she was gifted. She was also the youngest, twenty-four, and the best looking.

Teaching these people gave me the urge to get back to work myself and I started by doing some carvings in wood. The first of these was a life-sized squatting female figure which I called 'Akua Ba'. It was purchased by Sir Michael Sadler. The second, based on the form of a violin, was bought by Mrs J. B. Priestley, the novelist's wife. The third was a larger-than-life-sized horse which Liz helped me to rough out.

This was a colossal undertaking. The head and body were carved out of a two-ton trunk of mahogany, and the legs out of a harder wood called pinkardo which was dowelled into the body. Dowelling consists of leaving a peg on the extremity of the piece of wood which is then fitted into a slot cut in the piece which is going to receive it. This makes a very strong joint when glued. In order to avoid inevitable splitting, I cut the trunk in half, lengthwise, and hollowed it out with an adze. Having joined the two halves together, I proceeded with the carving. The finished work took three months in all.

Liz had fallen in love with me and I took advantage of this as I was badly in need of someone to love me. I hoped it would help me to get over my love for Eileen, who was always at the back of my mind, despite the fact that I hated her.

Juliette Huxley came to the Central School to learn wood

carving from me. She had a good deal of natural ability and made rapid progress. It was through her that I met her husband Julian, who was interested in and most knowledgeable about sculpture and art in general. The meeting with Julian was a landmark indeed and our close friendship lasted until his death in 1974. Not only did I learn much from my association with him but he introduced me to many of the great people of the day. Although a scholar of renown, he had a most delightful sense of humour, with a unique repertoire of really funny stories and a mischievous sense of fun.

Not long after I had met Julian he was appointed Secretary to the London Zoological Society. The first thing that he did was to have a studio built in the Zoo for animal drawing. It was like a small theatre, the stage being a cage, with bars down the front, in which any animal could be safely kept. I had for years been taking a group of students from the Central School to the London Zoo for animal drawing and this innovation of Julian's was ideal for the purpose.

Whipsnade Zoo really got going under the imaginative guidance of Julian, and he asked me to do a fresco of animals running all round the walls of the new restaurant. Above it, he had a flat where we spent many happy weekends together.

He kept two Iceland ponies at Whipsnade to transport him on his tours of inspection. Early in the morning, before any visitors had arrived, we would saddle up these ponies and ride around the Zoo. Julian would give me a scholarly dissertation on all the animals, their ways and peculiarities, some of which he would demonstrate. He would gallop past the lions' enclosure, whereupon they would leap towards him, roaring and crashing against the bars. Passing the ostriches, he once asked me if I had ever noticed how closely a running ostrich resembled a running man who at the same time was trying to stop his trousers from falling down. When I said that I had never noticed it, Julian promptly gave me his pony to hold whilst he leapt with great agility over the high fencing (he had at one time held the high jump record at Oxford) and lowered his trousers, holding on to them with one hand and waving his long woollen scarf in the other. The ostriches ran off with Julian in pursuit. His imitation of their running was perfect. After this performance we set off again towards the flat for breakfast.

Passing the giraffes' enclosure, Julian then asked me if I knew why the body of a giraffe sloped downwards at an acute angle towards the rear end. Adding yet another piece of biological information, he explained that this unusual formation was to facilitate copulation which was executed at the trot. One of the reasons that giraffes rarely bred in zoos was because they had not sufficient distance to get going in small enclosures. He added that if a giraffe was to say 'Someone has run away with my wife,' it would not be a figure of speech, but a fact.

I know Julian enjoyed taking me around with him. I was an animal lover and knew enough about them to understand what he was telling me, unlike the King of Portugal, who was known to be slightly more than eccentric, and once had to be shown round London Zoo. Julian gave his usual learned discourse on each animal as they came to it; the King's only comment was to raise his walking stick, point it at the animal in question, and say 'Bang!'

Occasionally I would be invited to a dinner party given by Julian and Juliette in their apartment at the London Zoo where such celebrities as Bernard Shaw, Arnold Bennet, H. G. Wells, and also distinguished biologists of the day like Sir Ray Lancaster, would be present. I would sit quietly and listen to the banter of their conversation, which was often far above my head and highly competitive, one vying with the other for *prima donna* position.

Shaw, with his caustic penetrating sallies, would always get an argument going, shooting down the statements of the others with some destructive remark. Such was his talent for debunking and exposing fallacy that at times he would even shoot down his own ideas himself. Whilst he could devastate the ideas expressed by others, I noticed he rarely, if ever, offered a constructive alternative to take their place.

Wells was a more gentle wit but none the less sharp for that. He had a great reputation as a lady-killer for which he himself was largely responsible and this, as I was informed by some of his female contemporaries, was to cover up his inadequacies in this connection. One night at dinner, a young lady who was seated next to him, having heard of his vaunted prowess, was making every effort to draw him out, but Wells, either not interested in this lady or not wanting to be cross-examined, was making little conversation apart from a few caustic remarks. Finally, feeling frustrated, the lady said after one such remark of Wells's: 'I can give you tit for tat, Mr Wells.' 'All right,' said Wells, 'Tat'. This terminated the discussion!

It is a peculiar thing that one often finds in men of great learning and wisdom an inexplicable childish streak. Sir Ray Lancaster's peculiarity was an irresistible desire to play practical jokes on people whenever the opportunity arose. His best known performance was when he walked into the 'Fifty-Shilling Tailors' and ordered himself a suit, they having advertised that they would fit any man for this modest sum. As Sir Ray weighed a little over eighteen stone, this presented problems.

The manager was called to explain to Sir Ray that, owing to his exceptional dimensions, it would require twice as much material to clothe his body as it would for the average man. Therefore they would have to charge him double the fee. At this Sir Ray blew up and staged an angry scene, quoting back at the manager the wording of their advertisement which said they would fit 'any man' for fifty shillings. Unless they made him a suit for fifty shillings he would expose their advertisement as fraudulent. If, on the other hand, they made the suit, he would send them another client. They agreed to this suggestion.

The suit made, Sir Ray then sent his brother who weighed twenty-two stone! This time the manager threw a fit, whereupon Sir Ray said: 'An agreement is an agreement, I have kept my promise in sending you another client, now you must keep yours,' adding, 'Don't worry, I promise I will send you yet another client'. Reluctantly this was agreed to and the suit duly made.

Sir Ray, now in his element, took a month off from work and toured the British Isles with his brother until he found a man in a circus in Scotland who weighed forty-four stone! They sent him to the tailors. This time, oddly enough, they made no complaint and fitted the suit without a murmur, but what they did do was to obtain photographs of all three men, which they made into a poster saying: 'We fitted these three men each for fifty shillings'.

*

Life was once again very exhilarating. I was working well, surrounded by good friends, and had Liz as my devoted lover. Marion Hart generously lent me her car whenever I wanted it. I could spend my weekends at 'The Pound' and had my horse to ride when I went down there. But despite all this I was still haunted by my past follies and had not fully recovered from my disastrous love affair with Eileen.

Liz was a great companion and ready to have a go at anything, from helping me with my work to going out at night busking. I would play the accordion and Liz would collect the money. I wore a mask so that I would not be recognized, but Liz didn't give a damn and went as she was. We had one highly successful night when I played outside a pub in Jermyn Street frequented by continental prostitutes, who kept coming out with requests for me to play tangos, *paso-dobles* or some trendy song, and invited Liz to go into the pub with them for a drink. Three-quarters of an hour later Liz came staggering out of the pub with a hat full of money, so drunk that I had the greatest difficulty in getting her into a taxi to take her home.

Aided by Liz I had now done sufficient work to put on a show at Tooth's where Barbara and I had previously exhibited together. The show was a sell-out apart from the big horse. Later on Julian raised a small sum from Bernard Shaw, Wells and some of his other friends for its purchase, and it was then beautifully sited on high ground at Whipsnade, overlooking the Dunstable Downs. Many of the Council members disapproved of the horse being placed there and after Julian's retirement it was found some years later lying on a rubbish heap in a lamentable condition. Somehow or other it found its way into the basement of the Tate Gallery where I eventually had it repaired by Alan Coleman, an expert wood carver. It was then loaned to Coventry Museum for a year and has since been relegated to the Tate Gallery basement once again, where it will probably remain.

Despite the success of my show, the liquidation of long accumulated debts left me with little money. I have spent, and always will be able to spend, more than I earn in the pursuit of pleasure.

I now spent a good deal of my time in the country, whipping-in with the Essex and Suffolk hunt. It was with this pack that I first came across Sir Alfred and Lady Munnings, who turned out regularly. Sir Alfred looked like a sack of potatoes when mounted on his thoroughbreds, over-fat because they didn't get enough exercise at the slow pace at which he jogged along. He was too insecure to go any faster. On the other hand, Lady Munnings was a first-class horsewoman and looked wonderful riding side-saddle, taking any obstacle that presented itself. I continued to ride at country meetings and even made the odd excursion to Ireland to indulge in my favourite sport of race riding.

With this extravagant way of living I was soon in debt again and the need to raise money was urgent. Cedric introduced me to a wealthy lady who used to visit 'The Pound' from time to time, suggesting that she might be persuaded to come to my aid. Having neither scruples nor morals I made an immediate play for this target and made the required score, which was of course a loan. I promptly bought myself a fast car and with equal rapidity dropped poor Liz in the most callous way possible. This is something for which I will never forgive myself. Liz had done so much for me and all she received in return was a broken heart.

It was so despicable that I cannot bear to think or write about it even now, although it was over forty years ago.

Marion Hart was very fond of Liz and did her best to comfort her. I, too, still saw her quite often when I went up to work at Tom's yard. Despite all, Liz never quarrelled with me nor made scenes of any kind, which made me feel even more of a bastard. My affair with the rich lady was not of long duration, being brought to an end by the appearance on the scene of the Rector of Langham's daughters, Morwenna and Winsome, who were frequent visitors to 'The Pound' – known by Cedric's Welsh maid as 'those hot-assed bitches'.

Morwenna was a handsome girl with fairish hair and hazel eyes, about five feet seven in height. I remembered having seen her at a party with Lett Haynes some two years before and at the time being struck by her appearance and movements when she danced. She had been Dalcroze agent in Ireland for three years teaching eurhythmics. Artists tend to look at people as potential models, first of all taking in all their physical characteristics, their qualities and defects. Although Morwenna had a lovely face and moved well her legs were too heavy. She was, however, very attractive, and surrounded by male admirers, so I was flattered at the interest she showed in me. In contrast to Barbara and Eileen she appeared gentle. A good pianist, she talked knowledgeably about Stravinsky and Bela Bartok, still at that time only known to musical intellectuals. I found her company refreshing and we started going around together in my sports car.

In order to see more of her I started to do some work down at 'The Pound', which also gave me more time for riding. I hunted my mare Jenny despite the fact that she was an uncomfortable and tiring ride. She knew only two paces, either a constant jig-jog or a flat-out gallop. I had hurdled her quite a bit but she pulled like a train. Racing, this didn't matter so much, but trying to hack or hunt her was another matter. All she really wanted to do was to run away with me, and up-sides with other horses she was quite impossible to hold. Her one idea was to get in front of everything and occasionally I found myself up-sides with the fox when out hunting. My relationship with the master would become strained on these occasions.

I thought I might cure her by letting her run away until she became exhausted and would then stop. I had a field exactly one mile round where I used to train her. I took her into this field and let her go. She ran thirteen times round it, getting slower and slower, losing so much weight in the process that I had to tighten her girth three times to prevent the saddle slipping. As she stumbled and staggered into the fourteenth lap I pulled her up and dismounted. Leading her back to the stable she could scarcely put one foot in front of the other and once in the stable she stiffened up and was unable to move for about two weeks. Had I not pulled her up when I did, she would have gone on until she dropped dead.

Marion Hart came to see me at 'The Pound' and fell in love with the beautiful countryside. Shortly after this she rented a nearby house where she spent her weekends, often coming down with me from London. On one of these trips we fell to talking about my very sticky past. She had met Morwenna and knew I was seeing a lot of her. She had also heard about the rich lady from Liz. Marion, given to making snide remarks, implied that I was up to my tricks again, wrecking the lives of still more women. I protested that I had given up my evil ways, to which she replied: 'Leopards never change their spots,' or words to that effect. Resolved to reform, I decided there and then to ask Morwenna to marry me. I proposed that night and was accepted immediately.

In reality this was the most immoral thing to do. Morwenna was in love with me and I was incapable of being in love with anyone at that time. After three years I still hadn't got Eileen out of my system. I was thinking of myself and nobody else.

Having been accepted by Morwenna I felt that I had a chance of stabilizing my life and recovering something from the wreck I had made of it. We were married in St Ethelberger's Church in the City, the only church that would marry divorced people at that time. Morwenna's father performed the ceremony.

Despite the fact that Marion hated Morwenna's guts, which I only discovered later, she lent us her car to go on our honeymoon in Wales. On our return she invited us both to go out to France and stay with her. She had recently bought herself a lovely house with a swimming pool and big studio in Montfavet, just outside Avignon, having given up her place in Suffolk, and she offered me the studio to work in whenever I wanted it. Why she invited us, loathing Morwenna as she did, I shall never understand. Was it out of extreme kindness to me or was she a glutton for self-punishment, a masochist?

Naturally had we known of this we would never have accepted her invitation. Not having an inkling of it we had a most wonderful holiday in the land of Cézanne and Van Gogh. Seeing Provence for the first time I developed a better understanding of what had contributed so greatly to the genius of these two fine artists. The sunlight, the cypress trees, the villages and people, the mountains, yes, and even some of the actual trees – the cherry tree, the apricot orchard and the old bridge that Van Gogh painted – were still there right before my eyes. This was magic and most inspiring. I couldn't wait to get down to work.

I drove all over the countryside making pastel drawings of the rocks and trees and drawings of the Camargue horses and bulls. I also bought a large block of stone from Fontveille and carved a figure in it. There is no doubt I have always done my best work on the impact of a new excitement and this occasion was no exception. All the work I did at Montfavet was good.

We were there from April to July 1934, after which Marion suggested we should go off and make a round-trip of Spain. She was, at that time, madly keen on bullfighting, and Morwenna and I both had a passion for Flamenco music. Never having been to Spain we jumped at the idea and within a few days were on the road.

We drove over the Pyrenees and down into Santander, where

I saw the Altamira cave-paintings. Having only seen reproductions of them I had not realized that they were not painted on a flat surface but on boulder-like forms hanging down from the ceilings of the cave. The artists had selected stones which most resembled the forms of bison, colouring them and adding such details as horns, feet and tails, in the same manner that a child, finding a projection on a rough wall resembling a head, will draw eyes, nose and mouth and turn it into a human face.

Then it was Marion's turn to indulge her passion, bullfighting. There was to be a Grand Corrida the next day. We had good seats not far from the barrier, too near in fact, as we were to witness some horrifying sights at much too close a range for my liking. However, not knowing what was to come I was very excited, stimulated by the typical Spanish *paso-dobles* being played by the band. Now I was seeing the world through the eyes of Goya, who has always been one of my favourite artists. There were Goya subjects everywhere, dark-haired women with flashing eyes wearing brightly coloured shawls, men wearing *sombreros* to protect their heads from the sun, which beat down with great intensity into the arena.

Suddenly the doors leading into the bullring opened. The *matadors*, leading the *paseo*, stopped and crossed themselves before proceeding, followed by the *paeons*, *picadors* and bullring servants. As they walked across the ring in their shiny gold-braided *traje de luces* they were greeted by thunderous applause. Having obtained the traditional permission from the President to commence the fight, the *cortège* dispersed, leaving only the *matador* and his immediate assistants in the ring who took up their positions behind the *barrera* awaiting the bull's entry.

A dead silence fell, just as though one were in church, afraid to move for fear of making a noise that would echo round the building. Then the trumpet sounded, the doors of the *toril* were flung open and in rushed the bull. A magnificent jet-black beast, he stood still for a second whilst looking to see from where the danger was to come. For the next five minutes I was back in the

Altamira caves whilst I watched the dramatic charges of this creature. The *matador's* graceful movements reminded me of Massine when dancing the leading role in the *Three Cornered Hat* to the music of de Falla, with Picasso-designed costumes and scenery. The *matador* was Juan Belmonte, making his last appearance before retirement from the ring.

Then the *picadors* entered, mounted on poor old wrecks of horses, blindfolded on the bull's side and their ears plugged up with cotton wool so that they could neither hear nor see where the danger was coming from. Beauty was rapidly replaced with horror as the bull was mutilated with the sharp point of the pike and the horses thrown to the ground by the powerful upward blow of the bull's horns.

The next stage was a combination of beauty of movement and horror as the most famous *banderillero* of the day, Bienvenida, placed the *banderillos* in the bull's shoulders, mutilating still further this one-time magnificent creature. This was followed by the final stage of the fight where the *matador* works with the *muletta* finally to bring the bull to the correct position to receive the *coup de grâce*, his head lowered and his front feet touching,

leaving the shoulder blades well separated, so that the sword can penetrate deep into the animal's heart.

The bull was standing near the barrier, not far from where we were sitting, but he was not in the correct position, his fore-feet being too wide apart. As the *matador* made his thrust the sword, instead of penetrating the animal's body, hit the scapula, bent like a spring, and flew out like an arrow into the audience where it penetrated the chest of one of the spectators, killing him outright. The bull was finally killed and his body dragged out of the dusty ring by two horses, whilst the dead man was removed from the scene. Although I had experienced the height of almost every human emotion during that afternoon I was in no hurry to see another bullfight, my nerves couldn't stand another such experience.

We left Santander that evening and headed south for Madrid, stopping only for a short time for dinner, then on again into the early hours of the morning. It was an ink-black night, the only illumination coming from the stars and the headlights of the car.

It was about two-thirty in the morning when all of a sudden there appeared, coming out of a side turning, a mule drawing a cart with a lantern swinging underneath it. As it pulled right out in front of me I braked violently and swerved across the road trying to avoid it. Safely past, I stopped the car and we all got out to see what had happened. Not only was there no sign of the cart, but no side turning from which it could have emerged! Where had it gone? This mystery was inexplicable. We got back into the car nonplussed and drove on until we reached Madrid. The roads were appalling in those days, most of them being unpaved, bumpy and full of deep holes. There was no danger of falling asleep whilst driving, for every few minutes we would strike a pot-hole which would throw us all up in the air and off our seats.

Whilst in Madrid we went to the Prado to see the fabulous Goya Collection. What a painter! What a draughtsman! His later works, painted after the age of seventy when he was suffering

right: With Paul,
aged about six months.

below: Morwenna as she was
the first time I saw her.

right: Myself in the SAS
during World War II.

above: Potters at Coyotepec removing one of my works from the kiln.
below left: Lupe   *below right:* Aurelia, Lupe's mother.

from the effects of syphilis and probably with his mind tormented as a result, were like the bullfight, a combination of horror and beauty. Goya was a man after my own heart, moved and inspired by what he saw and had experienced during his life, expressing in a most dramatic way all that was Spain.

The following day Morwenna and I went in search of gypsies. We asked a waiter in a café if there were any Flamenco performances to be found in Madrid. Our Spanish was anything but fluent, the only word we were sure the waiter understood was 'Flamenco'. Perhaps in Madrid this word has another meaning for we were directed that night to a broken-down music hall in the rough quarter of the city. On arrival there I recognized the doorman chucker-out, who was none other than Firpo, the one-time world champion heavyweight boxer. He was flattered when I spoke to him, telling him that I knew who he was. He gave us special attention and we were placed in the front row of the gallery.

This was one of the last of the old-time music-hall cafés run by prostitutes. There is still one in Barcelona today called 'El Molino'. The turns were somewhat monotonous as they were all performed by naked ladies who could neither dance nor sing very well. However, there was some comic relief. They all had artificial bushes attached round their waists on elastic, which they pulled out and let snap back against their stomachs every so often. This received great applause from the all-male audience, who were shocked to see two women, Morwenna and Marion, in the audience – an unknown occurrence in such places.

I was given VIP treatment by the star whore who had a particularly good shape and sang fairly well. She had no bush at all, having shaved it off, but she carried a gigantic magnifying glass, about two feet in diameter, which she used with great skill and dexterity to magnify intimate parts of her body for my personal benefit. This required very fine adjustment in order that the object on display should arrive at my eyes in perfect focus.

Diverting as this was it wasn't what we were looking for.

Afraid to make further enquiries in Madrid concerning Flamencos, and there being no bullfights on there that week, we moved on again down through the centre of Spain. We visited the interesting towns such as Toledo, Cordoba and Almeria, landing up in Malaga, where both Morwenna and Marion got stoned for going into the sea in bathing costumes instead of wearing the then customary ankle-long dresses and straw hats.

The rough roads had given the car considerable punishment and I took advantage of there being a Buick agent in Malaga to get it serviced and overhauled. Everywhere we went we continued to ask people where we could find gypsy singers and dancers, and the Buick agent told me that there was a fair taking place at night in the park outside the town where the gypsies would be congregating. However, he warned me not to take my car there as I would probably find it with no wheels and all removable parts taken. Instead he made a suggestion: 'My father is Chief of Police here. He will round up the gypsies for you. You can go to the fair in a police car, which will be safer.'

A rendezvous was arranged, and we were taken to the fair in a huge black Maria with a uniformed *guardia* at the wheel. We were dropped off at an outdoor café, which we found had been cleared of its tables, chairs and clients. There was one table for us with a couple of bottles of wine, and on the other side of the café were seated on the ground some thirty gypsies of all ages ranging from young children to men and women of about eighty years old. They, too, were generously supplied with drink.

Amongst them were some of the most famous Flamenco singers and dancers of the period. Slowly they started to play and sing and move around, and as the wine began to work on them they burst into a furore of music, singing and dancing. The ballet they were performing was the one from which de Falla took the music for his *Three Cornered Hat*. I had already seen these same gypsies perform in 1922 in the special Diaghilev presentation, *Quadro Flamenco*, which ran for two nights only. Diaghilev complained that the gypsies were impossible people to control, and this was doubtless true. A more compelling reason for cutting short the run, however, was that the gypsies' performance, by its spectacular nature, totally eclipsed the Russians'. It received standing ovations such as I have never heard before or since.

On our return journey we stayed the night at a town whose name I cannot remember. There was an English-speaking hall porter. We asked him about Flamenco and bullfights, also asking if there was a swimming pool anywhere in town where ladies could go. His reply was splendid and went as follows: 'Here we have no bullfighting, we are impassionated by the football, we are very modern here, we have a *piscine*, and every Thursday we have the pissing ladies who can piss in the piscine without molestation!'

From here we moved on to Granada. We walked into a café where we sat down to have a glass of wine and enquire about the gypsies who lived in the caves on the outskirts of the town. In the café there were two broken-down pianos with no fronts to them. Sitting at these pianos were two men in their shirt sleeves who, in spite of the inadequacy of the instruments – some of the notes were missing, while those that remained were badly in need of tuning – were producing the most stimulating sounds. The waiter, who was a gypsy, put down his tray and started dancing. After half-an-hour of this fantastic display the two men got up, put on their jackets, paid for their drinks and went out. The waiter mopped his brow with his napkin and came over to us. I complimented him on his dancing, saying that I would not have missed that performance for anything. He replied by asking me if I knew who the two pianists were. I said 'No', and he told me: 'The little one on the left was Senor Ravel and the other man was Senor de Falla.' I hung around that café for the next two or three days, but they never came back.

It was time to think about returning to France and then home to England. There comes a point when one has seen so much that it is impossible to take in anything else. To continue under such circumstances only serves to dim the impressions one has already received.

For one thing I was anxious to get back to work, being full of ideas I wanted to carry out whilst they were fresh in my mind. For another, as we moved further and further north, there was a strong feeling of unrest in the country and signs of the coming revolution.

Back again in Provence we had a last look round, and I decided that here was the place where I would like to spend the rest of my life. With this obsession in mind we returned to London.

VIII

Horses and Granite

Once back in London after the carefree time we had spent with
Marion in France and Spain, I had quickly to get organized.
We rented a charming flat over Hampstead Public Library in
Stanfield House, Rosslyn Hill. I started doing my own work up
at Tom's place and returned to my teaching job at the Central
School. Now a married man once again, life was urgent and I
had to get down to work.

First of all I wanted to find out what had happened to Paul,
as I had not been in touch with Barbara for some time. I rang her
up and made a rendezvous on Hampstead Heath one afternoon.
She brought along her triplets, now three years old. She was
very amiable and we chatted away, telling each other what we
had been doing since we parted. But she gave what was to me bad

news about Paul. According to her account he had become an unmanageable, problem child and she had been obliged to send him away to Dartington Hall School the year before, at the age of five.

At the time I married Morwenna she had promised to take Paul and look after him, but when I reported to her what Barbara had told me she flatly refused to have him in the house. We had our first serious rift over this, which exposed a new side of her character of which I had been unaware. She was selfish and was not prepared to put herself out. This criticism could also have been applied to myself.

When I went down to see Paul, it was apparent that I didn't really mean anything to him; after all he hardly knew me, we had seen so little of each other. Dartington was a non-correctional school and far from helping him over his understandable rebelliousness he had become an unmanageable monster. What was I to do? If I left him there he was going to get worse. Morwenna wouldn't have him, Barbara had thrown him out. I just had to leave him there until such time as I could make other arrangements. I blamed Barbara, I blamed Morwenna, and I also blamed myself. All I could do was to put it out of my mind as far as possible, at least for the time being.

Then came a welcome diversion. I was asked by Gracie Fields, the famous comedienne, if I would go to Ireland to take part in a filming of Synge's play, *Riders to the Sea*. She wanted me to play the accordion as background music to the film and double for Denis Johnson in the horse-riding parts.

I jumped at this chance and Morwenna and I took off for Ireland, taking with us our newly acquired poodle puppy, Pooh. My pay was fifty pounds and expenses. As was to be expected in Connemara, it rained most of the time and we were confined to St John Gogarty's Renvile Hotel. We were there for a month and I played poker with the crew whenever we were not filming or I was not fishing. During the month I won several hundred pounds at this lark, which was a windfall for me.

I returned to England with money in my pocket and a longing to return to Ireland in my heart. I had enough money to buy myself a horse over there. I knew I could get one for twenty-five or thirty pounds which would be good enough for me. At the first opportunity I returned taking two or three hundred pounds with me. Morwenna stayed in London as she did not fancy bumming around with me in Ireland. Anyway, she now had enough money to live on and Pooh to keep her company. She wanted to go to stay with her parents down in Langham.

The first thing I did on arriving in Dublin was to go to see a horse coper I knew in Ballsbridge to seek his advice about the purchase of a horse. We went to a pub and over a few draughts of porter discussed the matter at great length. He was a fairly honest man as horse copers go, but he trusted nobody, not even me. His advice was to keep away from horse dealers and racing people and go wandering around the farms and out into the bog. 'Take your time,' he said. 'Take your time' was music to me for I was in no hurry to go back.

We decided that the best thing for me to do was to hire a pony and trap from him and drive across the bog in a westerly direction. I was to pay him fifty pounds for the hire, and on returning the pony and trap to him in good condition, he would give me back forty pounds. Back again in the yard, he showed me a smart black Connemara mare and a nice, well-sprung trap. 'Come back after you've had a bite to eat and a pint and I'll have her ready for you.'

I went off and did as I was bid. I got together a few necessities for my journey which included a second-hand fly rod with which to do a little poaching *en route*. When I returned the pony was already harnessed-up and in the trap. A bale of hay was roped on to the rail-board and a small sack of oats placed under the seat. I gave him the fifty pounds in cash, for which he gave me a receipt, and a sixpenny piece for luck. 'She'll trot until the cows come home,' he said, adding, 'Be lucky.'

Out of the yard I turned towards the west and away we went

at a beautiful trot. Don't ask me what time it was for this was of no consequence to me once I had set foot on the Emerald Isle. Even the date didn't matter and I couldn't tell you that either. I was on the 'pig's back' as the Irish say. All I know is that as the sun settled down into the horizon I was well out into the country and travelling on a lovely peat track. The pony had been trotting all the time and we must have covered some forty or so miles. It was time to call it a day and find somewhere to spend the night.

It was nearly dark and time for the 'little people' to come out, when I came up to a hovel, the only building of any kind I had seen for miles. It didn't look very promising but having no choice in the matter I stopped, threw the reins over the pony's back and got down. There was no fear of her going off as she, like myself, was dead tired.

I tapped on the door – there was no answer. I tapped louder and heard some movement inside, then the clanging of chains and bolts and groaning like a rheumaticky old man. The door opened about three inches and a hand appeared holding a candle which was thrust into my face. A soft voice said, 'What do you want?' 'A night's rest for myself and a bait for my pony,' I answered. 'Fine for the pony,' she said, 'but yourself?'

Having thoroughly scrutinized me through the chink of the open door, she came out with the candle in her hand, shutting the door behind her, and went straight over to the pony.

'It's a nice mare you have there.'

'It is,' I said, 'and she's trotted all the way here from Dublin today.'

'Is she yours?'

'No,' said I, 'I hired her from Mr Hogan at Ballsbridge this morning.'

'Ah! You did, did you?'

Then she started to take the pony out of the shafts and tie it up in a 'lean-to' at the side of the hovel, throwing down on the ground an armful of hay.

She then returned to me and the questions continued. 'Who

are you?' 'What are you doing here?' 'Where are you going?' 'And for why?' I did my best to satisfy her on these points.

This over, she asked me if I would be wanting a cup of tea. Would I indeed! I was invited in at last, and was seated on a wooden box in front of a peat fire above which hung an iron kettle. In the dim light I could see no furniture or any other sign of habitation, but I did see in one dark corner of the room something that looked like a donkey. Closer inspection showed me that the donkey was leaning up against a straw-filled wooden bunk.

The woman pointed at the bunk saying: 'You can sleep there.' 'What about the donkey?' I asked her. 'Where will he sleep?' 'Sometimes he stays where he is now and sometimes he goes outside,' she replied.

Pushing the donkey to the side I climbed into the bunk. Despite the donkey leaning up against me all night and snoring, I slept like a log.

Very early the following morning the woman gave me a lovely cup of tea and some soda bread. She had already been out to feed my pony and her donkey. When I was ready to take my leave I asked her how much I owed her. 'Nothing at all, at all,' she said, 'and I hope you'll be after having a good night.'

Harnessed up and away we did not stop until eleven o'clock when we came upon a ford crossing a small river, where I gave the mare a drink. So far the only animals I'd seen were a few sheep, one or two donkeys and the odd heron or crow. Life was so blissful that I had forgotten everything of my past life; I had almost forgotten what I had come to Ireland to look for.

It was not until I got in the region of Ballinasloe that I saw some horses. Apparently they were collecting in the district for the famous annual horse fair which opened on 4th October and lasted for several days. I decided to go into the town and spend a few days there, looking around and asking questions. This would also give my mare a few days' much needed rest. There was only one hotel as far as I can remember and I was lucky enough to get the last room. I had still over two hundred pounds left and could well afford this luxury.

The gypsies and the tinkers started arriving and camping on the common. They brought their horses with them and soon there were more horses in Ballinasloe than there were people. On the first morning, by nine o'clock, the bar was packed with buyers and sellers. Aided by a Guinness or two I rather unwisely divulged the reason for my coming to Ireland. From then on I was struck by the great generosity of my companions who kept standing up pints for me on the counter. They, of course, were the 'sellers' who were hoping to get me into a spending mood. With slightly dimmed vision I would be less likely to see any defects that their wares might have.

When they thought I was 'ripe', one of them moved in on me and said he had a real bargain, a chance of a lifetime. For me, as I was such a nice fellow, he would make a special price. Grabbing me by the arm he pushed me through the jostling, singing, happy crowd, out of the smoke-filled bar and into the fresh air of the entrance hall. There, tied to the hat-stand, were two ponies – were there two, or was I seeing double? Twin greys, two-year-olds, as alike as peas in a pod. 'They're beautiful,' I said. 'How much are you asking for them?' 'To anyone else I would be after asking one hundred pounds but for you I will take half that amount – fifty pounds only.' Struck by his generosity I handed him over the money, we slapped hands and he gave me back the customary sixpence for luck.

The next thing I knew was the hotel proprietor was asking me to remove my purchases before the bar closed down for the night and at the same time to clear up the large heap of manure which they had deposited on the flag stones during the long day.

Shocked and faced with reality I started to come to my senses. What had I done?! These two animals had only been handled but not broken. What was more, where could I take them to at that time of night and what use could they be to me? I finally decided that there was only one solution – take them out and let them go on the common. They might stay out there along with the others and that would give me time to work things out over night.

I untied these two youngsters who were by now raring to go and took them outside. Before I had a chance to remove their halters they had pulled themselves free of me, galloped away towards the common and disappeared in the darkness.

All night long I lay in bed afraid to move, for every time I did so it felt as though my head would come off, roll off the pillow and under the bed. Next morning I had a cup of tea, so strong that the spoon would nearly stand up in it without touching the side of the cup. Then into the bar for a brandy and a chat with the proprietor. 'What had happened yesterday?' I wanted to know.

'Well,' he said. 'Those ponies you bought won't be out there now for they will have galloped straight back to the gyppo you bought them from and he'll be on his way to the next fair where he'll find another sucker like yourself. That's the third time he's sold them to my knowledge and he'll do it yet again. They're worth a fortune to him.'

Taking pity on me, he put me on to a farmer friend of his who was there at the time. He told me he had a five-year-old for sale. I wasted no further time and went out with this man to see his horse. It was out in the field and, as far as I could see, a bay. It was so covered in mud that I could hardly tell what colour it was.

Having a real good look at it, I could see that it had good bone, stood about sixteen hands and appeared to have nothing wrong with it. I asked the farmer how much he wanted for it and why was he selling it? Twenty-five pounds was the price, cheap enough in all conscience. He told me his reason for selling it was merely that he wanted to make room for other horses. He had had it in training with a Mr Mullins last year when it ran two or three times in one-and-a-half-mile hurdle-races. It had jumped well and had been close up in all three events.

The long and short of it was that I bought it. I went with him to see this Mullins and arranged with him to take the horse and get it going again during the winter. The horse's name was *Cnámh* (Fishbone).

The meeting was successful and I think the fee for training was three pounds per week, two months payable in advance. I could see my way to managing this, or at least took the risk, thinking that I might win a race, which would pay all my expenses. Mullins was to let me know when *Cnámh* was ready, enter him somewhere, and I could come over again and have a ride. I then drove back to Dublin, returned the pony and trap and regretfully left for England.

Back home everything seemed to be going well: work, teaching and home life. Teaching is always a pleasure when one has talented students and I had several. Two in particular, Ferelyth Howard and Laura Palmer, were excellent wood carvers. Ferelyth was to become perhaps the most knowledgeable person on this subject. She has written a book on wood carving which is a classic and of inestimable value to anyone wanting to take up this branch of sculpture. But I had other students, some ordinary and some extraordinary.

One day I was approached by a Harley Street mental specialist who asked me if I would go to see him. What could this be about? I wasted no time in finding out. He had a patient, recently released from an asylum, who was under his care: a woman doctor who had been shipwrecked on some remote island in the East Indies, along with forty men of the ship's crew to whom she was doctor on the voyage. They were not found until four years later when half the crew had died of starvation or disease. Those who remained alive had all gone insane, this woman included.

During the time she was in the mental home she had proved to be most helpful to the medical staff. Having the confidence of the inmates, they told her things which they would never have imparted to members of the staff. She acted as an intermediary, translating into medical terms what the 'nutters' had said to her.

The specialist then went on to explain what he wanted of me. The woman was in need of occupational therapy and the best possible thing for her to do was to take up clay modelling. 'She is not dangerous and is highly intelligent,' he said, and then added, 'You must encourage her in what she wants to do. Give her no adverse criticism, only encouragement.'

I was not altogether unfamiliar in dealing with unusual characters, there are plenty of them in the field of art, and I felt confident that I could easily cope with this problem. On meeting her when she came to the Central for the first time, however, having previously received detailed instructions from the specialist on how I was to behave, I realized that I had a problem on my hands requiring a great deal of tact.

After a few meaningless pleasantries, showing her round the school, the stone carving room, the life classes etc., I asked her what she would like to do. She said she would like to model a candlestick, the ordinary sort of candlestick which is like a saucer with a handle and a centre piece in which the candle could be placed. Fair enough, she could do this and I showed her where we kept the clay, opening a bin which contained three tons of this material. She looked at it for a moment or two and then said, 'There won't be enough clay there for what I need, I want to make a *big* candlestick!' I showed her another bin containing an equal amount of clay. No, not even these two combined would be sufficient. But on being shown a third bin she said that with all three she might manage.

Remembering my instructions not to frustrate this lady I gave her an empty class room where she could work undisturbed, in the meantime making a frantic call to Fulham Potteries to send up another nine tons of clay as soon as possible. On surveying the large room she said that it might be big enough for her project. She would clear the room of all furniture and make it on the floor.

What had I let myself in for? I gathered my students together to explain my problems and begged them to adopt the same line as I, should they get involved in conversation with the lady. They readily agreed, thinking that it was the most hilarious situation that had ever existed.

As the days went by and the whole of the floor was covered by a gigantic circle of clay, the doctor, now bare-foot, marched about ankle-deep in the clay and erected the centre piece, which was some six-feet high and about fifteen inches in diameter. The work completed, the moment of truth arrived. Would I look at it and give her my opinion? She might have been out of her depth in clay but that was nothing compared to my predicament. I was more than out of mine in bewilderment.

I went into the room with the doctor, as far as the candlestick permitted. It was about twenty feet in diameter.

'It's very nice,' I said. 'Do you really think so?' she replied. Then I went on, saying what an excellent idea it was to make such an object, not realizing that I was being led into a trap. The doctor then asked me innumerable questions, such as what use could a candlestick of that size be put to? After I had made a number of fatuous remarks in answer to her questions, she suddenly turned on me saying, 'You think it's good, you think it was a sensible thing to do, you like it, eh? You must be mad!!' – This situation was always arising. She would lead me on to make idiotic remarks and then accuse me of being off my head. Fortunately, before this became a reality, her mental state improved greatly and she left.

I kept on working up at Tom's yard where I now stabled my mare Jenny, having brought her up from the country so that I could keep up my riding practice. One of my students, an ex-Australian horse-breaker, used to look after her and keep her exercised for me. His name was John Downey. One-time rodeo champion, he had been smashed up whilst breaking a wild horse; then, giving up the game, he came to England to learn animal drawing from me. A wild character, he used to bring his saddle to school every day and amuse himself by lassoing either the students or a peg in their easels, pulling it out and causing the board to fall to the floor.

Then one day I heard from Mullins, telling me my horse was fit and that it had been entered in a race. Would I come over about a week before as he had news for me? I went, and over breakfast Mullins told me that the true reason why the horse had been sold to me was that it couldn't stay more than a mile-and-a-half. It was a front runner and would hold this position for that distance, thereafter it would run out of 'puff' and be tailed-off. However, it was useful to him as a pacemaker and this was to be the plan for the forthcoming race.

Mullins had two horses entered in the same race at Mullingar; both their chances he estimated to be good, more particularly as the other entries were not up to much in his opinion and half of them would be ridden by their owner-riders, 'bumpers' like myself. *Cnámh* was to go into an immediate lead, and stay on the rails, where they existed. As he ran out of steam I was to look round and see what horse was tracking me. If it was one of ours, I was to leave the rails and let it through, impeding the opposition by 'dying' in front of them, if necessary meandering about the course to render this operation more effective. If, on the other hand, it was not one of our pair, I was to stay where I was and deny our rivals the inner position.

This event was to be a big coup for one and all connected with the operation. Our two horses opened up the betting, one at six-to-four favourite and the other at five-to-two second favourite. Our connections backed the second horse down to even money, allowing the other horse to drift out to nine-to-two, since everyone concluded that it was a non-trier. Then they proceeded to plunge on the other horse. The final result of these manoeuvres was that the horses ended up at six-to-four each of two. My reward, for my part in the affair, was to be on the odds to a 'pony', a great deal of money at that time. But being over-confident as to the outcome of this stone-wall certainty, I threw my total wealth into the gamble.

The race started in pouring rain. I got a 'flyer' and took up my position. Once off, the going was like Fowler's Black Treacle, the rain deluging down. I was doubtful if I could hold my position long enough to be of any use. My horse hated the wet.

If the reader has ever galloped in porridge-like mud he will know that the thrash of the horse's hooves makes an infernal noise. Despite this, passing the stand on the first circuit, I could hear a lot of shouting from the patrons. This caused me to look around before the appointed moment, when I made the horrifying discovery that I was the only one out of the eleven runners left standing. Two had fallen early on, bringing down half the field. Running out and slipping up had accounted for the rest. For my own personal safety I slowed down and miraculously kept *Cnámh* on his feet until the last fence. He trotted up to it, slid over, landed safely, and ambled past the post, the winner.

It was well known that his chances were nil, all things being equal, and anyone could have had two hundred-to-one on him had they wanted. As I unsaddled my horse in solitude – the trainer and stable connections were out in the country picking up the pieces, and probably had no intention of showing up in order to avoid financial embarrassment – a little old woman came up to

Paul at the time of my return from Mexico.

The crucifix in burnt wood
which I made after Paul's death.

me waving a ticket, and congratulated me on my performance. She was the only person who had backed *Cnámh*, and I could have killed her. *Cnámh* was sold immediately. In his first race in new ownership he fell and broke his neck, thus ending this tragic story.

I was forced to give up riding for the time being, having neither horse nor money to continue. Some months later I was offered a chance ride at Totnes in Devonshire. Morwenna, who now enjoyed racing, decided to come down with me as she had never seen me performing, always fearing that I might have an accident. The horse I rode stood a long way back from his fences. This had been discovered by the jockey who was on the favourite and, as I was up-sides with him for three-quarters of the trip, he decided to shake me off. Moving up half-a-length in front of me he took off for the open ditch and my horse, taking off at the same time, hit the top of the fence. Both my mount and I fell back into the ditch and as the horse struggled to get out, it kicked me on the head.

Like all concussed people I was very obstinate. I refused aid from the ambulance people, and walked back to the dressing-room. Morwenna then took me home, disobeying the course doctor. For six months afterwards I suffered the effects of delayed concussion, some of which were odd. Once I telephoned the police to report the theft of my car. They found it next day parked in Bedford Square. I had absolutely no recollection that I had left it there myself the night before and come home by train to East Molesey, where we were now living.

This experience broke my nerve for racing and in future I confined myself to show jumping, particularly the bareback jumping competitions which were popular at the time. At this lark I could hold my own and was successful.

Morwenna and I were now getting along fine. She agreed to having Paul come to live with us, so I duly went down to Darting-ton to collect him. I don't think the Dartington people were sorry to see him go, for they had found him unresponsive to their system of education. His housemother gave me an example of this lack of response. During a biology lecture on how fish managed their various manoeuvres, propelling themselves backwards or forwards by the use of their fins, Paul had appeared to be taking no interest, standing at the back of the room with his back turned to the lecturer. When asked by the lecturer why he had paid no attention – was it that he was not interested in the subject? – he said that he was interested. Well, she asked him, what had he been doing all the time she was talking. Paul pointed to an aquarium in front of him where all the fish were swimming vertically. As she had mentioned the various fins and their uses he had taken the fish and cut off that particular fin with a pair of scissors and then replaced it in the tank to see if what the lecturer was saying was actually true.

Horrified at this barbarity and unable to punish him, as that would have been against school principles, it was decided to shame him by making him get up on the platform in front of the class and ask a question – one of a biological nature of course. Without the slightest embarrassment, he said he would love to do so. Mounting the rostrum he asked 'Do spiders fart?'! All the kids collapsed into roars of laughter whilst the lecturer retired from the battle, defeated. When I told the story to Julian Huxley, he said: 'The child is a genius. This matter has never before been raised in scientific circles and no one knows the answer!'

I took Paul away from Dartington and brought him back to East Molesey. The house was large and there was a fair-sized garden where he could play. Like all so-called 'problem' children, what he was suffering from was insecurity, lack of affection and a feeling that he was not wanted. He had every right to protest. He made rapid improvement at home, got on well with Morwenna and gave her little trouble. We did not send him to any school; had we done so it would have put him right back to where he was before I took him away from Dartington.

This problem settled, everything seemed now set for a run of peace and prosperity. Work was going well and one or two good commissions were in the offing. The first of these was to paint a fresco about one hundred and twenty feet long by ten feet high on the British Pavilion in Paris for the 1937 World Fair. Assisted by Michael Foley, a student of mine, and using spray guns, the work was completed in four weeks, for which I was paid the handsome sum of one thousand pounds.

Morwenna's mother lent us her cottage on Dartmoor for the long summer holidays and whilst we were there I made the acquaintance of Bert Gratton, a granite carver, who had his yard by the roadside down in Sticklepath. Seeing this wiry little man knocking great lumps off a block of granite as though it were no

harder than stale bread made me want to try my hand at it. Bert agreed to teach me.

I had cut some hard stones in my time but never anything approaching granite. My first efforts felt as though I were trying to remove the rock of Gibraltar with a tooth pick. To give some idea of the hardness of granite, were this to be measured by figures the ordinary Portland building stone would be two hundred and fifty, whereas the reading of granite would be one thousand three hundred and fifty. At the end of three months I was getting the knack of it. Brute force alone would only break off the ends of the points, leaving the granite slightly scratched. I felt I could tackle a piece of sculpture. Up to now I had only been carving granite curbs for tomb-stones.

Life on Dartmoor was bliss. It provided me with everything I wanted in life. I wandered over the moors fishing for mountain trout, which abounded in all the little streams. All I could hear were the larks singing as they soared up into the sky, accompanied by the ripple of the waters. I could ride a pony over the moors to the Warren Inn where a peat fire burned in the open grate – it had stayed alight for over one hundred years – have a pint and ride back home. The only person I would ever meet would be 'old stony Adders' who used to get out blocks of granite for Bert Gratton. He wore an old bowler hat which was green with lichen, in the band of which he had stuck a remembrance poppy probably dating from the end of the 1914–18 war. He slept and lived up on the moor, never appearing in the villages. Happiness is as contagious as disease. Morwenna, Paul and the poodle loved the place as much as I did and we all resolved to return the following year and stay as long as possible.

Back at East Molesey I took up my teaching job at the Central School. About this time I was commissioned to carve some large relief panels in wood for the Cunard liner *Queen Mary* being built on the Clyde. These panels, representing deer in flight, I carved at Tom Gumbrell's yard and finished off when *in situ* on the ship, assisted by Jim McPherson, who was one of my best students at the time. Jim had come to me from New Zealand, where he had formerly earned his living fishing for shark and selling their skins.

Whilst finishing off the panels we heard that King Edward VIII was to make a tour of the ship. Jim, like myself in my youth, had no idea how to behave in such circumstances and I had to brief him. In answer to his questions, I said: 'It's quite simple, all you have to do when you see the King arriving is to stand up a little distance away from your work. Only speak to him if he speaks to you and then only to answer his questions.'

I saw the King accompanied by his *entourage* enter the saloon. I stopped work at once and stepped back. I was horrified to see that Jim continued to hammer away. The King went straight to him and I heard him say: 'How are these panels going to be treated when they are finished?' Jim just gave him a dirty look and carried on working. As soon as the Royal party left I went to Jim and said: 'Why the hell didn't you stop working when the King came along and why didn't you answer him when he spoke to you?' Jim replied: 'How the hell did I know it was the King, he had a bowler hat on? I didn't answer his question because I thought it was a stupid one.'

Now that I was fully occupied with teaching and commissions I could see a possibility that I might be able to re-establish myself in the world of sculpture, particularly in the field of granite carving, as there was no other living sculptor who had attempted to work in this stone. One of the essentials in sculpture is respect for the inherent quality of the material in which you are working. Because of their unco-operative nature there is a better chance of producing really good sculpture in the hard stones than in the softer ones.

Louis Osman, a young architect for whom I was doing quite a lot of work, commissioned me to carve two gigantic granite tortoises for a pool he was building in the grounds of a house in Savernake Forest. They were going to take a few months to carve and before starting them I wanted to get further experience in working this material. I took time off from my teaching and went down to Dartmoor in the spring of 1938. 'Old stony Adders' got me out a lovely block of granite in which I carved a torso about three foot six high down in Bert Gratton's yard. It was a good piece of sculpture, I knew it. I did not need anyone else to tell me so.

Now at the age of thirty-seven I really knew something about myself – my strengths and my weaknesses. It would be futile to try to change my character but I could make the maximum use of my strengths and this I firmly resolved to do. Had I given sculpture my undivided attention, as Barbara and Henry Moore had done, I know I could have made an important and individual contribution to the art.

This resolve to concentrate on my work did not mean that I had to cut myself off from all the other joys of life. I bought myself a pony or two to run on the moors and I continued to fish and ride over the hills when I had finished the day's work down at Sticklepath.

I was ready now to take on the two tortoises. The two blocks required were too big for 'old stony Adders' to handle and I got them from Blackingstone quarry near Moreton Hampstead. On surveying these two gigantic blocks of granite I could see that it was going to be a long job. I had one or two small stone carving commissions to do – a tomb-stone in Ancaster, and some Portland stone carvings for a building. They were of little interest to me and I was anxious to get them behind me, leaving myself free to embark on the road to artistic recovery.

As soon as these dreary jobs were done, I applied for a year's leave from the Central School, which was granted, got rid of my rented house at East Molesey and set sail for Devonshire. We had all agreed that Dartmoor was the place for us – ideal for Paul, he loved the village school; ideal for Morwenna, she had been given a poodle bitch and wanted to start breeding them and, of course, the perfect place for me to live and work.

The first thing I did on arrival was to go over to Sticklepath and see Bert Gratton and my two blocks of granite which had been waiting for me since the autumn of the year before. Bert and I went down to the Cawsand Beacon pub in South Zeal to discuss the problem facing me – the tools I should need and the best way to tackle this work. Bert made a list of the tools and undertook to get them for me – two three-pound steel hammers, a dozen steel punchers and a pair of granite axes, one coarse and the other fine.

Returning to the yard I sat myself down in front of the two blocks as though I had come to worship before an ancient shrine. Ancient they were, for they had taken somewhere around three hundred million years to form and that alone demanded some considerable respect and reverence. Inside those blocks were my two tortoises, or for that matter thousands of other objects if I chose to imagine them. A mountain of stone contains all the sculptures that have ever been, or ever will be done. It is merely a matter of which one of them you decide to release by knocking away the rest of the stone.

Whilst waiting for the tools to arrive I bought a live tortoise from a pet shop, which I thought might help me to crystallize my idea. Before one can start a direct carving it is essential to have a complete mental picture of the finished work, otherwise one would not know what size pieces of stone to cut away or where they were to come from. The tools arrived, the idea formed in my mind, I was ready to start.

The first task was to knock the corners off the blocks. There were always a few tough old Dartmoor types sitting round in Bert's yard talking of this and that. Amongst them was an old retired ploughman, who, although crippled in his legs with rheumatism, had a pair of shoulders on him which enabled him to swing a sledge-hammer with great force. Bert held the steel wedge in place whilst the old ploughman swung the hammer. The impact of his well-directed blows split great lumps off the block and within half an hour the first one was roughed-out and ready for me to make a start on the carving.

When working granite it is essential for one's own safety to direct all pieces away from the body. They come off like bullets shot from a gun and have razor-sharp edges that can cut through almost anything, ligament and bone alike. One also had to watch out that none of the old men sitting around Bert Gratton's place got struck by flying pieces of granite. They sat there talking amongst themselves and watching me from dawn to dusk, droning away in that lovely Dartmoor dialect where all words are joined together, sounding like bees hovering around a flower-bed.

I let my tortoise roam freely round the yard. All of a sudden one morning the conversation stopped abruptly as the old plough-man got up from where he was sitting, having caught sight of my tortoise for the first time. Grabbing it by one leg he said: 'Cor bugger, this be a thing of the devil, a tater with legs!!' and he threw it as far away as he could. I never saw it again.

Every lunch-time Bert and I would go down to the Cawsand Beacon for our bread and cheese and a beer. One day a man came in leading a lovely greyhound bitch which he wanted to sell. I couldn't resist her and bought her for a fiver. I had great fun with 'Fly', as she was called. She was cunning enough to catch a hare single-handed, and Purse Tucker (a local farmer) and I used to go ferreting with her up on the moors. We needed all the rabbits we could catch as Morwenna had bred her first litter of poodles, which meant that we had eight dogs to feed – Fly, Pooh, Sally and her five pups – not to mention ourselves. There is nothing I like better than 'bunny' stew, but it must be a wild rabbit to make the genuine article.

I found out that there were two greyhound tracks in Exeter, Marsh Barton and the County Ground. Morwenna and I trundled off to inspect them, taking Fly with us to try her out. Sure enough she knew what it was all about. We got Fly entered up for a trial and eventually for a race at Marsh Barton. Although she ran well, she was getting on in age and was not fast enough. Now thoroughly bitten with this game I started to get a few greyhounds together. Dartmoor was an excellent training ground, up hill and down dale, ideal country for building up their muscles. Besides there were plenty of rabbits and hares around whenever they needed a gallop or sharpening up.

I started to win races with my greyhounds. They were better fed and trained than those of my competitors. People started giving me their greyhounds to train, until I had a kennel of about ten. This meant getting a kennel-boy and fixing up 'traps' from which to release the dogs during training. I became absorbed in the training and, getting up early, would think nothing of walking four greyhounds together over a distance of ten miles. They would pull on their leads in front of me and I would watch the action of their rippling muscles, just as I used to watch the plough-horses when I was young.

Even though I was spending more and more time walking with my greyhounds my thoughts were not idle. Wasn't it Leonardo da Vinci who said: 'An artist does most of his work when he is not working.'?

Eventually I got the tortoises finished. I was justly proud of the accomplishment. Although they would never be on public display I had satisfied myself that I could carve granite, something no other living sculptor could do. I made a lot of good drawings of the dogs and the Dartmoor ponies, and turned once again to wood, carving a twice life-size recumbent hound and a running hare. But it was not my nature to give sculpture my undivided attention as perhaps I should have done. I was always too attracted to the joys of living.

Julian Huxley came down to stay with us. He had recently suffered a slight nervous breakdown and wanted to get away from his worries. What better place than to stay with us on the moors? He took up painting and even came greyhound racing, which he had never seen before in his life. This complete change worked wonders, and he returned to London a new man.

Listening to the radio the news was disquieting. Hitler had already invaded Poland and Czechoslovakia. He certainly was not going to stop there. Was all this going to bring to an end my hopes for the future? Was there going to be a repetition of my childhood experiences that black day of 14 August 1914, when I sat up in the birch tree and heard the horses going along the highway? There were my own ponies out on the moors. What would happen to them? Would they get involved in some way if war were to break out?

Horses once again became an obsession. Thinking of them and my childhood, I decided to write a book for children on *How to Draw Horses*. I showed it to William Gaunt, editor of *The Studio*, who was delighted with it and undertook to publish it. It was an immediate success, being bought by thousands of parents for their children, selling in England, America, Australia and New Zealand. Eventually it was translated into other languages, and it continued selling for years.

One day when Morwenna and I were having a drink in the Cawsand Beacon it was announced on the radio that war had been declared with Germany. Although the bar was full of all my old chums – Bert Gratton, Edwin Vegas, the Endicotts, Billy Rowe, the butcher, amongst others – not a word was uttered unless it was to order a drink in which to drown our sorrows. Morwenna and I walked the four miles home across the moors in dead silence. What was there to say? Even the one-time gay sounds of the singing larks and the rippling streams now seemed like a funeral march and the flowers seemed to be bowing their heads in grief.

Not long after this there was to be further bad news. A soldier came into the Cawsand Beacon one morning saying he had just returned from France and that the French could not last for more than two weeks. I could not believe this possible, but he was right. Within two weeks the great Dunkirk epic was under way.

Optimism was replaced by pessimism. It was feared that England would be invaded by German parachutists. The Home Guard had been formed, and I joined the mounted section to keep guard up on the moors. What on earth one could do against such an eventuality, armed only with sticks I cannot imagine. I, at least, was equipped with an antiquated revolver and was given thirty rounds of ammunition. Realizing the futility of the whole idea I used up my ammunition shooting at rabbits. When I applied for further supplies my crime was discovered and I was immediately discharged as a saboteur, even, possibly, a spy. It was known that I had been in Italy, spoke Italian and played the accordion, and that I was friendly with Rudolph Messel, a man of German origin. My playing the accordion in the garden in the evenings was obviously a method of signalling to Rudolph, who only lived eight miles away from me.

I tried to join the Intelligence Corps as an Italian linguist. Italy had not as yet come into the war and my services were not required. Eventually I got into Air Force Camouflage. We decided to move to London as I was to be based at the Air Ministry. My parents had left their house at Chalk Farm and moved down to Epsom, lending us their London house. Paul was sent to H. S. Neill's school at Blaenau Ffestiniog in North Wales. All the dogs were disposed of in one way or another, excepting for Fly, Pooh and Sally.

My best greyhound Slim I gave to Peter O'Sullevan who was working with the Light Rescue Squad in Chelsea. Peter was very keen on greyhound racing, having kept two greyhounds racing on a local track when he was a schoolboy at Charterhouse. I had been given a horse which Peter and I registered together under the name of Light Rescue and gave to Charlie Bell to train at Epsom. Unfortunately all racing was stopped on account of the war and we had to have the horse destroyed.

I cannot remember how I met Raymond Carr, who came and lived with us at Chalk Farm, but forget him I never will. Raymond was a brilliant scholar who had just finished his time at Christ Church, Oxford University, where he had gained a distinguished first in History. He was the one bright spot on the horizon. Brilliant, eccentric as a clockwork orange and delightful company, before going up to Oxford he had played the clarinet in a Swedish jazz group. We passed many a happy evening playing together, Raymond on the clarinet and I on my accordion. Two drinks and Raymond was out of control. I shall never forget as long as I live the evening when Morwenna, Raymond and I went out to dinner at Maxim's restaurant. Two or three drinks before dinner and Raymond was well away. Crossing the restaurant he went up to a couple he had never set eyes on before, saying to the woman: 'How the hell you can go out with this monster of a man I cannot imagine.' There was an immediate brawl and Raymond was dragged away by the waiters and taken back to our table. We were asked to pay the bill and leave forthwith.

We went to Leicester Square Underground to catch a train home to Chalk Farm. An old tramp was sleeping on the station platform under a poster he had torn off the wall as a bed cover. Raymond went straight up to him and started to recite the famous soliloquy from *Hamlet*. The tramp was quite unmoved, but when Raymond forgot his lines and could no longer continue, he rose slowly to his feet and in a magnificent theatrical voice took up the speech where Raymond had left off and continued it to the end. Long before the tramp had finished Raymond was stone-cold sober. He had unknowingly hit upon a down-and-out Shakespearian actor.

Within a week of this epic, I was offered a direct entry commission in the Intelligence Corps, Italy having come into the war.

IX

World War II

All my friends told me that I would never be able to stick army discipline with my unconventional upbringing and lack of discipline within myself. This was anything but the case. 'Bashing my tabs' on the parade ground was a novelty, a new experience, and I found barrack life great fun.

I was sent up to Oxford on a three months' Intelligence Course and general army training. I had had a good deal of experience riding motorcycles and at this I excelled above many of the men who had never ridden before joining the army. Physically I was quite tough, in fact I was a lot tougher than many of the young men in their early twenties; but I was hopeless when it came to learning all about German Army formations. I could never remember how many bicycles there were in a Panzer division – I couldn't understand why they wanted bicycles at all. Anything to do with Army Law or the theoretical stuff floored me, and it was quite clear early on that I was not destined to be a Divisional

Intelligence Officer. But there were plenty of more exciting activities in the Intelligence game, far more suited to my temperament, and it was one of these courses that I pursued. When the final sorting out came to decide where we should be posted, my cockney Regimental Sergeant Major was asked for a personal report on us to go with our written papers. He said: 'Give this geyser something special to do, he can use his loaf'.

I was posted to Political Warfare, and installed in a 'secret house', with two other Italian-speaking officers, for intensive training under the direction of an ex-headmaster Lieutenant-Colonel. After three months of this we were considered proficient enough to be posted. Long before the time came I had reached the conclusion that this was a phony outfit which was highly unlikely to speed up the end of the war.

We were to be sent out with the First Army to the November landings in North Africa. The moment arrived and we were put on a troop train going north to where the convoy was assembling off the west coast of Scotland. Here we boarded a ship, the *Strathallan*, which finally put to sea with six thousand, five hundred troops aboard. In the Bay of Biscay, where weather conditions kept up their reputation, we broke a crank-shaft and could no longer proceed with the rest of the convoy. The repairs took twenty-four hours, while we drifted towards the French coast. You can imagine the relief of everyone aboard when we heard the engine throbbing once again and the *Strathallan* pointed her bows seaward. She went ahead at top speed, and when after three days the convoy and the warships escorting it came into view our joy was complete.

I had taken my accordion with me, and in gay mood we danced to its accompaniment with some of the nurses who were going out to set up the field hospital. As we turned into the Mediterranean the aircraft-carrier, which had formed part of our escort, left us, heading for Gibraltar. Although it was already November it was a lovely day, the sun was shining, and I watched the dolphins playing around the bows of the ship as she forged her way along. We were due to dock at Oran the next morning.

At half-past two that morning we were still up on deck, dancing with the nurses in the moonlight, when we decided to turn in. I was sharing a cabin five decks below with my two companions from the 'secret house'. Disobeying regulations, I undressed completely and put on my pyjamas, as I wished to pass what was left of the night in comfort before the landings next day. Sound asleep, I was suddenly awakened by a terrific crunch. I thought we must have hit a rock. I sat up in bed and nearly fell out, for the ship had keeled over at an angle of thirty degrees. I went to switch on the light, but there was none. We had been hit in the engine room by a torpedo, which knocked a hole in the side of the ship big enough for a London bus to drive through, killing ninety men in the engine room and blowing all the electrical installations to pieces.

I never dressed so quickly in my life. In a flash I was up five flights of stairs and standing at my boat station, along with the troops who were rapidly assembling on that side of the deck.

The crew were Goanese, and therefore neutral. By international law they were the first to take to the lifeboats, followed by the three hundred and fifty nurses of the field ambulance, and other persons who were considered of maximum importance. Since the lifeboats would only accommodate one thousand, seven hundred people, the remainder of the six thousand, five hundred were left standing bewildered on the deck. To say I was frightened is an understatement, for as the lifeboats pulled away the rest of the convoy, including the escort, scattered and disappeared from sight. We were left alone to what appeared to be our inevitable fate. I managed to keep some sort of control over myself, although I had no control over my legs, which were like jelly under my body. I carried out my instructions, which consisted of telling the men that if any of them lit a cigarette they would be shot immediately, as a lighted match could be seen some miles away at sea and we would be likely to receive a second torpedo which would surely send us straight to the bottom.

By now the scene on deck was one of profound despair. After the lifeboats left a great many of the men had jumped over the side with their tin hats on and broken their necks on hitting the water. A thousand or more were killed in this way. For those who remained the prospects were little better, and the atmosphere was not improved by the overpowering smell of shit which pervaded the decks, for almost to a man the troops had messed themselves in fright.

From the moment I realized that our position was practically hopeless I regained my equilibrium and accepted the likely outcome of this disaster. As dawn broke a low-flying German aircraft came over the ship and was shot at with our Bofors guns. It went off, as I thought, to give information of our whereabouts in order that the Stukkas could come out and finish us off. The captain gathered a few of us together and told us that, as the ship had fifteen water-tight bulkheads, she was likely to remain afloat for some hours, but she would nevertheless continue to sink slowly. When the water-level rose to a certain height, the oil in the bilges would ignite and the five thousand tons of twenty-five-pounder shells which we were carrying would probably explode. These shells were situated in a certain position, from which he recommended us all to keep well away.

Whilst waiting for this happy event I went down below into the now flooded cabin and rescued my accordion and a drawing pad which I had brought with me. Back on deck I set about making some drawings of the groups of desolate men standing like statues as though petrified. I even went down the rope-ladder over the side, and taking up a position on a raft made some drawings of the foundering ship. There was nothing brave in this, rather the reverse – it was all part of a scheme to give myself a feeling of false security. After an hour or so I climbed back on to the ship and went up to the forepeak, where I found my two chums sitting with a member of the crew. I took up my accordion and we started to sing a lot of the old dirty army songs which we had learned at home.

Then, sure enough, the horror of which the captain had warned us took place. There was a colossal explosion and shells started to fly up into the air and through the deck, bursting as they went. The centre of the ship became a raging inferno, and the heat began to melt the superstructure, which collapsed into the well of the ship. How many more men were killed by this disaster I do not know. It was now fourteen-and-a-half hours since we had been torpedoed, and the ship was going further and further down. She was already well down by the stern, when our old-timer said to me: 'Don't go over the side until I tell you to. This is the eleventh time I have been torpedoed and they haven't got me yet. That life-jacket you are wearing will only keep you floating for twelve hours, so don't go over until the last possible moment. When you see large bubbles about a yard across coming up around the ship, take off your boots, put your life-jacket under your arm, go over the side and, if you can, swim out fifty yards – that's far enough to stop you being sucked under. Then put your life-jacket on, lie peacefully on your back and hope for the best.'

He had hardly finished giving these instructions when five puffs of smoke appeared on the skyline, and he said to me: 'Those are destroyers: if they're German, we've had it, if they're British, we're saved.' By God, they were British. They came full-speed and one by one drew alongside, firing steel nets on to the ship so that we could slide down the sixty feet to their decks. As each destroyer loaded, she moved away, and another took her place. Such was the panic and the scramble that some of the men jumped straight over the side and broke their legs, crashing on to the steel decks of the destroyers. It was a terrifying sight to see men who had behaved with calm and dignity as long as there was no hope at all become like wild animals now that there was a chance of survival, pushing anybody out of the way in order to be saved themselves. We four still sat up in the forepeak, when our chum suddenly said: 'My God, I've forgotten the cat.' He went down

D.F.L.   K below and brought up a small ginger cat tucked in his battledress, saying, 'This is the third generation of cats that has never been ashore, and I'm not going to let this poor bugger swim there.'

As the *Lightning*, the last of the destroyers, pulled alongside, I and my two chums hurried along the deck to get aboard her. We were nearly the last off. We had in the meantime lost sight of our friend with the cat. As we pulled away from the sinking ship the crew of the *Lightning* were fishing bodies out of the water with boat-hooks and working with artificial respiration on any of those who appeared to have a chance of surviving. I shall never, as long as I live, forget the case of one man they pulled unconscious from the water. They worked away at him until he regained consciousness, when he asked in a feeble voice, 'Where am I?' When being assured that he was safely on a British destroyer, he passed out again. Aided by the ship's doctor, he regained consciousness once more, and he asked another question: 'Where am I going?' They told him, and he lost consciousness yet again. By now he was wrapped in blankets and had been given a shot of some kind by the doctor. His first question on coming round for the third time was: 'Is it true that you can get a woman for forty-five francs in Algiers?'

Eventually we docked at Oran, where we were given dry clothing and food. During the meal a sailor walked into the hall and shouted out: 'Is there anyone here called Scramplings, Sheepskin or Shirting?' As I thought this might be a corruption of my own name I spoke up, and he said: 'Does this belong to you?' handing me my accordion in its case. It had, apparently, been rescued by the crewman who had also rescued the cat because, he said, it had given him so much fun and there might always be a chance of having another sing-song. And that was where he had gone when we lost sight of him on the boat – in search of the accordion.

That same night we survivors from the disaster were put aboard a warship and taken on to Algiers. The First Army, to which our convoy belonged, was to press on from Algeria and join up with the Eighth Army under Monty's command, coming up the other way through the desert. Its operations were, as I discovered for the first time on arrival in Algiers, under American command. The head of the Intelligence Section was an American West Point colonel, who, in my view, was not the greatest expert in this field of activity.

The first thing that he did was to recruit local beauties to work as secretaries in the top secret department. It did not take long to discover that many of these girls were not the most loyal people in the world, particularly the dark-eyed beauty with pearly-white teeth and a gardenia in her hair who was the colonel's private secretary. When I told him with fear and trepidation that she was a Vichy agent, he was furious, and replied that all the girls employed by his department had been vetted for him by the French police. That in itself confirmed my gravest suspicions, for the police in Algiers were Vichy supporters to a man. I was only a lieutenant at this time, and there seemed to be nothing I could do about the situation. Worried to death, I spoke to a very charming American brigadier, who was the chief of the medical section, and asked him what could be done. He was most sympathetic and said: 'There are more ways of killing a cat than drowning him – leave it to me.'

The next day there appeared an order demanding that all civilian employees present themselves for medical examination owing to the outbreak in the district of a highly contagious skin disease. All the girls were examined and found to be in need of immediate treatment. The brigadier had all their hair including their eyebrows shaved off, and their bald heads painted with that fierce-looking purple disinfectant. They all got the sack at once. I think the colonel had just enough intelligence to realize that I was at the back of this manoeuvre, for my already waning popularity declined still further. I did my best to keep out of his way and spent my time doing intelligence work on my own account.

Nosing about in the Casbah I noticed a nun-like character, whom I was told by the local Arabs was a holy woman, addressing groups of men in one corner of the market. I listened out of curiosity, although not understanding Arabic I could make nothing of it. One day I asked a bystander what she was talking about, but he confessed that he understood no more than I did, as she was speaking in classical Arabic. One thing which struck me was that she frequently mentioned place names in the field of battle that were familiar to me. This made me suspect that her activities were not entirely confined to religious matters.

I had to find someone to check on her that I could trust. I knew of a Bedouin aristocrat living somewhere outside Algiers who spoke excellent English as well as other languages, and I made up my mind to find him as soon as possible.

Away out in the back of beyond engaged on this task I met and was accosted by an Arab clad in rags. I was in uniform, of course, and he addressed me in the following manner: 'You English? I have five children, too much, a lot. You give me English half-crown.' I asked him how he came to speak such good English, to which he replied: 'I go to Manchester, Birmingham, Liverpool, Bristol, Cardiff. I sell the carpet, the woollen, the necktie, the rug. You give me English money.' I gave him some money and he thanked me, saying: 'You go fuck Hitler and Maccaroni and Jesus Christ for you every day.' I didn't know if I should offer him Allah once a week in return or not. However, he was able to help by telling me where I should find the man I was looking for. I contacted him and he arranged to have the holy woman's little talks monitored for me. The results were to confirm my suspicions: she was a runner carrying information to the enemy, and she was duly disposed of.

What increasingly undermined my confidence in the set-up was that the head of the Department seemed quite out of touch with what was going on. On the night that Darlan was assassinated we were all in our headquarters. The next morning we were called in front of the colonel and told that something terrible had happened, so terrible that no one was to go out. It was likely that there would be an uprising which would imperil the whole operation. It was so serious, he said, that he could not tell us anything for the moment. We pressed him further on the subject but he would not talk. We could, as a matter of fact, have told him all about it the night before, but it seemed more discreet not to do so.

Despairing of any progress being made on the official front, I carried on with my private investigations. During the course of these it came to my hearing that there was a prison camp out in the desert containing some ten thousand men of different nationalities, Americans, English, and Spaniards amongst them, who were prisoners from the Spanish Civil War and had been there ever since. There was no way of identifying any of them for all their passports and identity papers had been taken away and destroyed. They were in a lamentable condition, both mentally and physically, and half-starved.

When I reported this matter to the colonel he merely said: 'This has nothing to do with us. It is the concern of the French and we must not interfere.' I tried to object, but he cut me short and went on: 'Our landing on the Algerian coast was facilitated by our co-operation with the French, who were prepared to help us on condition that we did not interfere with their Civil Administration. This was the agreement.' It was abundantly clear to me now that I was going to be frustrated at every turn and that what I had found out would be totally ignored. I was wasting my time.

I wrote out a long report of my findings and took it to the RAF Station at Maison Blanche, where I gave it to the CO to read. He was horrified, and arranged to have it flown to England immediately. In London it was placed in the right hands and prompt action was taken. Within three-and-a-half days a 45-knot mine-laying cruiser called the *Abdil*, under the command of Captain Orr-Ewing, arrived in the Mediterranean. It carried a top-secret message for me to the effect that an immediate investigation was to take place, and that it would be advisable for me diplomatically to remove myself from the scene.

I had been wanting for some time to get into Spain in order to investigate a rumour that the Germans were trying to bribe the Spanish government to let them come down through Spain so as to get control of Gibraltar, thus cutting off all supplies to the First Army. My insides were giving me some trouble, so I suggested to the colonel that it might be a good idea for me to go to Gib. for a check-up in the army hospital there. I knew he would be glad to see me go and would facilitate my departure. I hopped into a Dakota and was flown to Gib., where I entered hospital for a couple of weeks.

Whilst there, I discovered that an arrangement existed with the Spanish authorities whereby English soldiers and sailors could borrow civilian suits and obtain a day-pass to cross the border into Spain. This enabled them to visit the brothels in La Linea, a matter of some moment, since all the women had been evacuated from Gibraltar. The pass was stamped with the date of issue and had to be handed in by the bearer on his return the same day. I duly furnished myself with a book of passes and a stamp, together with one of these civilian suits. I crossed over and into Spain, where I was free to stay as long as I liked. All I had to do was to stamp a pass in on the day I wished to return, and no one would be any the wiser.

I got a good deal of my information by working on the escape line along which pilots, shot down in France, were being passed on their way to Gibraltar. Some of them were flown down by the Spanish Air Force, who being very co-operative supplied me with much of the information I wanted.

La Linea was a hot-bed of espionage, both German and English; the Germans watching Gib. and the entrance to the Mediterranean, and the English watching the Germans. We spent our spare time in the cafés, feeding the German agents false information by means of 'careless talk'. Y Signals would then monitor the messages they were sending out, which gave us a good idea what lines to plug.

Not being attached to any unit and receiving orders from no one I was free to do as I liked, and when I thought I could no longer serve any useful purpose where I was, I decided to return to England. At that time the Americans were ferrying Flying Fortresses to England via the West African route, stopping off in Gib. to refuel. I hung around the airfield and made contact with some of the pilots, and offering my services as a flank gunner hitched a lift back to Cornwall.

Back home I was appointed to a branch of the Intelligence Service which suited me down to the ground, for it was so very top-secret that nobody but myself was allowed to know what I was up to. There were the 'high-ups', or course, who knew what was going on, but they 'did not want to know' as officially they would never have been able to condone it.

Interrogation of Italian prisoners was one aspect of the job. I was not surprised to find that they were terribly depressed. They had never wanted to go to war against England, and were ready to do anything to get out of it. I understood their philosophy of life, and went all the way with them when they used to say: 'Pass in front of mules, behind guns, and as far away from superior officers as possible.'

Their first request on entering the 'cage' was always the same, 'When can we have a woman?' This request was a little difficult to comply with, but I managed to supply them with other forms of distraction and in this way received from them the maximum co-operation.

Since we were stationed not far from Woburn Abbey, I organized a small pheasant shoot. His Grace the Duke not being in residence at the time, I was regretfully unable to ask his permission. We selected a pinewood plantation away from all signs of civilization and kept very silent, using catapults – guns were out of the question. Most of my party were Sicilian peasants and they handled their weapons with considerable dexterity and accuracy. Speed was essential, and in a short space of time we returned with six brace of pheasants, one of which had actually been hit on the wing. Although highly illegal and improper, this approach was far more effective than all the accepted Political

Warfare techniques in winning over the Italians to our side. There was nothing these chaps wouldn't have done for me, including murder, had I so wished.

One day, in conformity with my method, I took one of them out for a drive in a car. The car was an official one, provided for me by the Foreign Office, but bore no indication of the fact. At that time private cars were not allowed on the roads, unless the driver carried a special permit for his journey.

We were driving through Luton when I noticed that there was greyhound racing on at the local flapping track, and I asked my charge if he would like to see it. He said that he would; so I hid the car in a wood-yard beside the track, and in we went, spending quite a profitable afternoon on the premises. When we got back to the car at the end of the day there was a man of about six-foot-four standing by it in a grey mackintosh and with unusually large feet. It didn't need all my experience in the intelligence game to know what he was and why he was there. 'Is this your car?' he asked. 'Yes,' I replied. Inevitably, he wanted to know what I was doing in uniform with a civilian car, and why I had parked it in the yard. I told him that that was my business. He retaliated by asking me my name and the place where I was stationed, and the name of my friend. I replied that all the information he would receive from me was that I was a captain in the Intelligence Corps. I gave him my regimental number and told him that he could take the number of the car, but that he could not see the car papers. I refused to give him the name of my friend. Further to that I reminded him that, as a civilian police officer, he had no authority to arrest me, but that he was welcome to make his own investigations from the information that was available to him. I thought that he would have an epileptic fit, he was in such a rage.

We got into the car and drove back to our secret site, but not without some fear that I might be in for big trouble. A week later I was sent for by General Brooks, the Head of Intelligence. I went to London in a state of real fear and trembling. I think I was more frightened then than I had been on the sinking *Strath-allan*.

I was shown into Brooks's office. I had never met him before. I clicked my heels, saluted and sat down at his desk. Brooks pushed a paper in front of me with a full report from Scotland Yard of what had happened, saying, 'What do you know about this?' I told him exactly what I had done and why I had done it, explaining that I was well aware that I was contravening regulations when I took this personage out for the day. He said: 'What made you think of taking the man greyhound racing?' I told him that I happened to notice that there was racing at Luton as I passed the track, and as a keen follower and former owner and trainer of greyhounds, I was very pleased to go. Brooks then asked: 'Do you ever go to the White City?' 'Often,' I replied. 'Whenever I can get up to London.' At this he pulled open a drawer in his desk which was full of White City race-cards, and drawing one out he said, 'Were you at the White City when this favourite ran such an appalling race?' I said that I was indeed there, and had lost my money on this particular dog. 'So did I,' said Brooks. 'If ever I saw a dog "stuffed" it was this one.'

He rang a bell, and a corporal entered. 'Bring in some whisky,' said Brooks. That done, we sat down to a good half-hour's talk about greyhound racing. Then Brooks said to me, 'What was it you came to see me about?' I pointed to the paper from Scotland Yard lying under a pile of race-cards and said, 'It was about this, Sir.' Brooks snorted, took out his pen, wrote across the form: 'Mind your own bloody business,' and dumped it in the out-tray.

I said goodbye to the general with increased confidence in my ability to get out of any situation, no matter what. I felt prepared to take even greater risks in future.

As our house was 'secret' we were entirely cut off from the rest of the world and had no social life. Although I was probably not so keen as the Italians were on finding women, I, too, was longing for some female society. I did have a girl friend, a tiny little thing, also in Intelligence, and I was dying to be able to spend an evening with her. Talking to the Italians one day about the womanizing problem, I mentioned her, and happened to describe how small she was. They interrupted me at once, saying, 'Oh, that's fine, we can get her in for you. We can put her in the laundry-basket.' I said, 'Do you really think we can do it?' They were captivated by the idea, and said: 'Come on, let's have a go.' The girl was consulted and she was willing to try – she was a splendid person and would have a crack at anything. So it was arranged, and the next time the prisoners and I went to collect the laundry we removed the contents of the basket, put the girl in their place, and covering her over with a few bits of linen carried her off back to the 'secret house'. There we were confronted at the door by the colonel, who seeing us struggling with this heavy load generously gave us a hand with it upstairs. God alone knows what would have happened had he known what was inside, but she never made a squeak.

Work increased and I was in need of a multi-lingual secretary, knowledgeable in matters concerning Intelligence work. Having applied to the Foreign Office I was called to London to interview a girl they thought might fit in well with my organization. I was ushered into a room where there were three people seated behind a desk. Two of them were Italian, while the person seated in the middle was the girl I had to interview. What I could see of her I found most pleasing. She had prematurely grey hair, being only twenty-three years of age, and although thin and hungry looking she was very shapely where it mattered most to me. As I explained what was expected of her, with certain reservations, I took stock of everything. She had large bluish eyes which stared straight at me and a strong nose. She was rather timid but I could see behind this screen an intelligent, vivacious person who would be ready to have a go at everything. Her name was Margery Scott. I engaged her there and then.

'Maggie' was a great success with my Italians, and also a steadying influence on me, which was a good thing. We all got on like a house on fire. But the work had become routine, and after six months I began to tire of constantly having to think up new ideas. In addition I found the security side was becoming a great strain on my nerves. I made several efforts to get out, but the security types were reluctant to release me. I knew too much to be let go. The only road open was to join a paratroop outfit, as they were known to be badly in need of men. I knew Colonel Ian Collins, the head of SAS, and he arranged for me to transfer to this splendid outfit.

During the early days of my association with SAS I spent a great deal of my time out at First British Airborne Corps Headquarters at Moor Park. General 'Boy' Browning was in command there, a fine man with an ingenious sense of humour which set the tone for my future experiences with SAS.

One day a Jewish gentleman, dressed up immaculately as a major, arrived at headquarters and explained to the general that he was a psychiatrist come to investigate the psychosis in parachutists of refusal to jump. Browning asked him if he had ever had any experience of jumping himself, to which he replied that he had not. He assured the general that it was not necessary, as he could get all the information he required by interrogating men who had themselves refused.

Browning said: 'But how on earth can you get anywhere with this project unless you have jumped yourself and witnessed at first hand how these men react?'

The major still protesting that personal experience was quite unnecessary, Browning went on: 'For a start the troopers will be most unlikely to talk to you as an officer, still more as one who has had no personal experience himself. You would be most suspect.' He then continued: 'Look, I've got an idea. You'll go up to Ringway, our training airfield in Manchester. We'll dress you up as a trooper and you will go up with a stick on a training flight. You'll be number five. When it comes to your turn to jump, you refuse; then you'll be able to observe what effect your refusal has on the man who is to follow you.' This idea struck the major as a good one and he readily accepted.

The day arrived and the major went up to Ringway. He took up his number five position, as arranged, and they became airborne. When they reached the dropping zone the first man was ordered to jump: 'Number one, jump!' He did. 'Number two, jump!' and away he went; and so on until it came to our major's turn. When the despatcher said, 'Number five, jump!' number five refused in a hysterical way, saying 'I can't jump, I can't jump.' Whereupon number six put his foot up number five's arse and, kicking him out of the plane, said: 'You fucking well can!' The major's descent was the last we saw of him.

Working with SAS was more like being on the music-hall stage than in the army. It was an enlarged form of *The Crazy Gang*. This is not to belittle the great contribution that its members made to the war effort – they were very brave men – but they achieved the impossible in making it all fun. It was a real pleasure to work with people possessing intelligence, courage and a sense of humour, and there was never a dull moment.

I flatter myself that I was well suited to the role in which I was cast. From top to bottom individuality was predominant. It was the one thing which everyone in SAS possessed, although in other respects they were a most diverse collection of characters. Esmond Baring, who was a great wit, heightened the effect of comic opera by coining absurd names for all the principal characters, which stuck. Ian Collins, who was always thinking up bloodthirsty operations for the Brigade to carry out, was dubbed 'Brides-in-the-Bath'; while Major Shaw, whose wife gave birth to a son when he was over fifty, became 'Many-a-good-tune-played-on-an-old-fiddle-Shaw'.

Christopher Sykes was another intelligent and humorous person who contributed much to the entertainment value of SAS. His stutter, which could at times be very bad, was if anything an advantage. One night when I was sitting in my office in the SOE building the telephone rang. I picked up the receiver, and a voice said: 'Is th-th-th-th-that you, J-J-J-J-John?' 'Yes', I said. There was no need for me to ask him who he was. He went on: 'I-I-I-I'm at K-K-K-K-King's C-C-C-C-Cross. I'm g-g-g-g-going t-t-t-t-to c-c-c-c-catch t-t-the last t-t-t-t-train to Gl-l-l-lasg-g-gow'. 'How long will you be away?' I asked. 'Well I-I-I-I d-d-d-d-don't ex-ex-ex-ex-exactly kn-kn-kn-know.' Then there was a pause in the conversation, after which Christopher started up again: 'Are y-y-y-you st-st-st-st-still t-t-t-there, J-J-J-John? I've m-m-m-m-m-m-missed the b-b-b-b-b-bl-bl-bloody tr-tr-tr-tr-train.'

My field of activities widened as I was now supplying intelligence to other airborne outfits including the American 82nd and 101st Divisions. I was at the same time liaising with SOE, where I had my office. In this respect I was in a unique position. So secret and complicated were my activities that not only did my left hand not know what my right hand was doing but no one, no matter how high their rank, could touch me. My office became a sanctum and in quieter moments I could set up my easel and paint without fear of being disturbed. Even generals who knocked on my door would apologize for interrupting me and admire my painting before mentioning the business on which they had come.

Attached to SAS were French, Belgian and Dutch paratroopers, and odd characters recruited from the French Foreign Legion. One such character was Ramon Lee. We needed not only intelligent and able men, but fearless gangsters for infiltration and scullduggery. Lee was definitely in this category. After the collapse of the German Afrika Corps, General Rommel was based on Paris and Fontainebleau, and his movements were known to us. I think it was 'Brides' who thought up the idea of sending Lee out with a party to try to capture him and bring him back to England. Lee was duly despatched, and I received many messages from him saying that he had just missed Rommel by the skin of his teeth. Then there was silence. What had happened to Lee and his party?

Some days later Colonel Brian Franks, who was manager of the Hyde Park Hotel and provided us with accommodation there, walked into the hotel lounge and there, sitting on a couch with a blond German boy from the Hitler Youth, was Ramon Lee. It seemed he had taken a fancy to him and brought him to England instead of Rommel, who was proving difficult to capture and was, in any case, not so good-looking.

The ability required to pull off a stunt like this was extraordinary; put to good purpose it made SAS the unique organization that it was, capable of carrying out operations which no other outfit could have undertaken. It could, on the other hand, in the case of a man like Lee produce quite unpredictable results.

The mixture of opposites contained in SAS was well represented in the commanders of its two regiments, Brian Franks and Paddy Maine. Brian was a kindly and considerate man. Paddy, an ex-Irish Rugby International of great physical strength, was as mad as an Irishman can be. Towards the closing stages of the war our brigadier, McLeod, was replaced by another Irishman, 'Mad Mike Calvert'. Calvert and Maine met for the first time in years in a hotel in Brussels which we were using as our headquarters. Delighted to see one another, they embraced, and then Paddy said to Mike: 'God, Mike, we must have a fight'. The room was cleared and they set about one another with bare fists, refusing to stop until they were both exhausted and had smashed every piece of furniture in the room.

As the war entered its final phase SAS was left with nothing more to do. My stomach trouble had returned due to the nervous strain, and I decided to quit. Going before a medical board I was 'Y' listed, which meant that I was no longer fit for military service. I got out as quickly as I had got in.

I turned in my uniform and equipment, and was given in exchange a 'ready-to-wear' suit. The term 'ready-to-wear' did not specify by whom. In order for it to have fitted me I should have had one arm six inches longer than the other and legs the length of a dachshund's. I wore it only once – to go down to Langham where Morwenna had been living with her parents throughout the latter part of the war. It was on this trip that I first got a glimpse of the twins who had been born on 18 June 1944.

Morwenna and I agreed that it would be better for her to stay on at Langham until I could get organized and find some place where we could live. I then went up to London.

X

Return to Devon

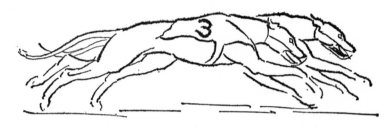

My first disillusionment on returning from the war came when I tried to get my teaching job back at the Central School. Jowett had become the head of the Royal College of Art and had been replaced by Tomlinson at the Central School, a one-time Art School inspector, the sort of man that I always despised and disliked. They were usually unsuccessful artists who wanted to take the micky out of the others who had succeeded. Jowett, on the other hand, was a charming, sensitive person, a good artist and amateur pianist. Instead of an open-armed hero's welcome I was confronted by a cold inspector-minded person who informed me that my place had been taken by a younger man who, incidentally, had kept out of the war, as a great many of them had. I was not alone in this situation; most of the artists who had dodged military service were doing quite well thank you, and those like myself who had been in the army during the whole of the war were disorientated and not wanted, least of all by some of the other artists who had cornered the art world.

London, wrecked by bombing, was a sorry sight, and I felt as if I was a part of this total destruction and desolation. I wanted to get out of it and away into the country where I could hear the birds singing and the rivers of Devonshire rushing over the granite rocks, see the sun rise over the moors and smell the heather and all those lovely things which are indescribable.

I had neither house nor studio, and little wish to return to sculpture, as four years in the army had completely cut me off from anything to do with art or the art world. I hadn't an idea in my head except a wish to escape and I felt as James Thurber says in one of his proverbs: 'If you know of a desert island, don't walk to it, run to it'. That's really what I did when I went down to Dartmoor to look for a house.

Maggie had returned from the war, and meeting up with her again gave me back some faith in humanity. I soon regained my joy of living, and that was all I wanted; to live and to forget. I had a small army gratuity and an army pension – a disability pension for having been 'Y' listed at the finish of the war.

Morwenna was quite pleased with the idea of going to live in Devonshire. She liked Devon and she remembered the pleasant times we had spent there in her mother's cottage. I would have been very happy to return to the cottage on the moors where we had spent a great deal of our time before and during the early part of the war, but Morwenna had other, less humble ideas, and wanted a big house with room for a nursery and a nanny. Who she thought was going to pay for all this I cannot imagine. My total assets were somewhere in the region of £2000.

So Maggie and I went out to find a house somewhere on my beloved Dartmoor. We looked for a big house with all the necessary requirements. After a bit of a search we found a nicely situated house – big and ugly with about fifteen rooms, just outside the village of Chagford.

The name of the house was 'Puggiestone', a corruption of the word Puckiestone or Fairy stone, because of a three-hundred-ton granite rock which lay close to the kitchen window, believed to have been thrown there by an enraged giant. At one time there was a phallic cross mounted on the top of this rock, said to have been used by the Druids as an altar. The house itself was substantially built, with thick granite walls, standing in about six-and-a-half acres of ground surrounded by woodlands and with a salmon river running through it. I thought to myself this is it, this will do me a treat. It had stables, kennels and everything that I liked, and I could see myself running a sort of small-holding there, keeping chickens and a cow and raising my own vegetables and fruit as it had a useful sort of garden. But I hadn't the money to buy it.

During the war I had become very friendly with David Astor. David, without hesitation, lent me the money to get this house. We bought it, the papers were signed, and Maggie and I moved in. Needless to say Morwenna did not know that she was there with me, as I was supposed to be getting the house ready for her to come down and live there. It was in a chaotic state and it was a question of doing odd things and shoving it around, but I was quite happy to camp in it like a gypsy. I was not anxious to set up a big domestic operation and earn a living, which would have meant teaching, doing hack jobs, anything that came along.

Anyway, we were in. Of course the first thing I did was to go back to the Greyhound Stadium. Maggie, like myself, loved sport of this kind, any form of racing and above all any form of gambling, and greyhound racing offered a splendid opportunity.

I took up with all my old contacts – Nat Smith, the bookmaker, other characters I knew connected with greyhounds, and I started to collect together one or two dogs. I not only collected one or two dogs but I found two very sympathetic characters who were working with greyhounds, training and racing them. One was a chap who had been on the run throughout the whole of the war. He was known as Big Johnnie. His real name I never knew. He had volunteered at the beginning of the war to join the Royal Air Force, but was refused, so he said to himself, if they don't want me in the air force I'll not join anything. He disappeared along with many others like him, managing to survive without rations or identity cards and dodging the police through the whole of the war, training and racing greyhounds on unlicensed tracks. Big Johnnie, like most of the others on the run, could only earn a living in illicit ways and one of these, of course, was on the unlicensed dog tracks where even the dogs had false names and identities.

Every now and again the police would descend on these meetings in search of such people, who had a very good early-warning system. As the police entered the track a swarm of men would disappear over the wall, and occasionally an unfortunate one would fall into the arms of the law waiting on the other side. Big Johnnie had been one of the fortunate ones and got away with it.

The other boy, Johnnie Rowe, had been a barrow-boy before joining the Merchant Navy during the war. This Johnnie was a delightful character and apparently, whilst a barrow-boy, had frequented the Opera House, as he adored music and was always singing arias from *Tosca* or *La Bohème*.

Both of them cheerful characters, it was not long before they joined up with me and moved into Puggiestone with their dogs. They, like us, were very glad the war was over and that they could get back to greyhound racing without fear of arrest and live in peace and quiet, if not in comfort. We set up the kennels and started to train the dogs. We used to walk over the moors exercising them; the dogs were happy, the dogs were well, we were happy, we were well. We were living like fighting cocks on God alone knows what. But what was really keeping us happy was the *joie-de-vivre* of the whole set-up.

Paul came down to spend the summer holidays with us and help with the greyhounds and household chores. His one contribution to the commissariat department was cooking stewed apples. Collecting them from the orchard he used to stew them by the pailful. We ate stewed apples until they were coming out of our ears. The dogs fed a lot better than we did. Rabbits abounded and I would go out at night with a battery strapped on my back and a car headlight on my front. Suddenly switching on the light up the side of a hedgerow, the rabbits would be immobilized by the glare and I would release two greyhounds simultaneously. In this way it was easy to catch thirty rabbits in less than half-an-hour.

We also fed the racing dogs on good red beef, which I used to get from old Collins, the village butcher. I went into his shop one morning to order the meat, on my way home from walking two greyhounds that were fighting-fit. Old Collins had just got out a side of beef, which was lying on the block, and before you could say 'sit' the dogs had the side of beef on the sawdust floor and were tearing off great lumps of steak, whilst the butcher stood back and laughed his head off. Having eaten about ten pounds of meat each the dogs were separated from the side of beef. Collins refused to let me pay for the damage. 'Just tell me when you expect these dogs to win,' he said. 'That'll do me. Give me a hand to put the meat back on the block, we'll dust it off and clean it up and the clients will never know the difference.' Both dogs won next time out and old Collins was on the odds to a tenner with both of them.

There was a curious carefree atmosphere in the country generally, at least outside of London. I think all that people wanted to do was to forget and enjoy themselves and not to think of tomorrow. There was a good deal of money about. There were fellows with their army gratuity who did not know what to do with it, except just squander it. There were black-marketeers with pockets full of immoral earnings and bookmakers, as there was plenty of scope for betting.

We were successful with our greyhounds. Big Johnnie really knew how to get a dog fit, and we pulled off some splendid coups. I was using my army gratuity for betting purposes. On one occasion we took four dogs into Exeter to race, knowing that three of them would win for certain, and we backed them all. We came home that night and I remember sitting in our squalid old kitchen, with ashes lying in the grate and the smell of an old, burnt frying-pan, and out of a sack we pulled ten-shilling and pound notes until half-past-two in the morning. Counting out this money we found that we had won £750. This we shared out. Life was bliss. We were neither short of money nor pleasure. I bought an old van to take the dogs into Exeter to race them, and we started taking them further afield. I had really no desire to hurry on with preparing the house for Morwenna's arrival with the children. To all appearances I was trying to do something about it, but deep down I was stalling on the whole thing. I knew that once she got there the Johnnies would have to go and in all probability the greyhounds would be at least reduced.

Finally the day came and the house was more or less ready. All the furniture arrived from the depository in Exeter where it had been stored during the war. I went to London to interview Katherine Graay who had been Nanny to Barbara's triplets. I took to her immediately and engaged her. She went straight down to Langham and shortly afterwards, Morwenna, the twins and Nanny arrived at Puggiestone.

Maggie, of course, had disappeared, so once again I was confronted with a return to horrid reality. What did I have to do? I had no studio. The only thing I had was an old Nissen hut, but it was no good starting to work, I hadn't an idea in my head, and I had no market. I had no contacts. They had all gone. The galleries that used to take my work were not interested. When I went in to Tooth's with some of my animal drawings, I found that they had gone all modern and did not want anything of this kind. There was this mad modern craze everywhere. An artist, like myself, who was producing realistic or romantic works was completely out of fashion. It was an awful shock. I decided to look for some teaching jobs.

I got two appointments, one in Exeter and another in Newton Abbot. These brought in a certain amount of money, but having to keep this extravagant place going was too much of a drain on my finances. I slowly started to get more and more into debt. Morwenna had some money of her own; she was loathe to part with it, but she did, at least, guarantee me an overdraft.

I kept on with some of the greyhounds but I had to cut down their numbers on account of shortage of money and help. Morwenna enjoyed a gamble, she enjoyed racing, and was very fond of dogs. That was one of the things which she had in common with me. She had kept up her interest in breeding poodles, and was eventually to make a name for herself in the standard poodle world. She preferred poodles to greyhounds, as much as anything, I think, because the poodles were hers and, possessive by nature, her interest always lay in things which belonged exclusively to her. I battled on and started to do some wood carving and to become once again interested in my work. I returned to granite carving, which was exciting. Here was something that was connected with the moors, with my salmon river, with the realities of the earth. It was a great solace to me and my enthusiasm was rekindled.

I still kept on with a few of the greyhounds, and finally got an Irish woman, Kathy Rochford, who had been with greyhounds all her life, to come and look after them. She was a splendid character. When she walked into the yard not a single dog barked, not a sound did they make. She was indeed a greyhound herself, and the dogs knew it. They took to her immediately, charmed by her Irish magic.

The twins, now two years old, were beginning to be very entertaining and a great joy to both Morwenna and myself. Despite the past, the future looked bright for us all. Now that everything seemed to be going well I wanted to get my smallholding under way. The first thing I did was to buy some chickens. For some reason Morwenna was not too pleased with this, still less so when I bought a cow against her wishes. She said: 'You will have to look after it yourself, I am not going to do anything about it.' Nevertheless, as we all did, she enjoyed the products of my hens and my cow.

Not unnaturally, I suppose, Morwenna enjoyed success but had no time for failure. When things went wrong or were difficult, as they frequently were, she was of little help to me. I began to feel that there would come a day when our temperamental differences would make it impossible for us to stay together. Always at the back of my mind was the shining star of Maggie, not quite three million light years away, but far enough to make her almost impossibly remote. I knew that there would come a day when Maggie and I would be reunited. When we were, it would be for ever. To be fair to Morwenna I think that her selfishness was to a large extent activated by my own unsympathetic and unco-operative attitude towards her.

Eventually I decided to take out a private trainer's licence. This was quite difficult to obtain. It meant that I could not go racing on 'flapping' tracks, but only on those licensed by the National Greyhound Racing Club. Lord Astor gave me a letter of recommendation, which got me my licence, and I started to train dogs for open races. Eventually I was made a member of the NGRC, and later on a steward, not so much because I was a competent trainer but because I was a well-known artist and so was acceptable to the Club. Furthermore, I was an asset to them, as I knew the seamy side of the game and the malpractices that were involved, as well as knowing a good deal about the animals themselves.

Apart from the secretary, Col. Forsdike, the veterinary surgeon, and myself, the rest of the stewards were 'gents' or generals who knew little or nothing about greyhound racing and merely voted 'yes' or 'no' at enquiries conducted almost entirely by Forsdike. As time went on new and more knowledge-able stewards were elected, until it became a really efficient body.

But the snob aspect was not yet dead. When the Marquis of Carisbrooke was elected Senior Steward on the death of Lord Denham, he was asked by the Catford Greyhound Stadium to go down to present the 'Stewards' Cup', which the NGRC gave every year. There was, at this time, a young lady known as Sabrina who used to appear on the halls. She was famous for possessing one of the most aggressive busts of all times. The first and only time I saw her, she came strolling on to the stage and in the dead silence which followed her entrance a youthful cockney voice from down in the pit exclaimed at the top of his voice, 'Cor'.

Lord Carisbrooke, only surviving grandson of Queen Victoria, graciously accepted the invitation, only to find on arrival at the Stadium that he had this lady seated next to him at the dinner table. He was justifiably annoyed, for he had not been told that she was to be there, and when the manager told His Lordship that Sabrina would go down on to the track with him when he went to present the trophy, he exploded. 'Had I known that this was to happen I would not have dreamed of coming here,' he said. 'Why didn't you tell me? Why did you do it?' The confused and now scarlet-faced manager blurted out: 'Well, my Lord, we did it because it was cheaper than fireworks!'

The Stewards' meetings were held once a month. Apart from going to London for these gatherings I stayed down in Devon getting on with my wood carving. I carved mostly animal subjects, many of which were successful, particularly one of a cow which I carved in chestnut wood and exhibited at the Royal Academy. It was afterwards on loan to London University and has since been lost, like so many of my works, through my own negligence.

I dug some bog oak out of the moor. Bog oak is wood about fifty thousand years old which is on the way to turning into coal. In this I carved a running hare, which is now in the possession of my son Nicholas. I then carved a life-size salmon in mahogany, flanked by two sea trout, now owned by David Astor. None of these works was realistic, in the generally accepted sense of the word, as I was making forms which revealed the inherent qualities of these beautiful materials.

It was during this time that Paul left school and came down to live with us in Devonshire. I found him an excellent companion, as like myself he loved Dartmoor and was mad-keen on fishing. We spent many a happy hour flogging the water together. I had two very good holding pools for salmon and sea trout on my stretch of the River Teign, one in particular excellent, known as 'Blacksmith's' because the village blacksmith had drowned himself in it.

After several months of this life Paul began to get restless and wanted to do something apart from fishing, but like a lot of youngsters of his age – he was now about eighteen – he had no idea what. I got an introduction to Miles, the man who owned the aircraft factory of that name, and we set off one day for the factory, near Reading, in the old Ford van which I used for the greyhounds. We were shown round the whole place and finally Miles took Paul up for a flight to demonstrate the end product of the combined departments of his factory. Paul was delighted with this and accepted a job as a workman there. He attended night classes to study draughtsmanship and aero-dynamics, getting promotion after promotion in the factory.

One weekend when Paul came home he told me that he had decided to go the whole way with flying and that he would join the RAF, with the final goal of going into civil aviation when his time in the air force was up. My feelings were mixed, as I knew the dangers of flying from some of my war-time experiences, having walked out of two 'prangs' myself, but on the other hand I was delighted to see that Paul at last knew what he wanted to do and was as keen as mustard. He went off with my blessing, and that was that. He joined, and was sent to South Africa to an Elementary Training Flying School.

I missed Paul's company very much, particularly when I walked along the banks of the moorland streams fishing in the evenings and when I brought home my catch. If either Paul or I killed a salmon we would give each other a detailed account of where and on what fly it was caught, how it ran up-stream and tried to break the line on Otter rock and how it was finally gaffed and landed after half-an-hour's fight. Now when I brought one home no one was interested in the fisherman's story. All that mattered was how it would be cooked and when we should eat it. Once an object of pride and beauty it had now become a purely gastronomic problem.

The temptation to go fishing was lessened – perhaps a good thing as I spent more time at my work, in which I was becoming more and more interested, regaining some of my pre-war enthusiasm. I did, however, feel slightly out of touch with the art world. Devon was beautiful but at the same time a cultural desert. I felt the need to renew my acquaintance with the museums and galleries, so I started going to London more frequently. On one of these trips I met Robin Darwin and he asked me if I would like a job in the Royal College of Art School of Sculpture, where Frank Dobson had just been appointed Professor. I readily accepted the invitation.

Where to live when I went to London was no problem. Maggie had a flat in Sloane Street and on her invitation I moved in straight away. We renewed all our old activities, going dog racing, dancing at the Caribbean Club in Soho and paying weekly visits to the Chelsea Palace, where the old-time music hall still survived. Being back again with Maggie compensated for all I was missing away from my beloved Devon.

XI

Mexico

After nine months as assistant to Frank Dobson I was anxious to get away and do my own work. There were many experiments I wanted to make and London was not a congenial place for trying out new ideas for which I needed peace and quiet.

Although I had been eager to get back into the art world, having done so I was disappointed. It all seemed artificial, pretentious and pseudo-intellectual. I began wondering what was the attitude of primitive peoples towards art and felt I could gain a great deal by going to live with the Indians of southern Mexico, who were as yet uncontaminated by so-called civilization. I started to think about going there.

It was at this time that Katherine Dunham brought her negro dance group to London. Maggie and I went to the first night. Immediately I felt that this wonderfully creative woman had something for me. I returned to her show on fifteen consecutive nights and finally persuaded David Astor to do a profile of her for his paper, *The Observer*. I went with him to the interview and in this way I made her acquaintance. We hit it off straight away. I told her of my plan to visit Mexico, and she gave me every encouragement. She knew the country well herself and said that I couldn't do better. Going to Mexico was the obvious solution to my problems both artistic and domestic. Although happy living with Maggie in London I did not feel able to make a clean break with Morwenna and the children at this time, which left only one course open to me – to get right away from everyone.

Having made up my mind, I took another necessary decision; to go into hospital and have my duodenal ulcer fixed. It had played hell with me ever since the war, and I had had enough of it. The operation was a big one, and I emerged from hospital a complete wreck. I was horrified when I saw myself in the mirror for the first time to see how old I looked. But I was determined that nothing should stand in my way and after three months convalescence, which was not nearly enough, I set sail for Mexico, having obtained leave from the college for an indefinite period. I left Maggie with Dunham, who had taken her on as her secretary.

David Astor had arranged for me to stay in New York at the Ritz Carlton Hotel, which belonged to his family, and I spent three weeks there looking up friends and people to whom I had introductions. I travelled from New York to Mexico City by train. The journey was long and tiring, but it gave me a chance to see a great deal of the American countryside and observe its transformation from the rich and fertile land of the Central States to the deserts of Texas; a dustbowl punctuated by solitary cacti and with no sign of life save for two dust-laden cowboys I saw riding across the plain.

Once over the border into Mexico the heightened sense of desolation and poverty was a great shock to me. The country is an uninterrupted volcanic desert, totally infertile, with no grass and no trees. As we passed the isolated villages inhabited by poorly clad, miserable-looking Indians and their scrawny goats and donkeys I saw only one redeeming feature, the morning glory climbing up the walls of the adobe huts, which contributed an unexpected splash of colour to the scene.

Approaching Mexico City the train came to a grinding halt which threw everyone off their seats. After about half an hour it slowly moved on again and I saw, out of the window, the wreck of a car lying by the side of the track. It had been hit by our train at a level crossing and literally flattened. You could still see the corpses of the four occupants trapped inextricably in what looked like a tin of sardines run over by a steam roller. I was relieved when I finally got out of the train at the end of the journey. My legs and feet had swollen up from sitting so long in one place but I had not dared take off my shoes as I should never have got them on again.

Installed in a hotel in Mexico City I chased up the two introductions I had been given, to John Grepe, by my sister Mary, and to Miguel Corvarrubias, the artist and author, by Katherine Dunham. I went first to see Corvarrubias, who was an authority on Indian folklore. I told him what I wanted to do, that I planned to go and work with the Indian potters down in the State of Oaxaca. He was extremely discouraging and stated flatly that it would be impossible. In the first place the Indians, who were primitive and dangerous, disliked white races, and their way of life was so alien as to be intolerable to civilized people. Added to this was the certainty that a westerner living in these conditions would become infected with intestinal amoeba, which for someone in my state of health would be fatal. Even if these dangers were avoided, the potters were notorious for guarding their ceramic secrets with a furious jealousy. I would become suspect the moment I started watching them, let alone asking questions.

With my usual over-confidence I was rather encouraged than otherwise by what Corvarrubias told me. One thing emerged clearly from our conversation, and that was that the Zapotec Indians of Oaxaca had remained primitive and untouched by civilization. This was the most important thing as far as I was concerned. I was still confident that I would find a way to get in with them.

John Grepe, my other introduction, was kindness itself. He gave me a room in his house and a place to work in while I made preparations for my great adventure south.

I decided I would need a car, so I bought a second-hand Chrysler off the street. This is standard practice in Mexico. Any used cars which are for sale are parked in the road with a notice on the windscreen giving the address of the vendor and the price. The next step was to get a driving licence. I was told I would have to go to Police Headquarters for this, taking my car with me.

On arrival I presented myself to a police sergeant who was leaning up against a wall in the courtyard.

'What do you want?' he asked me.

'I've come for a driving licence,' I explained.

'Have you got a car?'

'Yes,' I said. 'It's outside.'

'Bring it in then.'

I went outside to where it was parked and drove it into the yard. 'What do I do next?' I asked the sergeant. He pointed to some skittles standing in rows in the middle of the yard and said: 'You see those markers over there? You must drive between them without knocking them down, and then in one movement reverse between those others without knocking them down either.' I took a look at the markers and saw at once that they were too close together for my car to go between them. I pointed this fact out to the sergeant, who simply replied, 'Yes, I know.' I asked him what happened if I did knock them over. He said: 'You come back in a month's time and try again.' 'What happens,'

I enquired, 'if I keep on knocking them over, as I presume I will if they are still in the same place?' This time the answer was more illuminating. 'You just keep on coming back until you get it into your fat head that there are other ways of getting a licence.' I cottoned on at once to what this meant, and started to pull some bank notes out of my wallet, asking the sergeant how much it would cost. He shook his head and pushed them back at me, saying, 'Not to me, to that man over there,' indicating a civilian who was lurking in the background. I approached this man, who said: 'Give me four hundred pesos, and come back for your licence bringing a passport photo of yourself.' All parties to the arrangement being now satisfied, I got into my car and drove off.

I quickly realized that for the Mexicans bribery was a way of life – strictly bribery, as distinguished from bribery and corruption, for there were fixed rates for bribes in most areas, which were generally known and respected. If, for instance, you were involved in a car accident and the police turned up on the scene, for a fee of two hundred pesos you were innocent and let go on the spot, for one hundred you would have to contest the case, and for any lesser sum or nothing you were guilty, no questions asked. The system was time-saving and I found that for a foreigner like me it worked well. You always knew exactly where you stood.

The real start of my Mexican adventure came after two months in Mexico City when I travelled down with John Grepe to establish myself in Oaxaca. It was a fabulous drive through five hundred and fifty kilometres of wonderful, ever-changing scenery, mountains alternating with plains, fertile land with tracts of dramatic soil erosion where the dust was a fiery red when caught in the light of the setting sun. It gave the appearance of a vast field of burning embers.

Poverty was in evidence everywhere; the hot dusty roads were empty save for the bent forms of men tramping along with great loads on their backs, or women with bundles on their heads. Outside every village there were children standing by the side of the road holding an egg or a piece of fruit in their hands, waiting to sell it to some passing traveller. The only animals were lean cattle and half-starved donkeys, trailing along slowly amid clouds of dust. Once we passed a hat maker with three hats on his head. He was busy making a fourth as he walked along. These men walk backwards and forwards between two towns some fifty kilometres apart. Making the hats as they go, piling them up on their heads, they sell them on arrival at their destination. We asked this man how far it was to the next town to which he replied 'Pues, un sombrero o un sombrero y media' (a hat or a hat and a half), a customary way for these ambulatory hat makers to measure distances.

I had been warned that there were still bandits about and told that if ever I saw a man lying in the road, apparently motionless, I was not on any account to stop but to run him over if necessary as this was a ruse to trap the unwary. If you stopped the bandits came out of their hiding place and robbed you of everything you had. Should you resist they would have no scruples about killing you. Fortunately I was never called upon to test this theory.

We arrived in the main square of Oaxaca in the evening and installed ourselves in a café opposite the Cathedral. The Cathedral was undergoing repairs, and there were some stone masons working on it. I have always found it a good policy to go to craftsmen for local information; they are, as a rule, intelligent and kindly. My Spanish was not fluent, but it was good enough to make myself understood. I went up and introduced myself to the Indian foreman explaining that I was a fellow stone mason, and arranged with him to rendezvous at the café at seven o'clock that evening when he had finished work.

I returned to the café later on to await seven o'clock. The town *marimba* band was playing on the square – what an enchanting sound this instrument has! The nineteenth-century bandstand was surrounded by huge laurel trees where the vultures were pitching in for the evening, beating their great wings against the leaves as they settled down. Every sound, sight and smell, of which there were plenty, ranging from the scent of honey-suckle to the stench of sewers, was new and stimulating to me.

Seven o'clock came, and the old mason turned up. I explained to him what I wanted to do, and he suggested that I should go out and see a young friend of his, an architect of Spanish origin called Martin del Campo, whom he thought might provide me not only with living quarters but with all the information I needed, for he was well-liked and on good terms with the Indians in several villages around. Unlike Corvarrubias he was encouraging about my plans and told me that I could accomplish anything if I went about it very slowly and just lay around, as most of the Mexicans did, until the Indians got to know me by sight.

He introduced me to Martin, who was a genial fellow, married to a rich American who was able to support him in idleness. He offered me a room in his house, together with the use of his studio which he no longer wanted, and said I could move in whenever I liked. I wasted no time in taking him up on his offer.

Martin liked the Indian people and understood their curious ways. He took me around the countryside, showing me the beauty spots and sites of antiquity. Amongst them was the village of El Tule, out on the Pan American highway, where stands one of the oldest and biggest conifers in the world. It is known to be at least two thousand years of age and measures forty-four feet around its trunk and one hundred and forty feet in height.

Sitting at its foot were little girls who came out from the village to sell *tortillas* and limes which they gathered in the forest. They were most attractive children and seemed to be friendly. I took to going there every day and buying articles from them.

There was one girl who was always there whom I thought most attractive. She had a beautiful head, and I wanted to make a drawing of her. I had so far had a great deal of trouble finding models amongst the Indians, and I suggested to Clothilde Schondube, a potter friend from Mexico City who had joined me in Oaxaca, that she should come and help me persuade the girl to sit for a portrait.

D.F.L.   M

We drove down together to the tree and were immediately surrounded by children screaming and fighting to sell their goods. We had to buy everything they had to offer – it didn't amount to much – before we could get a hearing. When the excitement had died down, Clothilde explained to them why we had come: I was an artist and hoped to find someone who would pose for a drawing. Clothilde asked the girl if she would do this, but she seemed mystified. It was quite clear that she did not understand the meaning of the word 'drawing'. She said that she would have to go back home and ask her parents, and ran off into the village. Ten minutes later she came back screaming to the other children: 'Don't let him do it, don't let him do it, mother says he will take you away and boil you down and turn you into aeroplane oil!'

At this many of the children scattered and disappeared into the village. We obviously couldn't leave the matter there. The only thing for it was to try to persuade the little girl to take us to her mother, so that we could explain to her exactly what it was we wanted to do. This we eventually managed to do.

She led us into the village, a conglomeration of adobe huts and tall spiky cacti with scrawny pigs and stray dogs running about in the dust. The yard was hidden from view by the tall organ cacti with which nearly all the houses are surrounded. When we entered it, followed by a bevy of children, we were confronted by a group of fierce looking Indians, some with *machetes* in their hands. In the middle stood the father, in a particularly aggressive pose with his *machete* clenched in his fist. He asked me to tell what this 'drawing' was. I did my best to explain and added that I was willing to pay the child for sitting. It was impossible to make them understand about the drawing, but at the mention of money the mother came to my support, saying: 'This man is a simpleton and means no harm and is willing to give us money. Let him show us what this drawing is and we will see if it is dangerous or not.'

A conversation took place in Zapotec and the child vanished. Her mother said she had gone to get ready. Fifteen minutes later she returned looking just the same – apparently she had been away to wash her feet. She was pushed into the hut, which was quite dark inside, and I was told to draw. This I proceeded to do although I could not see the girl at all as the only light, which came through the door, was blocked out by all the family watching me. They saw what I did, and although they couldn't make head or tail of it – they are incapable of interpreting anything two-dimensional – they realized that it was quite safe, and asked where the money was. I gave them ten pesetas, which was more than they would have earned in a whole week making *tortillas* to sell in the market, and left, not without a great sense of relief that I hadn't been run through with one of those villainous looking *machetes*.

As we walked to my car a little girl of about twelve approached me and said: 'You have always been nice to us – come to my house and meet my parents. They are more intelligent than these people. You may do what you like and we don't want any money from you.' All my confidence and hope returned. I felt I had stepped through the barrier. Moments before I had been conscious of the vultures perched in the dead trees, the evil thorns of the cactus plants, the scorpions and poisonous insects, the burning dust under foot. Now the scene had changed completely – I saw the morning glories growing over the huts, heard the charming piping sound of the long-tailed blackbirds and the friendly clucking of a hen who had just produced an egg for some child to sell under the big tree. We went with the girl, who told us her name was Sabena, and met her family. Her mother, Aurelia Pablo, made us a cup of hot chocolate flavoured with cinnamon to drink, and this combined with the charm and simplicity of the whole household put us entirely at our ease.

Aurelia told us that the house was ours, we could come and go as we wished. This meeting marked the start for me of a friendship with the Pablo family which was to become extraordinarily close over the period I stayed in Mexico. From then on my life revolved around them, and I paid them almost daily visits.

Meanwhile I had still to carry out my original plan of getting myself accepted by a community of potters. Clothilde, like Martin del Campo, was fond of the Indians, and being a potter herself she was interested in my project. By making enquiries in the market we found out that the best of the black pottery, which is characteristic of the region, came from the village of Coyotepec, some thirty kilometres from Oaxaca City. We drove out there in my car to investigate. The track was appallingly rough, full of gigantic pot holes, but this was ideal from my point of view as it put the place out of reach of tourists.

Coyotepec turned out to be perfect in every way, but it needed patience before my plan could be realized. In primitive communities a stranger is always suspect. I took my time getting to know the inhabitants, merely showing myself in the village at frequent intervals, waiting for them to approach me. This eventually happened when they could no longer contain their curiosity as to who this stranger might be and what he wanted.

I had stopped one day outside a potter's yard where a man was busy moving some logs of wood. Without a word I turned to and helped him. When all had been stacked in silence, he invited me to sit down and have a drink of *pulque*, a distillation of the Magay cactus plant which abounds in that region. No sooner was I seated on the ground with a jar of this concoction in my hand, than the interrogation started.

'Where do you come from?'
'England.'
'Where is that?'
'Across a great stretch of water on the other side of the world.'
'How do you get there?'
'By boat.'
'Is it your boat?'
'No, it belongs to a company.'
'Would it hold eight people?' When I said that it held about two thousand I did not realize that he could not think in these astronomical figures, and he stopped asking questions.

Eventually his curiosity again got the better of him and he asked:

'Do you live in the country or in the town?'

'A big town called London.'

'Is it as big as Oaxaca?' In order to give him some idea of the enormity of London, I cited a town called Mitla some fifty kilometres away from Coyotepec and said: 'If you were to walk from here to Mitla, and you know how far that is – well, if you were to start from one side of London and try to walk to the other side you would have to travel the same distance.' After a silence he said: 'Ah, when you did that you must have been going round and round without knowing it.'

I told this man that I also made pots, and before I left he had invited me to come and work with him in his yard. This was, of course, just what I was hoping for. His family were all potters, each member with his or her own speciality. His wife and daughter made cooking pots and kitchen utensils, he himself made big pots used either for decorative purposes or for burial with the dead, while his son, Valente, specialized in the making of night watchmen's whistles. These are shaped in the form of birds, and the watchmen blow on them whilst touring the buildings in their charge, so that their employers can hear for themselves that they are on duty. It gave one the weirdest sensation, when on the outskirts of the town at night, to hear these owl-like sounds of different pitches coming out of the darkness.

I did not want to make pots myself but I was interested to learn from these people their techniques in the use and the firing of clay. The skill of the Coyotepec craftsmen is amazing, and their methods unlike any other that I know of. There is no such thing as a potter's wheel in Mexico. In its place the potters use two saucers laid back to back on the ground. A ball of clay is placed in the centre of the topmost, upturned saucer. A hole is punched in the middle of the ball and as the saucer is spun round on its partner the clay is pressed upwards and outwards from the hole in the centre, to which more pieces of clay are constantly added. When the pot is judged to contain enough clay, the walls are worked still further upwards and outwards until their thickness is reduced to that required in the finished article. The final stage is to make the outside smooth by the application of a piece of damp leather as the pot is revolved. Pots of quite large dimensions were made in this way, although there was little variation in the shapes.

In firing the pots they broke all the rules of pottery as I had been taught them. They allowed the flames to play directly on to the pots throughout the firing. They burnt damp wood in the fire which created a good deal of steam inside the kiln. They didn't wait for the pots to cool but took them out of the kiln when still nearly red-hot. All these things I had been told were impossible.

Whilst their technical knowledge in many fields is considerable, the Indians are totally incapable of explaining anything. Children following their parents' profession are not taught, they learn by imitation. The way the Coyotepec children learnt the art of pottery was a clear instance of this. They were given a piece of clay and sat down beside the mother to reproduce what she was doing in miniature. I had to adopt the same approach myself, since it was impossible to gain information by asking questions. I did once ask Valente to what temperature the kiln was fired. He simply said, 'Very hot'.

On this site alone there was evidence that the pottery had been handed down in this way from father to son, mother to daughter, for at least sixteen hundred years. Planting a tree in the yard before I left, I unearthed a kiln full of pots identical to the ones that were still being made in the village, which were subsequently dated by archaeologists at 400 AD. It is no wonder that they had attained such a standard of perfection in their craft.

I used to make my models at home and take them out to Coyotepec to be fired. They included forms of animals and birds as well as human heads and figures, many of which were not what could be called realistic. Although the potters had never seen anything like my work they never asked any questions about it. All they would do when I presented a new work to be fired would be to take it in their hands, lift it gently up and down as if to weigh it, then draw their own conclusions as to the firing, making comments such as: 'You have too much clay in this for its size. We will not be able to fire it as black as you wish for it will have to be placed in the top left-hand side of the fire or it will break. So it will turn out slightly greyish here, more on one side than the other, perhaps. Don't make them of too much clay next time.' It was most refreshing not to have to explain one's works or apologize for anything one had made.

They were, however, most interested to know how I made my objects. One of the techniques I had learnt, while visiting some other potters outside Mexico City, was that of mixing bullrush seeds with the clay to strengthen it. It enabled me, for instance, to make animals which stood up on their own legs while the clay was still wet. This was quite new to the Coyotepec potters and they were curious to see how it was done. Of course the only way it could be explained to them was by demonstration, so I made several animals in front of their eyes. They were also most intrigued by the technique I used to burnish objects to a high degree of polish with a smooth pebble or piece of agate when the clay was leather-hard, something they had never seen done before. Valente tried it out himself on one or two pots, and became most excited at the results he obtained.

I was a little apprehensive at showing them processes alien to their traditions, as I did not want to corrupt them in any way. It seems that my fears were to some extent justified, as I have recently heard from a friend who returned from a visit to Mexico that it is now almost impossible to find any pots in Oaxaca which have not been burnished!

I was still living at Martin del Campo's but a lot of my free time was spent with the Pablo family at El Tule, helping them to harvest their maize and taking the girls to market in the car to sell their *tortillas*. I had been doing this for some months, and had become close to the family, when one day the mother came to me and said that her two eldest daughters, Lupe and Sabina, were seriously ill, and would die unless I could save them.

I said I would do all I could, and immediately went to see an army doctor friend of mine in Oaxaca. I explained the symptoms of the girls' illness, which he diagnosed as typhoid fever. He provided me with a hypodermic syringe and an American drug which had recently been developed and was very effective. He told me what to do, but said that under no circumstances was I to allow the Indians to see me give the injection as they would be certain to think it was something evil. I might, in consequence, find myself in great danger.

I returned to the village with the equipment and explained to the parents that I could do nothing unless left entirely on my own, and that on no account should anyone come near me while I worked my magic. They readily agreed to this condition and after a few injections the girls recovered. In consequence I began to be regarded by them as a man with supernatural powers. A few weeks after the cure, during a religious ceremony on Palm Sunday, I was installed as spiritual godfather to Lupe, the eldest girl, and thus *compadre* to the father, Prudencio. Whilst this was very gratifying, it placed an enormous responsibility on my shoulders, as I was soon to find out.

I did all I could to help these extremely poor people. Amongst other things I tried to teach Lupe the principles of marketing. The Indians have no idea how to conduct any form of business. Once when I was in a village market I saw a girl selling oranges. She had ten of them placed on the ground in front of her. I asked her how much they were, and she said: 'Ten centavos each'. 'How much would they be,' I asked, 'if I were to buy all ten?' She answered, without hesitation, 'One hundred and twenty centavos.' I pointed out to her that ten tens were a hundred, to which she replied: 'Yes, I know, but if I sell them all at once I will have nothing left to sell'.

Some village markets would sell mostly tomatoes, while

right: My bust of Lester Epstein

below: The three wooden figures after their installation in Lincoln Cathedral.

left: On horseback in the Camargue

below: My statue of Mill Reef with his first foal, at Rokeby, Paul Mellon's stud farm.

right: At work on the statue of Brigadier Gerard.

MILL REEF

BAY HORSE, 1968, BY NEVER BEND – MILAN MILL, BY PRINCEQUILLO
HORSE OF THE YEAR IN ENGLAND 1971
WINNER OF THE DERBY, THE ECLIPSE, THE KING GEORGE VI AND
QUEEN ELIZABETH STAKES AND THE PRIX DE L'ARC DE TRIOMPHE
BRED BY PAUL MELLON AT ROKEBY · RIDDEN BY GEOFF LEWIS
TRAINED BY IAN BALDING AT KINGSCLERE
JOHN SKEAPING, R.A. SCULPTOR, 1972

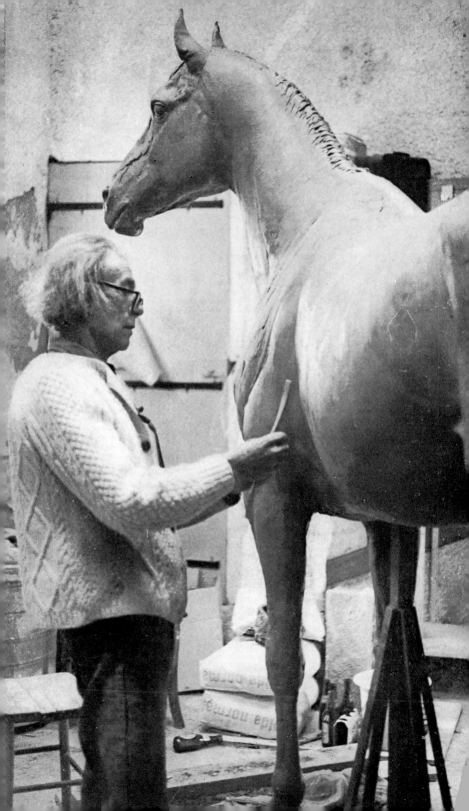

left: Maggie

below: Marion Hart
on her last trip.

others specialized in chickens or some other produce. I explained to Lupe that if she bought chickens in the chicken market, or tomatoes in the tomato market, and took them to sell in markets where they were not available she could make an easy profit. She seemed to understand and I gave her fifty pesos to finance the operation. But the venture never came to anything, for a few days later Lupe told me that she had lost the money.

It did, however, have another unexpected result. A couple of weeks after the disappearance of the fifty pesos she came to see me in Oaxaca and told me that she had got the 'fears'. When I asked her what she meant by the 'fears', she said she had head-aches, was dizzy, felt sick and could eat nothing. I didn't know what advice to give her. It was useless to tell her to go to bed as the Indians do not have such things. All I could think of telling her was to keep out of the sun and carry nothing on her head.

Every day she became worse, and eventually almost demented. I went again to see my army doctor, who was himself a *mestizo* (half-Indian), and asked him what I should do about it. He told me that it was a psychological problem and advised me to take her to a witch, as they were the only people who could deal with it. This posed a problem, for I knew no witches and was not sure if it was diplomatic to mention witches to the Indians as they were very much 'under-cover' people. However, it was the only thing to do, and I had to take the risk.

I went to El Tule to see Lupe's mother, Aurelia. I sat around for a while, talking of this and that, before coming to the point. It was wise never to rush anything but to wait for the right moment. This came while talking of the children. When the conversation came round to Lupe, I said that she didn't seem to me to be at all well. 'No,' Aurelia agreed. 'She isn't.' 'She tells me she has the "fears",' I ventured, as if I knew all about this ailment, adding that I thought something should be done about it. 'Well,' Aurelia said, 'it's for you to decide. You are her spiritual godfather.' There was obviously no way round. I had to brave it: 'I don't know to whom I should take her,' I said. 'Do you know someone?' 'Adela will take you to the woman in the village,' was the reply.

I set off, led by the hand of this dear little child who was accompanied as usual by a tame bird which used to perch on her head. I once asked her about the bird, and she said, 'I don't know where he came from, but he has always done that.' Occasionally the bird would fly up into a tree or dart off after insects, but it would always return to the child's head.

She took me to the outskirts of the village, where she pointed to a hut saying 'There she lives,' and bolted off like a little rabbit, kicking up a cloud of dust behind her with her bare feet. I went to the entrance where I saw an elderly woman arranging herbs and other objects on a rack. She turned to me and asked me to come in. I sat down on the ground, facing her, as I was bidden to do, and started to say who I was and for what reason I had come. She interrupted me before I had finished, saying: 'I know who you are, and all about you, and why you have come. It is about Lupe. Yes, she has the "fears". Bring her to me this afternoon when the sun is behind that tree.'

I waited until the appointed time, which must have been about four o'clock in the afternoon, and went on my way with Lupe, who was by now in a very bad state indeed. The witch told us both to come in and sit down on the ground. She sat opposite us, as she had sat in front of me that morning.

'Are you prepared to do anything I require of you?' she asked me. I said that I was. She then got up and fetched a small pile of charcoal and some herbs off the rack, two small earthenware bowls and a fan made of turkey feathers. She lit a little charcoal fire and on it she put the two bowls, one with water in it, the other containing some kind of oil. When the water came to the boil, she lifted it off the fire and crushed some dried leaves into it which made a kind of strong smelling tea. This she mixed with the oil. When the mixture was cool she gave it to us to drink, giving Lupe twice as much as she gave to me.

This potion, whatever it consisted of, had a disgusting taste, rather like camomile tea mixed with olive oil. However, I had little time to think about the taste before it started to act. As it went down I lost all contact with the ground and my body, and the woman, as she sat there opposite me, appeared to become smaller and smaller, turning upside-down and finally disappearing.

The state of trance I was in was similar to that experienced just before losing consciousness under an anaesthetic. I could hear the woman's voice, and indeed the vibrations of my own voice in my head, although I had absolutely no idea in what language she and I were speaking. It was like listening to a radio through the wall of a house – one can tell it is a human voice without being able to distinguish a word.

How long this situation lasted I haven't the faintest idea. Eventually the process of disappearance was reversed. First of all the tiny figure appeared upside-down, then, getting larger, it turned the right way round, and as the woman reappeared before me I regained the lost sense of my body and its contact with the earth. Then she spoke to me: 'As soon as you feel you can, go out and sit down under the tree, and I will come and fetch you when I am ready for you.'

I obeyed and fell asleep. The sun was well down at the base of the tree when the woman woke me, asking me to return to the hut. Then she began: 'Listen to me and I will tell you why and how Lupe got the "fears". She went into the hills to fetch wood and a serpent crawled out from under a stone and afflicted her with them. I will tell you why this happened. You gave Lupe fifty pesos and she told you she had lost them?' 'That is so,' I said. 'She didn't lose them,' she continued, 'but hid them, hoping that by telling you this she would get more money from you. To deceive your spiritual godfather is a great crime in the eyes of the Gods, and they punish the guilty with the "fears", often with ultimate death. It is an equal crime for a spiritual godfather to deceive the child put in his trust. You are innocent.'

This information had been extracted from Lupe and myself whilst under the influence of a powerful hypnotic drug. The

Indian witches are knowledgeable in the use of drugs, and this woman was no exception. She possessed a formidable array, as I later discovered, including some twenty derivatives of opium.

Lupe was still in a trance, but we got her to her feet. The woman handed me another mixture in a bottle and said: 'Now take her home and give her this potion to drink. She will be "dead" for sixteen hours. You will not see her breathe, but do not worry – she will wake up knowing nothing of what has happened, and the "fears" will have gone. Never mention it to her again.'

The next sixteen hours were some of the most anxious of my life. To all intents and purposes Lupe was dead. I saw no sign of her breathing, and could not feel her pulse. Nevertheless, she recovered as predicted, and that was the end of this strange story.

I had by now left Martin del Campo's house and was living in a hut lent me by Willi Ramirez, the *mestizo* proprietor of a café in Oaxaca. I felt I wanted to enter more into life as it was lived by the Indians. All the same, the state of my new home on my entry came as a shock to me. There was no furniture save an old iron bedstead, and most of the space was occupied by Ramirez's pigs, who were using it as a sty. The first thing was obviously to drive these animals out into the yard, which I proceeded to do. Then I set about cleaning away a pile of rubbish lying in a corner under an old piece of linoleum. In so doing I unearthed thirteen white scorpions as big as prawns. Worse still, in a fallen tree outside, I found a nest of widow spiders. There must have been at least a hundred of them living there. My first idea was to pour petrol over the trunk and set it on fire, but I was advised against it by an old Indian neighbour who pointed out that if they were disturbed the survivors might invade the house. I had to resign myself to sharing the garden with them.

I had been told by Willi that a boy called Carlos, who worked in his café, was using the hut to sleep in at night but that I was at liberty to turn him out. I spent the day making myself comfortable, moving in a few odd bits of furniture and bedding, a packet of candles, and some pots and pans. There was no sign of

Carlos. At midnight I was woken by the pigs grunting. Carlos had appeared with a sack of kitchen waste which he gave to them and then crept into the hut, where he lay down on the floor in a corner. I woke in the morning just in time to see him shoot out of the hut like a stray dog and disappear. I had wanted to tell him that he was welcome to stay but he hadn't given me the chance. That evening when I went to Willi's to eat, I saw Carlos and I told him he could stay on in the hut. He simply said '*Muchas gracias*'. These were the only words exchanged between us for three weeks.

The hut stood some way back from the road in what was once the garden of a large house, destroyed in the earthquake of the 1930s when half the town of Oaxaca crumbled. Four gigantic laurel trees, some sixty to seventy feet high, were all that was left of the original garden, along with a toronja tree that still bore a good crop of fruit. Behind the garden wall passed the single line track of the Oaxaca railway. Whenever I heard a train coming I used to run out of the hut and on to the road in order to avoid being suffocated by the dense cloud of smoke which enveloped the place. In the stillness of the air it was sometimes fully half an hour before I could return to work.

As a studio the hut was not ideal, but it was sufficient for my purpose. My first model was a pig, who had a peculiar habit of propping himself up on his haunches outside the door, waiting for me to give him scraps to eat. He was an excellent model, as he stayed in this position for most of the day. My next subject was a game cock, a present from Lupe. She had meant me to kill and eat him, but he was far too beautiful to destroy, so I kept him alive to serve as a model for a series of terracottas.

My life by now had evolved a more or less regular pattern of work, visits to and from the Pablos, and excursions to Coyotepec to get clay or take my works to be fired. I was developing the same attitude towards my work and life as the Indians, which was exactly what I had hoped to do by going to Mexico. My shack was heaven on earth, undisturbed by people and noise. Apart from the occasional train the only sounds were the grunting of the pigs, the crowing of my cock, the weird and exotic songs of countless birds chanting high up in the branches of the laurels, followed at sundown by the beat of the vultures' wings as they pitched into the tree tops for the night, when all became deadly silent, save for the hooting of an owl. This was the signal for me to go to bed, when I would read myself to sleep by the light of a candle. Sometimes the illumination was more exotic. Carlos would catch hundreds of large fire-flies and put them in a jam jar, where they would glow for about four hours, giving me just enough light to read by if placed fairly close to my book.

One of the things which had interested me most in my reading about Mexico was the description of the life in the Tehuantepec peninsula. I was ready for a break from my work, and I decided to go there.

The route to the isthmus was the most spectacular I have ever travelled. As I neared my destination, affected by the beauty of the surroundings I branched off the Pan American Highway and took a side track which led me through the jungle. The surface was appalling, and the cloud of dust I raised, together with the loud bangs from the bottom of my car as it struck a rock or a bump, sent flocks of screaming parrots into the air. My detour effectively doubled the length of the journey and it was nothing short of a miracle that I completed it with my car intact, for I more than once ran into a tree when taking my eyes off the track for a moment to look at some bird of fabulous plumage.

At last I reached the sea and a little fishing village called La Ventosa. It was like striking an oasis in a desert – the view suddenly opening out into a wide seashore, where pelicans, spoonbills and frigate birds in their hundreds plunged gracefully about in the air and into the sea, which rolled up the beach and broke in a crescendo of sound that drowned all others. As the waves receded they left all kinds of treasures behind them on the sand – sea shells, star fish, the odd spar from an old wreck – which were pushed further and further up the beach.

I drove the car axle deep into a dune and had hardly time to get out before I was surrounded by hordes of pretty children and women screaming 'Gringo, *gringo*!' This is the Indian name for an American. It is said to derive from the opening words of the song 'Green grow the rushes, o', sung by the American soldiers during their invasion of Northern Mexico.

I was taken in hand at once and led off in triumph to see the head man, who turned out to be charming. He told me immediately that another *gringo* had arrived in the village a month earlier and asked me if I would mind acting as an interpreter on behalf of the villagers. They had so far been unable to communicate with him at all, as he spoke not a word of Spanish.

I was taken to a hut, and from it there emerged a rough-looking fellow, who seemed delighted to see me and have someone to talk to at last. He launched at break-neck speed into an account of what he was doing in La Ventosa, why he had come to Mexico and how he had landed up in the village by accident. He was on a GI scholarship and wanted to be a painter, and his name was Lester Epstein. Lester's rough appearance belied his character. He was at heart an intellectual, and a good poet and writer. We were to become great friends.

Later I found out his earlier history. His parents' home was in St Louis, Missouri, and on coming out of the army (where he had had a distinguished career as the only recruit in the US Forces never once to have hit the target at rifle practice), he opened a bookshop there on money borrowed from his mother. He amassed a thousand or so volumes of the classics, shut the shop, and sat in it without once opening until he had read almost everything in it. It took him three years, by which time the business was bust.

When I had been in the village for two or three weeks I was asked by the head man to come to his house and confer with him on a matter of some urgency. When I arrived I found him and his brother in conference with a couple of other senior citizens of La Ventosa. He explained the situation to me. 'There is a *mestizo* who has arrived here from Tehuantepec with orders from the Prefect to the effect that all our children must go to school by next Thursday, or the police will come and we will all be imprisoned. I told him that we have no school here, and we don't want to learn to read and write. We have no books, and nobody to write to. Nevertheless he repeated his order and said we should use the little church as a school. This we refuse to do. If you would write and explain this to the Prefect, we will send a runner with your letter to Tehuantepec. None of us are able to write.'

I was glad to help with the letter and the runner left for the Prefecture with it later that day. A few days later the reply came back – the attitude of the Prefect was unchanged. The gist of the letter was as follows: 'The man who has been sent to you will be your children's teacher. You will have him and like him.'

Another conference was called, at which my presence was again requested. After a long and heated discussion between the two brothers in Naoia, not a word of which I knew, the head man turned to me and said: 'I expect you have understood what the matter is under discussion.' I replied that I supposed it concerned the schoolmaster. 'That is correct,' the head man went on, 'but do you understand our intention to dispose of this stupid tyrant in our own way?' I said that I did not, and the head man explained: 'My brother will deal with him in the same way as he dealt with the tax collector before,' adding, 'Do not mention the matter to anyone, above all not to the women. You know what women are, they talk, the man would get to hear of it, and it is much easier and neater to kill a sleeping man than one who is trying to run away.' I did my best to conceal my astonishment, and promised to mention the plan to no one, not even the *gringo*.

That night I took up my usual resting place in a hammock strung between two trees on the seashore, and was soon lulled to sleep by the rhythm of the waves breaking on the beach. At five o'clock next morning as dawn was breaking, I was woken by the words '*Buenas dias, Juanito*,' coming from behind my hammock. It was the brother of the head man. 'I hope you slept well and that I didn't awaken you? Or perhaps you heard something during the night?' he enquired. 'Not a sound,' I replied. 'Good,' said the brother. 'The schoolmaster will not awaken. When you are up my brother and I would be obliged if you would write another letter to the Prefect notifying him that last night the schoolmaster passed away in his sleep, and that he will be buried with all due ceremony. His grave will be open to the inspection of the Prefect whenever it suits him to come here.' They seemed quite certain that the Prefect would leave the matter there.

I wrote the letter, and another runner went off with it to Tehuantepec. Sure enough, there was no reaction from the Prefecture. The funeral was held in proper style the same day, with the traditional fireworks to scare away the evil spirits. Then the whole incident passed into oblivion.

My role in this drama being played out, I returned to Oaxaca. After my few weeks holiday I was feeling really well for the first time since my operation and I resolved to do my best to stay that way. I left the pig-sty house and rented a nice little cottage on the outskirts of town. It had a beautiful big garden, full of flowers and fruit trees, among them bananas and mangoes which were the feeding ground by night of a half-tame coati who would spend his days curled up asleep in the corner of my room. In the day the place was alive with the buzzing of humming birds hovering among the flowers.

I spent a pleasant winter and spring there, busying myself about my work which was going really well. I was steadily getting together a good collection of drawings and terracottas. Meanwhile I was still seeing a lot of the Pablos. I had been helping them to plant maize, the only crop which these Indians cultivate, and which forms the basis of their diet. The rainy season had just started, and I was talking to Aurelia, saying that the rain had come just right and that they should, in consequence, have a very good crop. 'Yes,' she agreed, 'and for that one of my children will die, maybe Roberto,' nodding towards the year-old baby she held in her arms, 'or maybe even Adela.' When the harvest was abundant, she said, the Eternal Father came to the villages and took children away to help gather it in.

The conversion of the Indians to Christianity had never been completed. Cortez's priests, finding that a religion of white people made no sense to the Indians, were satisfied with leaving them in a halfway state, having changed the names of their deities and dispensed with human sacrifice. Aurelia's belief, like many others still held by the Indians, was a hangover from the ancient Aztec religion, which demanded that children be sacrificed each year to the God of fertility, Xipe, in exchange for rainfall. The children were told of their fate in advance, so that their tears would be a portent of rain.

I had not been out of El Tule for a month, during which time it continued to rain, when one day Aurelia came to the house. I noticed as she approached that she was not carrying the baby, Roberto. She did not greet me, but walked into the house in silence, and then quietly said: 'This morning the Eternal Father came and took Roberto away.'

The reason she had come was to ask me to go to fetch Prudencio so that he could be present at the funeral which had to be held within twenty-four hours, so that the child's body remained in a perfect state for its entry into the New World. Of course I willingly agreed, but when I asked where he would be, all she could tell me was: 'Somewhere south of here.' This was of little help, as some three hundred miles, most of which was covered in dense forest, lay between Oaxaca and the Guatemalan frontier to the south. However, since they were by now convinced of my supernatural powers, it was no use showing any doubt as to my ability to find him. She did at least observe that I was slightly perplexed and offered to send her brother with me to help.

It was five o'clock in the evening when the brother and I set out for the Pan American Highway in my car. On hitting the highway we started out tentatively in a southerly direction. We had not been going more than an hour when one of the bolts stripped off the connecting rod and the front wheels began to wobble violently. This made steering extremely difficult, but it was still possible to proceed at a speed of about ten miles an hour. I explained to my companion that I could not go any faster as something had gone wrong with the car. Carrying on at this pace we arrived some six hours later at a small village called El Cameron, where we came across a group of some four or five hundred *brazeros* seated round fires in a clearing beside the road. During the season of heavy rain there were often falls of rock from the high cliffs overhanging the highway. Then gangs of workmen, named *brazeros*, would be called in to deal with the situation. Sometimes the blocks would weigh two or three hundred tons and could not be moved, and the *brazeros* would build a provisional road right over the top of them.

We stopped the car and got out, and I asked a group of these men if they could tell me where Prudencio Pablo could be found. One of them answered: 'He was here a few weeks ago, but he went further south and we have no idea where he went to.' I insisted that it was urgent that we find him, and explained why, at which an old man came over from another fire and said: 'In that case you will find him. Carry on along this road for thirty-five kilometres, then look into the hills on your left and you will see a fire burning. Beside the fire this man will be sitting.'

I must have looked helpless with astonishment, for the old man offered to accompany me. I now had two men in the car with me neither of whom had ever been in a motor car before, but they both fell asleep in the back unperturbed, despite the continuous wobbling of the front wheels. I kept an eye on the speedometer, and when I reckoned we had covered thirty-five kilometres, which took us the best part of two hours, I started to look out on the left as the old man had told me. It was not long before I could make out a glow coming from the general blackness of the hills in that direction. I stopped and my two passengers woke. I pointed to the light and asked the old man if that would be the place, to which he replied that it was and that if I waited in the car they would both go to find him. I was glad to be relieved of this particular task for at this point the forest was dense with thorn bushes and cacti, and infested with snakes and other dangerous creatures.

They were gone for what must have been half an hour, during which time I slept. I was woken by someone tapping on the window, and opened my eyes to see three men standing outside, one of whom was Prudencio Pablo.

They got into the car, and I asked Prudencio if he knew the reason for my coming to fetch him. He said he did not – the two men had simply told him that his *compadre* was waiting for him on the road. I told him about Roberto. He asked me how I had known where to find him. When I told him about the old man from El Cameron, whom I had met two hours before, he was amazed. He said that it was only half an hour since he had arrived and lit the fire.

The long journey back to El Tule was fraught with more disaster. We had to negotiate a rock fall just beyond El Cameron, and in so doing burst one of our tyres. We travelled the remaining eighty kilometres on a spare tyre which had worn through to the inner tube. By some miracle – the three men kept repeating that the Eternal Father was with us and we would surely return – we arrived in the village in the late hours of the morning, in time for the funeral. This ceremony passed off with the characteristic gaiety and joy which is expected of mourners at children's funerals in Mexico. The Indians think it the happiest thing that can happen to a child to depart to the next world before he has suffered any of the trials and tribulations of life in the present one. In fact any show of grief on the part of the mother is considered a grave offence, and any woman so weak as to give in to it is liable to be punished by her husband and relations with a severe beating.

There are things about these primitive people which I can never hope to understand. On the one hand the intelligence of the average adult is that of a seven-year-old child, on the other, they are capable of thinking in the fourth dimension – they have an extraordinary power of extra-sensory perception and a sense of direction as acute as a homing pigeon's. It is on these gifts that they rely for their guidance and indeed survival.

These people are 'absolutists' in the sense that they either believe in a certain thing or it simply doesn't exist for them. They are incapable of wondering what things would be like if they were different from what they are. They can explain nothing and have no wish to do so – they accept. Consequently argument and discussion do not exist for them.

My own mentality and way of thinking could not have been more distinct from theirs. One thing that was shared, however, was our understanding that there was an unbridgeable gap between our ways of thinking. The success of our relationship was based on the acceptance by both sides of the premise that we should never be able really to understand each other. Whenever we arrived at an impasse in our conversation, the matter under discussion would immediately be dropped and the subject changed. As Prudencio Pablo put it, when asked why a semi-idiot child kept on screaming; 'Some people are different to others.'

Early in July, quite soon after the episode of Roberto's funeral, Lester came up from La Ventosa to stay with me. I was delighted to see him, little realizing the trouble I was in for. Once transplanted from the calming environment of the small fishing village to Oaxaca, Lester unleashed all the furies of his artistic temperament.

Whilst down in the town one morning I bumped into a young couple I had known when I first came to Mexico City, an American artist and his coloured wife, who had posed for me as a model. They said they were hoping to stay around for a while. Should I be wanting a model, the girl would be happy to pose for me again. This offer I gladly accepted. She had come, as arranged, to sit one day when Lester's eyes fell upon her. Although he didn't join in the drawing, he made some designs – not on paper but upon her person – and it wasn't long before he started to cultivate her acquaintance.

The first anniversary of the couple's marriage was coming up and I invited them to celebrate it at my house. We would have a small party, drinks and some music. I left it to them to organize. Lester said he would give them some help with the arrangements, for which I was grateful as I wanted to get on with my work.

The day came, and the boy arrived at my house in the morning bringing the drinks with him. He told me he had got a Mexican friend to arrange for some *mariaches* to come and play in the garden while we had the party inside. These bands are traditionally hired at weddings and the name is in fact a corruption of the French word '*marriage*'. The arrangements sounded eminently suitable, and I left the boy in the house to supervise them while I went into town to buy some cakes.

In the square I bumped into Lester, arm in arm with the girl. They were both as drunk as could be, having spent most of the morning in a hotel bedroom fornicating and drinking *tequila*. I was dumbfounded but managed to elicit a promise from them that they would not appear at the house together and not before they had sobered up. I had my doubts, however, as they were obviously too sozzled really to grasp the gravity of the situation. I returned to the house feeling ill at ease and busied myself helping the boy to complete the arrangements for the evening. The party was scheduled for seven o'clock.

At six-thirty the band turned up and we seated them in the garden with a large measure of *tequila* per man. They managed to get through this while waiting for the guests to arrive. We had only asked one or two people as parties of this kind tend to get out of hand and go on for ever. Seven o'clock came and the guests started arriving, but neither Lester nor the girl had shown up. Meanwhile the band had run out of drink. They were supplied with more to give them something to do while they awaited orders from us.

It was about seven-twenty when Lester and the girl turned up, arm in arm and still very drunk. As they rolled up the drive towards the house the band, suffering under a delusion as to the identity of the husband, struck up vigorously with 'Here Comes

The Bride'. Now well oiled, they couldn't be stopped playing. As Lester walked into the house all hell broke loose. While he and the boy were fighting, crashing about the room and smashing the pots of flowers and the furniture, the band switched to 'Happy Birthday To You', playing louder and louder as the competition from the screams, yells and general fracas became hotter. It almost seemed as though they took this to be the usual proceeding at such functions.

The party finally broke up, leaving the contents of the house in a similar condition. Towards the end it became too dangerous to go inside, so I left without really knowing the outcome. All I know is that the place was a shambles when I returned. Fortunately I had taken the precaution of moving all my work out of the room, thinking that something might get broken – an estimate which in the circumstances was over-optimistic. I thought that if this was the behaviour of civilized people I would prefer the primitives any day and I wasted no time in returning to my Indian friends.

I felt that after a year and a half I had obtained my objective and had proved to my own satisfaction that true art flourishes much more in a primitive, unpretentious society than in the world of pseudo-intellectualism. I was now faced with a difficult choice: either to return to a phony world or to remain with the Indians for the rest of my life. I had written to Morwenna to ask her if she would consider coming out to live in Mexico, bringing the children with her. This she flatly refused to do, which left me with no alternative but to return to England.

In conversation with the Pablos I started to prepare them for my eventual departure. I had become so much a part of their lives that I knew my going would cause great grief to the whole family. They repeatedly asked me why I wanted to go away and if I went, where I would be going. The answers I gave in no way convinced them. To them the whole world was Mexico and they somehow got it into their heads that the country I spoke of returning to was another planet. Aurelia was most concerned for my safety and what would be likely to happen to me in this other world. She would ask me how long the journey would take. Did I have maize growing there, were there chickens and pigs, was there a well from which I could drink?

These gatherings were heart-rending and I knew when the fateful day arrived the strain on us all would be unbearable. All the Indians I had known were gathered in the garden having brought me gifts of one kind or another. It was as though they were all being sacrificed on my altar. All of them were crying.

Six months after I had returned to England I heard from Clothilde Schondube. She told me that Aurelia had walked five hundred and fifty kilometres to Mexico City, carrying on her head a large basket full of food for me. She found her way to the Shrine of the Angel of Guadalupe, where she remained for hours praying for me and then left the basket in the care of the Angel for her to send it on to me, wherever I might be.

XII

End of an Era

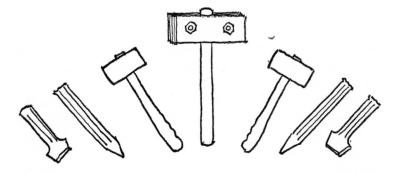

On my return from Mexico I was shocked to learn that although Paul had got his 'wings' at the end of the Flying Course in South Africa, he had been thrown out of the air force as unsuitable human material and was back in England heaving coal in Plymouth dockyard. I went immediately to see him and he told me what had happened. At the end of the course all the cadets were asked to write an essay on what they thought of it. Paul, in his usual outspoken manner, said exactly what he thought; that the school was badly run and that bad maintenance of the aircraft had been responsible for the death of three cadets. This report went directly to the CO responsible, and it was on this that he was discharged and sent home.

I immediately contacted David Astor, the owner/editor of *The Observer*, hoping he could have some influence in putting this injustice to rights. David passed the information on to Air Chief Marshal Sir Leslie Hollingshurst, who was in charge of air force personnel at that time. 'Holly', as he was known to his friends, sent for Paul immediately and told him to go on leave for ten days. He could consider himself still in the RAF whilst his accusations were investigated. The outcome was that Paul was proved to be 95% correct in what he had said. The immediate reaction was that 'Holly' sacked the CO in charge of the South African Flying School and sent Paul up to Cranwell, the Sandhurst of the air force, placing him under the care of his nephew who was chief Flying Instructor there. At the end of this course, Paul passed out with the highest marks in his group and was one of the first to do an 'eight-point roll' with a jet aircraft. On leaving Cranwell he was posted to Butterworth in Malaya with a photo reconnaissance unit which was making an aerial survey of the Timor Sea area.

I missed his company a great deal, more particularly when I would go down to fish in Blacksmith's pool alone. I remember one night particularly, when the moon was full and the sea trout were running – they could only be caught at night. All was silent save for the sound of the water tumbling over the granite rocks, the occasional mournful hooting of the owls and the squeaking of the bats, a sound I can no longer hear. I had caught several good fish which I wanted Paul to see, and went to the tree where he had carved his initials, wondering when would be the next time he would be there again.

I had to go to London to take up my teaching job at the college and I moved in with my sister who had a flat in Paddington. After living for a year and a half in Mexico, I found London life almost unbearable. The noise of the traffic, the smell of petrol fumes, the jostling crowds clattering along the pavements in hard-heeled shoes (we all walked bare-foot in Mexico), the cloudy skies. All this, coupled with the radical change in my outlook on life, made London intolerable.

Taking up teaching again was what saved me. I had so much

to tell the students, not only about sculpture but about life itself, and I was determined to liberate them from the pettifogging regulations which Dobson had established in the school. Male and female students were segregated. Women were not allowed to model figures of more than half life-size. A bell rang at six o'clock, when all the students would be turned out of the school like people being turned out of a pub after 'Last orders please'.

With a hundred per cent backing from the students I wiped away all these idiotic rules and established not only women's lib. but everybody's lib., my own as well, and did so with the backing of Darwin, the Principal, who, at that time, was very much on my side. I don't think, somehow, that he would have been if he had known to what extent I was going to carry out my experiment.

The school never closed, students went home when they liked and some of them even slept in the school after working until late. I often did so myself, furnishing my studio with a collapsible bed, a good record-player and my clavichord. The students often came into my studio to have a cup of tea, listen to a record, or just chat. I was more than a teacher to them, I was a father confessor, and they used to tell me all their troubles.

One of the best ways of teaching is by demonstration, and the students learned a good deal by watching me do my own work in the class-room. I did a lot of terracottas with my new-learned Indian techniques, which were a revelation to them. These I would take down to Devonshire and fire in a kiln I had built there after the Mexican-Indian pattern. The kiln was wood-fired; the flames would get directly on to the works and, by burning the green foliage of fir trees during reduction, the pots would turn black.

I also did several wood and stone carvings, forging all my own tools, and taught the students how to do this themselves. My methods of teaching were more like the old apprenticeship system, before Art Schools as such existed, where the pupils lived with their master. This is far more valuable than going round a class and expressing one's opinion on the students' work and ideas. Any such opinion is personal anyway and may not be of the slightest use to a student who is trying to do something totally different to one's own work.

My seven best students could not have been more different from each other, and none of them worked in the same style as myself. I in turn learned quite a lot from them. There was Ralph Brown, an excellent sculptor, who knew what he was doing and what he wanted to do. I never attempted to teach him as such, but we often discussed sculpture at great length.

Sally Arnup was an unconventional girl with a strong personality. She used to bring her baby into the school with her and keep it, like a puppy, in a cardboard box in the class-room whilst she worked.

Astrid Zidowa was a most talented and original person. Then there was John Paddison, a master marble carver, and Sid Harpley, the son of a Hammersmith taxi driver, who had a facility for modelling which was quite amazing. Jonathan Kenworthy used to come to the school on Sundays, brought by his father. He couldn't come during the week as he was still at school, being only twelve years old at the time, but on leaving school he became a whole-time student.

Robert Carruthers was an exception to the general run of students. Widely read and well-informed, he was not only one of the best students but he also became a close friend of mine, often accompanying me to Devon to help with the firing of the terracottas. Morwenna and the boys took to him, as I had done, and he made a great difference to the atmosphere at home. He began to take part in all my activities. He took up granite carving, working with me in the Devonshire quarries when I started to carve a big granite figure, one of the best carvings I have ever done. I brought the roughed out granite figure to London and finished it at the college in the yard.

Like myself, Robert became an expert salmon poacher, I teaching him the tricks of the trade that I had learned years ago in Ireland. There was a big oak tree down by Blacksmith's pool. Robert would climb up into the over-hanging branches and indicate to me where he could see a salmon lying on the bottom of the river. Then I would come into action. I would attach a large white chicken's feather to an outsize hook, tie a lead weight of about one ounce to the cast a yard above the hook, cast out four yards beyond and in front of where the fish was lying and watch the white feather drift and sink. As soon as the feather disappeared from sight, I knew it was immediately behind the fish. Then I would strike, foul-hook the fish and utilize the rush of the fish to swing it round to the bank where Robert would be waiting to gaff it. One September when the water was too low to catch them on a fly, we took twenty-five fish out of the river on my 'Irish fly'.

Life was good and full of joy, everything was going well. I had been elected an ARA (Associate Royal Academician) in 1951 and Robert was made an assistant teacher to me at the college. I was in demand as a lecturer and gave a number of lectures on my adventure in Mexico, showing some remarkable slides I had made whilst I was there.

I was invited to give a lecture on extra-sensory perception among the Indians in the Ashmolean Museum, Oxford, on Friday 13 February 1953. The lecture was a late affair, and whilst answering questions someone handed me a telegram telling me that Paul had been killed in a flying accident that morning. I read the telegram out to my audience and asked to be excused. I returned to London by the last train and on arrival telephoned Morwenna saying that I would come down next morning, bringing Robert Carruthers with me as he could give me moral support.

Robert had recently moved and I hadn't his address, so I went round to the college to try to obtain it from the Registrar. He didn't know it, and suggested I ask the Bursar. As I went into the Bursar's office, for some completely inexplicable reason I suddenly had a vision that if I ran, not walked, to the junction of Cromwell

Road and Gloucester Road, some three-quarters of a mile away, I would see Robert. Without a word, I dashed out of the office, down the stairs and into the street, running all the way. As I got to the road junction, a 74 bus pulled up at the curb-side and Robert stepped out of it right in front of me. I told him I had come to find him knowing he would be there. He had apparently just come there to collect some laundry from a cleaner in Gloucester Road, having been out of London all that week. I told him what had happened. Without waiting to collect his washing, he came straight away with me to Paddington and we caught the first train going to Exeter. Morwenna was at the station to meet us.

Robert was wonderful with the boys – the twins were nine years old and Nick only six. Paul had been their God, and this, their first encounter with death, needed delicate handling.

I was so distraught and helpless, literally struck dumb by the shock, that I could do nothing but wander about aimlessly. Everywhere that I looked there were things associated with Paul. In the garage was his jeep and the chimney where we used to smoke salmon. His fishing rods up in his bedroom, his photo on the dressing table, objects which had belonged to him were everywhere.

That evening I wandered down to the river, drawn as if by a magnet to Blacksmith's, to the place where Paul used to stand and cast his line. In a sense I was like a faithful dog who goes on looking for his master although he has seen him dead. I was looking for Paul.

The sound of the water flowing over the granite boulders, once a gorgeous symphony, had become a funeral march. The rock in the centre of the pool by which we used to measure the height of the water with such expectancy, turned into a tombstone. My mind turned to the name of this pool, 'Blacksmith's', and why it had been so named.

On coming away I passed the tree in which Paul had carved his initials some three years before. Lichen had grown over it so that it was scarcely visible. I returned to the house by way of the 'daffodil path', as we used to call it, which went up through the woods. When I got to the house I could not stay there and spent the whole night wandering about.

I cannot now remember how long I stayed down at Puggie-stone, a week perhaps. Morwenna was distraught. She had grown to love Paul as though he was one of her own children. I did what I could to comfort her but it was like 'the blind leading the blind', both so miserable that there was little we could do for each other. Robert held things together whilst I gathered my wits and got back some control over myself. We left, I never wishing to return, only wanting to remember the house, the woods and the river as the happy place it used to be. There was nothing for it but to get down to work.

The first thing I did was to make a large crucifix in wood. When I was in Mexico, wandering through the forest I had come across the wreckage of an aeroplane beside which lay the tortured, charred body of the pilot, the arms upstretched and the claw-like fingers in a grasping position. The head, burned to the skull, looked like one of those African shrunken heads, the white teeth showing under the contracted and shrivelled lips. Paul had suffered this same fate. Someone had placed a bomb in his plane which blew up ten minutes after take-off from Bangkok, killing him and his navigator. Only his charred and unrecognizable remains had been found.

To make this seven-foot-high crucifix, I got some branches of a cedar tree and joined two of them on to the main trunk to make the upstretched arms. This done, instead of carving the forms in a conventional way, I burned the wood away with a powerful blow-lamp, making the forms by scraping away the charred wood. When finished it was a good piece of sculpture, containing a great deal of significance to me, if to nobody else. It had real meaning. The students occasionally came and watched this awesome process with curiosity and respect, for they knew why I was doing it.

As time went on, keeping hard at work, I was able to regain my equilibrium. I had a Chinese student who was a brilliant wood carver, having spent fifteen years as an apprentice in China. He helped me to carve four hundred and fifty small panels for the British conference room in the United Nations building in New York. They were all animal and plant forms and were finished in a year.

The next undertaking was the carving of three six-foot-six-high figures for King's College Chapel to fill three niches behind the altar, which had been empty for one hundred and seventy-five years as the authorities, throughout this long period, had never been able to make up their minds who to commission to execute the work. The figures represented Christ the Shepherd, the Virgin before the birth, and St Nicholas, the patron saint of the College. Installed in the chapel, they were later removed to Lincoln Cathedral, as way had to be made for a valuable bequest of a large religious painting by Rubens and there was no other place for this painting to go. Noel Annan, the then Provost of King's, was most distressed, as it was he who had asked me to do the carvings, and they really looked magnificent where they stood.

I lent my studio to Jacob Epstein for a year to do the big group of figures which now stands at the Knightsbridge entrance to Hyde Park. Epstein was in sympathy with my ideas of teaching, and he used to invite the students into the studio to see his work and even ask some of them to musical evenings in his home.

I got professional musicians to come occasionally in the evenings to give recitals to the students in my studio; people like my brother, who came with his consort of viols and gave an excellent demonstration of ancient music played on the authentic instruments. Not only are my brother Kenneth and his wife excellent musicians, but they have four sons, Adam, Joseph, Alexander and Roderick, all of whom are equally talented. They perform on viols, crumhorns and other ancient instruments, making some of these instruments themselves, Joseph being a very competent woodworker and carver. Greatly in demand when authentic early music is required for films and the like, they have formed, together with other youngsters, some excellent groups. The latest one, 'The City Waites', has made a remarkable long-playing record entitled 'A Gorgeous Gallery of Gallant Inventions' which consists of ancient bawdy ballads, for which they had to do a great deal of research in the British Museum so as to obtain the correct wording and pronunciation.

Sir Malcolm Sargent lived in Queen's Gate, a stone's throw from the Sculpture School, and every now and again would come round to my studio on a Sunday afternoon and play on my clavichord or listen to a record and discuss music with me and any student who happened to be there. On these occasions he was very much at ease and dropped all his pomposity. In the outside social world he would hardly have dared to associate with us. He was, not without reason, known to orchestral musicians as 'Sir Self-Enlargement', though I personally always found him charming and intelligent.

The atmosphere was wonderful and totally unconventional; not a few of the other members of the college staff were envious of my set-up and would have liked to have had the opportunity to do likewise. I could do so because the Sculpture School was a separate building a quarter of a mile away from the college proper, and I was not being spied on at that time by the authorities – Darwin, the Registrar and other officials. This was to come later.

My last big job in the school was to carve a panel in black Irish limestone to go over the entrance to the New College of Science building in Prince Consort Road, Kensington. It was some forty feet long by six feet deep, or thereabouts, and consisted of incised forms representing the cloud chamber and other such phenomena together with mathematical equations: the formula for the H-bomb and such like. All the information was given me by Patrick Blackett, the rector of the College of Science, and an Indian mathematician called Salem. I worked out the design, but hadn't the faintest idea what the symbols meant. One day I was cutting one of the mathematical equations when Salem rushed into the room and stopped me, saying: 'Don't go any further with those numbers, I'm not sure whether that should be an eight or a nine, and I won't know for three years!' He may never have found out for he was killed in an air disaster some time afterwards.

Darwin was not happy with what he considered to be the undisciplined way in which I was running the Sculpture School. I later learned that he had questioned one of my assistants about a rumour that I had taken one of my girl students to Paris with me. This was confirmed by my assistant. It was true of course that I had done so.

Darwin's reaction was to install a security man to keep a check on the school at night. This man was so unpleasant with the students that on my recommendation Darwin was obliged to discharge him. In revenge the security man stole a photograph from my studio, of myself and a girl lying 'starko' on a Mediterranean beach. I later learned that he had made several copies of this, giving one to Darwin.

All this worry and anxiety made my duodenal ulcer flare up again and eventually I became so ill that I had to go to St Bartholomew's Hospital for an operation on my intestines. When I came out I was a wreck, physically and morally, and bordering on a nervous breakdown. I was by now worried to death because I was convinced that Darwin would give me the sack at the first opportunity.

Returning to the college was no pleasure at all, the best students had left and the new intake was a poor, talentless lot. They didn't want to learn, all they did was thumb through books on contemporary sculpture and pick out some gimmick which would be easy to imitate. The atmosphere I had created no longer existed.

A fortnight after my return I was sent for by Darwin. At this interview he told me that he had, locked up in his safe, a copy of the incriminating photograph which had been given to him by the night watchman. This he would show to the Council unless I resigned. He had, moreover, interviewed two of my assistants who had confirmed his suspicions regarding my taking a girl student to Paris. The interview turned into a slanging match. I had been longing to tell Darwin what I thought, and this I proceeded to do in no uncertain terms. Then, just before I left his office, having tendered my resignation, I got out of my chair and said: 'Robin, you are a great organizer but your only talent and claim to fame is that you could get shit out of a rocking horse'. He burst into tears as I left, for I believe at heart he was really fond of me.

What at that time appeared a disaster, was, in fact, quite the reverse, and I have never looked back since.

XIII

The Camargue

I had written to Lester Epstein in St Louis telling him of my predicament and what I planned to do – pack up and go down to the South of France for a year. I got an immediate reply saying that he was borrowing some money from his brother and was coming with me. A week later he arrived in England.

But things were not to go smoothly. I was struck by every kind of disaster. I had planned to travel down to France in my lovely old Rolls-Royce, one of my earlier extravagances, but coming back to London from a weekend at Easton Neston a couple of weeks before our departure was scheduled, batting along at a carefree eighty miles an hour, one of the pistons broke and shattered the engine. I realized when the breakdown truck came to tow the car away that I would never see it again. I sold it to the garage man for £250 cash, paid out of the till on the spot.

This accident had really thrown a spanner in the works. My only means of transport had gone, and I couldn't afford to replace it. Meanwhile Lester was at my home in Devon waiting for us to set off. What the hell was I to do? My total wealth was my college pension, which taken in one lump amounted to no more than £2000, half of which I had given to Morwenna. Add to this the £250 I had got for my defunct Rolls-Royce and I had £1250 on which to survive the coming year in France.

Brooding over my problems next day and feeling that the bottom had fallen out of my world, I happened to bump into an old friend in Queen's Gate. I must have looked the picture of misery, for he exclaimed at once, 'What the hell's the matter with you? You look ghastly – come and have a drink.' I followed him into a pub in Queen's Gate Mews, where I sat down to a pint of beer and related my sad story. His reaction was typical of him. When I had finished he simply said; 'Go and buy yourself a car, put it down to me and don't mention the subject again.'

My problems instantly assumed manageable proportions. I bought a Vauxhall Estate car, ideal for the job, and within three weeks we were on the road. On crossing the Channel, any shades of gloom that still clung to me were shaken off, and by the time the coast line of France appeared on the horizon I was a new man. We made straight for Paris and installed ourselves in the Hotel Royal in Montparnasse, the scene of my first experience of this city. I had stayed there with Barbara in the early twenties.

Just to walk the streets was heaven: the smell of black coffee and Gauloises cigarettes, the blasts of warm air blowing up your trouser legs from the *Métro* ventilators, the wafts of perfume picked up off a passing *cocotte* as she brushed by you – a whiff of 'Antelope' bought back vividly to mind a red-head I once knew. The names of the *boîtes de nuit*, too, conjured up memories: there was the 'Jockey' where the young Hemingway would enter with his band of toughs and would often start a brawl.

After a week in Paris we were on the road again, heading for Provence. It was bitterly cold, with snow on the ground, and the trees twinkled in the bright sun exactly like the tinsel on Christmas cards. After a couple of days we came to a stop in Beaucaire, another town of happy memories, to which I had returned many times since 1934, with students or lovers, sometimes combining the two. Here we put up in a cheap, broken-down, old hotel, cripplingly damp and without heating of any kind. It was so cold that we had to sleep together in our overcoats. In the morning, as soon as the first café opened, we would leap out of bed and run down the narrow streets, cut in two by the wind, to down a *café-cognac* as quickly as possible.

At night we frequented a café whose proprietor Cambi, a Franco-Italian, bred fighting bulls out in the Camargue, which was the rendezvous of the local *aficionados* of the *corrida* and the *courses libres* – the latter are the traditional games of the area in which the Camargue bull is used. Both the game and the bulls themselves with their lyre-shaped horns are said to derive from the Cretan occupation of this country over three thousand years ago. A group of men in white flannels, called *razateurs*, try to remove *cocardes* which are tied to the bull's horns with a comb-like instrument held in the hand, the *crochet* as it is known. As the game proceeds and the bull becomes more dangerous the prize money goes up and up and enthusiasm and tempers run high, with a corresponding increase in the noise coming from the supporters around the arena.

Cambi introduced us to a young boy named Gomollini, another Franco-Italian, who had a bungalow to rent at Fourques called '*Mon Rêve*'. The name had been chosen by his father, who built it as a secret love-nest for himself and a seventeen-year-old half-gypsy girl. Unfortunately old man Gomollini was over sixty at the time and was no match for the passion of this young girl. Within six months of installing her in '*Mon Rêve*' he dropped dead from a heart attack whilst 'on the job', as his son reported to me with a mixture of pride and humour.

It was into this love abode that Lester and I moved. It was unfurnished – even the kitchen stove had been removed – the electricity was cut off and there was no heating of any kind. When it rained the water ran down the walls into the two bedrooms and only the main room, which luckily happened to be the one room in the house with a fireplace, remained dry.

I furnished the whole house from a junk shop in Arles, buying for £12 two old box mattresses stuffed with hay, four chairs, a table, a few pots and pans, the odd knife and fork, a corkscrew and a box of candles. I found an old wood-burning stove on a rubbish dump which we brought home in the wagon and installed in the open fireplace.

This old stove was kept going day and night, and as long as the wind came from the north, the south, or the east, it worked a treat. Once the wind turned westerly all the acrid smoke from the pine wood we burned came belching out into the room, and we would have to open all the windows and sometimes put the fire out.

The place was lit at night by candles stuck in the necks of empty bottles – there was never any shortage of the latter. We had adopted a stray cat, which gave a homely touch to the evenings which we spent sitting in front of the open fire waiting for the dinner to cook. The standard of *cuisine* was extraordinarily high, considering the primitive set-up; my natural love for this art was reinforced by the fact that there was nothing else one could do after dark.

Despite the obvious discomforts of life at '*Mon Rêve*' Lester and I were radiantly happy and did a great deal of work. I was in my element, surrounded by horses and bulls to draw in their natural habitat and just twenty minutes' drive from Les Baux, a continual source of inspiration to me, with its extraordinary rock formations packed with natural sculptural forms. Lester scribbled poems and turned out collages by the hundreds. He would occasionally stalk round the village at night tearing strips off posters on the hoardings to use as material for his pictures.

Lester, by birth a Russian-Jew, combined a love of things pornographic and squalid with a strong streak of 'Russian depression'. He was happiest during this rough early period; being a kind of Walter Mitty, he liked to imagine himself in the role of

Van Gogh or some other struggling, unrecognized genius. I have met some perverse and complex characters in my time, but Lester was in a class by himself. However, his brilliant brain and occasional bursts of wit made him more than tolerable as a companion.

Lester had lived for ten years in Mexico and all he could say in Spanish was '*Buenas dias*'. He had a built-in resistance to language learning. For my own part I was keen to improve my French, and I took him with me to lessons I had arranged with an aged school mistress in Arles. Lester would sit there staring at this poor woman as though he was trying to mesmerize her, doggedly refusing to answer any of her questions. In the course of the lessons he did, however, produce one classic. We had been set some sentences from a children's story book to translate from French into English. One of these sentences, '*Petit François chasse une poule craintive autour du poulailler*', translated with reluctance by Lester, emerged as 'Little François chases the nervous whore around the poolroom'. The effort was obviously too much for him and after this he quit the French lessons.

Although it was hard going, I remained happy and wildly optimistic. To crown my happiness Maggie Scott turned up from Vienna, where the Dunham Company had been appearing. Katherine Dunham herself arrived soon after, looking for someone to translate a film-script into French. We found a French girl for her, Sylvie Devèze, whose boy friend, Jean Cendras, was a gypsy *rejoneador* – a man who fights bulls in the Portuguese style from horseback. It was through this contact that I made my entry into the true world of the Camargue. Cendras invited me to accompany him to a *ferrade* – a seasonal branding of calves, accompanied by a fiesta – to be held in the Crau, the rough scrubland which lies on the east side of the Rhône from the Camargue proper. He gave me a horse to ride and I joined the *gardiens* in rounding up the bulls. We had a great day. The whole spirit of the occasion was novel and exhilarating and I felt close to the real life of the place.

Towards the end of the morning, while standing beside the corral watching the bulls that had been brought in, I got into conversation on the usual subject, horses and bulls, with a young girl whose uncle, Louis Turquay, was bailiff at the bull farm, 'Les Trinitaires'. She introduced me to him and his wife Hélène. They were a splendid couple. We hit it off right away and I was invited to lunch. By the time I left they had given me an open invitation to stay and work with them on the farm.

The offer appealed to me strongly. I had become more and more interested in the life of the Camargue as it revolved around the bulls and the horses, and the opportunity to experience it at first-hand was irresistible. Besides, my relations with Lester were deteriorating. He had recently sunk into an unbroken phase of gloom, and my attempts to stop him finding comfort in the bottle led to frequent arguments. After some weeks of tension and fraught nerves on both sides he left for England. When I came to clean out his room I found countless empty Calvados bottles hidden in the cupboards and under the bed. As for the bed itself, I discovered, on trying to strip it, that the sheets had been nailed to the frame with three-inch nails to stop them sliding off – he obviously hadn't changed them once in the nine months he had been there. I burned the bed and bedding on a bonfire in the garden.

I was now free to take up the Turquays on their offer, and I moved in as soon as I could, impatient to start my life on the farm. Here a routine of work and rest soon established itself, and within a couple of weeks I felt completely at home. Every morning at 5.30 a.m. I would go down to the kitchen where Louis would be frying himself an egg in a filthy old frying pan which had never been cleaned since the day it was bought. He would break the egg into the pan and on contact with the burning fat it would turn black immediately. My own breakfast consisted of donkey sausage, dry bread and wine.

When our horses had been fed and watered we would saddle up for the daily round. This consisted of a twenty-five-mile ride before lunch over the whole of the property, through the swamps, water and thick scrubs, checking that all was well with the bulls and horses and doing the '*circuit*' of the boundary to see that the bulls had not broken down the barbed wire barrier and escaped into the open country. When this happened we were faced with real problems – where to go to look for them and, when we had found them, how to get them back through the space they had made in the barrier. It needed all the skill of horse and horse-man to achieve this last part of the operation and in winter it could be gruelling. Trying to drive a hundred fighting bulls, who are not in the best of tempers, through a small gap in a fence is no easy matter in the most favourable conditions – you can imagine what it is like doing it against a blizzard or a cold *mistral*, when the rain freezes on your clothing and your fingers can no longer grip the reins.

Fortunately for a novice, as I was at that time, the task is made easier by the horses which are trained to work like sheep dogs, needing practically no guidance. They know the difference between the sharp and blunt end of a bull and keep both themselves and their rider out of harm's way.

I remember once, in the early days, Louis asking me to saddle up Grisbi, one of the working horses, and go out into the country to bring in the twelve riding horses. They were away somewhere on the *manade* with the forty or so other horses of the Trinitaires herd. Louis's instructions were that I was to look out for the stallion. If he was near the herd I was to bring them all in and we would sort them out in the yard. If, on the other hand, he was more than three hundred yards away from the rest, I was to cut him out first, drive him right away from the others and then bring in the riding horses alone. This was all very well, but I had to confess to Louis that I didn't know the riding horses from the others. 'You won't need to,' Louis said, 'Grisbi knows them.'

I was not feeling very confident when I set off. Eventually a group of horses came into view, grazing way out across the plains.

On coming to within some six hundred yards of them, I spotted the stallion standing by himself at some distance from the others. I was just coming to the conclusion that it would be better to try to drive him away first, when Grisbi, without the slightest indication from me, suddenly took off after him and chased him a mile away from the others. Then he turned back towards the rest of the herd and, working like a sheep dog, cut out the riding horses before they knew what was happening to them and brought them back to the yard. I never once touched him, but sat on his back, a mere passenger, watching this display in amazement.

After I had been at Trinitaires a couple of months and had learned something about the game, Louis gave me forty-two four-year-old bulls to look after on my own. This meant that in the early morning I had to drive them out of a wood, where they were brought in for the night, into the plains beyond, and then fetch them in the evening, driving them to a clearing in the wood where hay would be spread out for them. The main object of this exercise was to get them used to being rounded up so that they would be easier to handle when the time came to ship them away in the bull-truck.

I had been doing this for some weeks and my bulls and I were getting used to one another, when one evening I was forced to break the routine – with somewhat hair-raising consequences. I had spent all afternoon out on an errand and did not return until late in the evening. Louis met me at the gate and said: 'Don't waste any time putting the hay out. The bulls are out there waiting at the barrier and if they are not let in soon they will smash it down. You had better go and get them in at once, and take the hay out to them afterwards.'

I jumped on my horse and rode out to the barrier where they were all waiting, just as Louis had said. Without dismounting I opened the gates. Immediately they charged in, heading in a rush for the clearing where they expected to find their hay. I did not wait to witness their disappointment but turned back to the yard where I harnessed up the draught horse, Olga. I loaded the wagon with hay and set off in fear and trepidation for the clearing. By now it was pitch dark, and on arrival at the scene all I could see were shining green eyes and the occasional flash of the white of a horn. As I led the pony along I was conscious of being followed by the bulls but I dared not look round to see how near they were to me. Then they started tearing the hay off the cart. One came right alongside me. Grabbing a handful of hay I held it out without looking at him, and he took it out of my hand.

After a while there were quite a few of the bulls I could feed by hand in this way without any risk of being attacked. Somehow I had managed to convey to them that they were not being menaced – which in the circumstances was lucky for me. Like most creatures bulls normally only attack in self-defence but, being short-sighted, they frequently think that they are in danger when they are not.

The farm itself was surrounded in the day by fighting bulls, who roamed about as they liked. This made visits to the lavatory at the back of the house a risky business. Sometimes, having gained the safety of the interior, it was impossible to come out again on account of a bull lurking outside the door.

Both Hélène and Louis had nerves of steel in this respect. There was a small red bull in the herd who was completely mad and would chase literally anything that moved. His favourite sport was to hide in the bushes behind the house and wait for someone to appear. Quite undaunted, Hélène would come out to spread her washing on the bushes to dry. Suddenly the red bull would appear from behind a bush and she would have to run for it – sometimes only gaining the gate by a short head! This performance took place regularly three times a week.

Louis combined fearlessness with a strength which was astonishing. I have seen him take a young bull by the horns when it was threatening to attack a fallen horse, turning it over into the mud so that its horns were stuck there long enough for the horse to get up and out of harm's way. His most spectacular display of bravery and skill has passed, with justification, into the annals of local history. One day a *rejoneador* came to see him wanting to buy a bull and borrow a good working horse for a *corrida* in which he was to take part in a nearby arena. Louis brought some bulls into a pen for his inspection. *Gardiens* like Louis who have spent their lives with a herd, have seen the animals grow up from calves and have watched the way they play and duel with each other, know exactly how they will behave in the arena – whether they are left or right hookers or straight chargers. It was a fine looking beast that the *rejoneador* picked, but he chose it mainly because it was cheaper than the others; the reason for this being that it was known by Louis to be a left-hooker. This meant that it was liable suddenly to swerve its head to the left under the cape, aiming at the man instead of following the cape's movements straight through. Of the bulls the hookers are by far the most dangerous and difficult to handle, for they are unpredictable.

Louis warned the *rejoneador* that under no circumstances was he to take the bull on the near side until he was sure he had him mastered. He impressed on him that he was lending him his best horse and did not want it injured. The man replied, somewhat touchily, that he had been in the profession for years and had coped with many a left-hooker in his time. Louis just said: 'Remember, I'm warning you'.

The day came for the fight and Louis delivered the horse and the bull to the ring. Then he took up a position in the area behind the barrier where he could see what was going on and be near at hand should anything go wrong. There he stood with his beret stuck Provençal-style on his head and his one good eye – he had lost the other in an accident – fixed on the *toril*. In due course the *rejoneador* entered the arena. He took the horse through a couple of fancy turns, then at the sound of the trumpet the gate of the *toril* swung open and in rushed the bull. At the first pass this conceited idiot took the bull on the near side, with the immediate and inevitable result – the bull swung his head inwards, caught the horse on the flank and turned the whole lot over.

Before anyone knew what was happening, Louis was in the ring with his beret in his hand, calling to the bull as he had always done on the farm at home. The bull promptly left the scene of the disaster and came straight for Louis, who stood like a statue holding out his beret in his hand, and just vibrating it gently.

As the bull charged he executed a magnificent pass, greeted by cheers from the delighted crowd. Now the bull was coming up on his blind side, but although Louis could not see it, he knew exactly what its next move would be. Still standing motionless, except for his extended hand, he brought the bull past him again, succeeding in holding its attention until the horse had been got up on to its feet and been taken out of the ring and the *peons* had come in to make the *quite*. Then, amid thunderous applause, Louis put his beret on his head and walked stonily out of the ring and round behind the scenes, where he dealt the *rejoneador* in question a blow that would have felled an ox. The man did not regain consciousness for several hours. Fortunately the horse, after attention from an expert vet, recovered and was none the worse for the experience.

Unfortunately I did not see this display myself since it took place some years before I came to France. However, those that did have told me that they would willingly have paid twenty times the price of their seats for the privilege of watching it.

Such men as Louis are the product of a unique and rapidly disappearing society where animal and man are on an equal footing. They despise any form of self-importance in a man, having particular contempt for those who try to live above their station, whom they usually describe in Provençal as '*Péta pus n'ant que soun quoin!*' – 'Trying to fart above their arsehole!' The Provençal language is full of such witty quips and no opportunity is missed to take down a peg or two anyone they think stands in need of it. Mison, the local saddler and incidentally the one-time elected champion saddler of France, is a master of this art.

In 1958 a film was being made in the Camargue. One of the actors came into Mison's shop in Mas Thibert to look at the saddles, which he had seen and admired on the ponies being used in the film. These saddles with their high decorated arches back and front are extremely fine pieces of work, taking a long time to make, and are very expensive, costing in those days as much as £120. After looking round the shop, the actor turned to Mison and said:

'I want you to make me a saddle.'

'Yes,' said Mison.

'I shall be leaving in three weeks' time and I shall want it finished by then.'

'Yes,' said Mison.

'How much will it cost?'

'It won't cost you anything at all,' said Mison.

'For nothing?' exclaimed the actor, imagining that he had been recognized as a famous film-star. 'You are giving me a present?'

'No,' said Mison, 'I'm not going to make the saddle.'

There were always splendid local characters hanging about Mison's place, many of them wonderfully out of touch with the modern world. I used to sit in there for hours chatting with the *gardiens* who came in and out. One day an old *gardien* came in on his horse to collect a small transistor radio which had been left there for him. It was the first radio he had ever owned and Mison had to demonstrate to him how it worked and how to switch it on and off. He then set off across the Crau with the radio strapped on behind the saddle. Halfway home his curiosity got the better of him and he reached behind him and started twiddling the buttons. Suddenly a blast of music burst from the radio and the horse, frightened by the noise, leapt into the air, throwing the old man off, and galloped away into the country with the radio blaring. It was not until late that evening that the horse was eventually found, traced by the mysterious music coming from behind the tall reeds in the marshes.

One would imagine from reading this narrative that I did nothing during my stay at Trinitaires but ride around on a horse. Fired by the excitement of my new experiences I did a great deal of my own work. Drawing and painting the horses and bulls out in the wild country was a real challenge and inspiring, despite the inevitable interruptions caused by the wind carrying off sheets of paper or an inquisitive bull forcing me to retreat at speed from the scene of activity. But this only made me feel I was following in the steps of Turner, who once had himself taken fourteen miles out to sea in a fishing boat in order to paint the scene of a lighthouse thrashed by monumental waves in a hurricane. Drama of this kind obviously has a profound influence on one's work, and gives it a vitality which cannot be achieved in the comfort of a studio. In my spare time I also produced a follow-up to my children's book on drawing horses for the Studio Series, this time on *How to Draw Dogs*. There were plenty of models available to me in the dogs that roamed about in the local villages.

At the end of the year I had enough works collected together to mount an exhibition in London, at Ackerman's. It was an immediate success. The clients, aided by the excellent champagne which I gave them at the opening of the show, entered into the carefree spirit of the works and bought them all before the last bottle had been opened.

XIV

... and they all lived happily ever after

While I was in England I was commissioned by Lord Derby to do a life-size bronze statue of Hyperion, possibly the most famous racehorse of the twentieth century – certainly the most famous stallion, having bred, in all, nearly nine hundred winners and made a unique contribution to the evolution of the modern thoroughbred. This commission was a great challenge, especially since the horse had been dead for six months. There were a few photographs but they were bad, and all taken from the same side. I was forced to resort to using his skeleton as a model, and

I applied to Professor Miller of the Equine Research Station at Newmarket for permission to borrow the bones which were being kept there in a tank of chemical fluid in order to harden them for posterity. Hyperion had not died until he was thirty, and his bones had deteriorated to a great extent.

Permission was granted and I took the skeleton away with me to the studio I had found in Devon in a beautiful house on the moors belonging to a builder named Jarvis. Once settled in there I set about examining the bones. They were certainly remarkable in more ways than one. Due to decalcification, some of them had become so porous that they were like lace when held up against the light. But the most interesting thing was the skull; when I put it on my lap to examine it, the teeth were so razor sharp that they cut through my trousers. I knew that Hyperion had always flatly refused to allow anyone to examine his mouth, so that his teeth had never been rasped down. Now, looking at the skull, I discovered the reason for this: one of the small bones which run down from the ear-socket to the tongue had, at some time, been broken and in mending itself had completely blocked the ear cavity. The horse must have been stone-deaf on the off-side for most of his life. No one at the stud could remember Hyperion having ever gone off his feed so there had been no way of knowing what had happened to him.

The skull gave me a fairly accurate picture of the head. For the rest I had to rely on photographs, such as they were, and the memories of those who had known the horse in his lifetime. I went to see 'Bunty' Scrope, stud manager to Lord Derby, in the hope that he might be able to give me some useful tips. Not only was he able to tell me a good deal about the horse, but I found him a charming man. I also talked to the stud groom who had looked after Hyperion, and got a tremendous amount of information from him concerning the horse's character, all of which was of great interest to me. I even got hold of Tommy Weston, the jockey who rode him in his three great victories. The meeting with him was rather less successful. I gave him lunch and a few drinks to encourage him to talk. All I got from him were a lot of incoherent, sentimental remarks and a tip for a horse, for which I paid five shillings. The horse in question was beaten out of sight.

I had now collected all the information I could lay my hands on. To inject some life into the work and to help me with the interpretation of the photographs, I had the loan of a horse which bore a slight resemblance to Hyperion. I set to work to make the maquette and, having got the approval of Lord Derby, I started the serious business of putting up the armature. This had to be exceptionally strong in order to support a ton and a half of clay. I had never before attempted a life-size figure of a horse in clay and I was to learn much from the experience. I had got the clay up, the model roughly in shape and proportion, and was working on it one morning when I became aware that it was moving slowly sideways towards me. I realized there was nothing for it but to jump out of the way, which I did, and the work collapsed in a heap on the floor. The armature had not been strong enough to hold it up.

I started again, the wiser for this setback, and within a year the work was finished. Lord Derby flew down to Exeter in his aeroplane and when he saw it he was delighted. On completion of the casting in bronze it went on exhibition at the Academy. It looked astonishing there standing in a room by itself surrounded by modern paintings. It was curiously out of place – like a horse that had broken loose and come into the gallery – completely unrelated to anything else that was there. However, it was much praised, and received a lot of publicity.

The statue was finally erected on Lord Derby's estate on the Snailwell Road, Newmarket. Mr Jarvis built the base for it, and it really looked most impressive. It was so realistic that, I heard later from people on the stud, horses passing by on their way to exercise would whinny at it and the mares in the adjoining paddock would come up to engage it in conversation. But the crowning compliment to both Hyperion and myself was paid by the unknown person who came out on a cold night and covered the statue with a hood and a rug.

The Hyperion bronze finished and paid for, I was in the money. I gave about a third of the cash to Morwenna. She was pleased, I was pleased, but what pleased me most of all was that now I could return to France and take up my life with Maggie. I bought myself a Daimler SP250 sports car, pointed it towards the South of France and went non-stop like a scalded cat until I got to Arles, where Maggie awaited my return in the penthouse she had fixed up.

Lovely as this little penthouse was, it was too small for me to do any sculpture. So eventually we bought and did up an old mill in the village of Castries, near Montpellier, consisting of a fourteenth-century mill tower, which at one time had been an olive oil press, three little rooms and a large sixteenth-century barn formerly used as the village slaughter house. We entirely reconstructed the building, turning the barn into a studio with a stable for two horses adjacent to it.

Castries, like most of the villages in this district at that time, was tenanted mostly by old people, and going down into the village was like going into a cellar only inhabited by black beetles. The women wore black clothing, as did most of the men. The difference between the Castriotes and black beetles was that beetles scuttle away and hide when approached, whereas the villagers just stopped and stared at us as though we were Martians. We were the object of much curiosity, invading as we were their sanctuary where they had been peacefully in-breeding for centuries.

Here I found much of the charm of my childhood days. Progress had by-passed Castries and the pace was slow and peaceful, an ideal atmosphere in which to work. There were still horses working in the vineyards. Come nine o'clock at night there wasn't a soul about in the streets, all was silent save for the church clock ringing out the hour and the occasional clatter of a dustbin lid which had been turned over by some scavenging dog or cat.

One would never know the time of day if it was not for the church clock, the cocks crowing, the clanging of copper bells from the flock of sheep passing the house morning and evening on their way to and from the *garrigue*, or the sunrise and sunset, which are always spectacular in the great expanse of sky.

Free from worry and my anxiety complex temporarily laid to rest, I got quickly back to work. I produced a number of imaginative bronzes for which there was a ready market in both England and America. My output of drawings, paintings and sculptures was prolific and enabled me to mount three exhibitions following one another in London, New York and Johannesburg, all of which were successful.

Maggie managed my business matters, untangling anything that showed any sign of giving trouble. Looking after me and my affairs was to her a 'round of drinks' compared with her last job trying to control a mixed bag of wild men from the jungle. But I should add that without her previous experience she might not have found the job so easy, as no one else has ever been able to do it!

My first break from work came when I accepted an invitation from the Union of Soviet Artists to visit Russia in 1964, along with my wife. Morwenna had completely accepted my living with Maggie and generously said herself that Maggie was much more suited to me than she ever was. It was, however, agreed that under the circumstances I should take Morwenna on this trip as she was, on paper, still my official wife. This may seem strange to some of my readers, but I cannot see why one has altogether to cut a person from one's life for no other reason than that one doesn't want to live with them.

This trip was very enjoyable. The Russians were charming, well-mannered people and we were allowed to go anywhere we wanted and take as many photographs as we wished, none of which were inspected. We visited the Kremlin in Moscow and the Hermitage in Leningrad, both too well known to need any description from myself.

There is no fear of getting into trouble in foreign countries provided one observes their laws and customs. In other words, 'When in Rome do as the Romans do'. There was only one practice in Russia which I found slightly embarrassing to comply with. Even in the grand hotels loo accommodation is eminently communist, for they are all six seaters. In you go, and wait in the queue until a seat becomes vacant. Sooner or later a gentleman will fold up his *Pravda* and get up. The lavatory attendant who is washing his socks in the hand basin will temporarily stop this operation to hand you a few sheets off a toilet roll, at the same time indicating that it is your turn next.

I had not been back in France for long when I received a letter from Lester Epstein's brother saying that Lester had died suddenly of heart failure at forty-four years of age. This was really sad news. He was just beginning to find his feet and get some recognition as an artist and I am sure that had he lived and got over his wild restlessness he would have made a name for himself.

*

Repose is never achieved whilst the brain remains active but now, for myself, without the many distractions common to youth, I have time to reflect and to revise my thoughts and ideas. This is the time when a true assessment can be made of one's contribution, where and why one made mistakes, succeeded or failed. The moment of truth has arrived. The uniqueness of man, unlike animals, lies in his ability to choose. I chose my way of life which has given me great pleasure, but I have paid dearly for it in that I have not achieved my potential as a sculptor. I know this only too well. Now, of course, it is too late to do anything about it and I have to content myself with the knowledge that I can model a horse and portray its movement better than anyone else.

Each successive horse portrait teaches me something, and when in 1965 I was bidden to London by Stanhope Joel to discuss the possibility of doing a life-size posthumous portrait of his horse

Chamossaire, I looked forward to the challenge. Stanhope was in bed with 'flu. I was ushered up to his bedroom in the Connaught Hotel to find the poor man looking very ill indeed and practically speechless. 'Sit down,' he said, in a hoarse voice, as he picked up the telephone and rang room service to ask for a bottle of champagne. Not until the first large glass was downed did our discussion commence. I found this a most congenial way of doing business.

Stanhope told me what he wanted and where he wanted the statue to go, and asked me how much it would cost. I told him the price to which he just said, 'OK.' I then asked him what position he wanted the horse to be in. 'You're the artist', he said, 'I'll leave that to you.' This suited me admirably.

Although the horse had been buried at the Snailwell stud at Newmarket I was not allowed to disturb the grave for sentimental reasons, so had to rely on the known vital statistics and the many good photographs available. It took me nearly nine months' hard work to complete and when the work was finished both Stanhope and I were well pleased with the result. The statue now stands at the Snailwell stud, a couple of miles up the road from the Hyperion statue.

It had been a long and arduous task and I was ready to relax for a while. One night after attending a gastronomic dinner at Aix-en-Provence, too tired to return home, we put up in a hotel in the town. The following morning Maggie and I went down to an oyster bar. The juke box was blaring out South American music and this, together with the oysters, suddenly reminded me of La Ventosa in Mexico where I had eaten oysters by the dozen for the first time in my life. We decided there and then to go to Mexico via California, taking up an invitation from our old friend Jo Cohn in Beverly Hills to visit him there. Within a fortnight we were on our way, together with my son Nicholas, and spent the first month with Jo visiting the Metro-Goldwyn-Mayer studios (Jo had been financial adviser to MGM) and racing at

Hollywood Park and Santa Anita. He was a wonderful host, knowing everybody in the film world. Living with Jo in his charming house in Beverly Hills was like being on the set of one of the great spectacular films of the past.

Nick was very restless and could not make up his mind what he wanted to do, so I bought him a second-hand car, gave him four hundred dollars and said: 'America belongs to you. Off you go.' He managed to stay in the States for the best part of a year, earning his living in devious ways – as a kennel hand, working in a candle factory, making leather belts, and as a golf caddy, a game he had never played in his life. Big and strong he could carry two sets of clubs at once, earning ten dollars a round. He was in great demand because of his English accent and his entertaining way of recommending a club for a certain stroke which was totally unsuitable and produced the most disastrous results.

Maggie and I set off for Mexico City in a car lent to us by Jo. He later joined us there and we continued down to the Guatemalan frontier stopping off at the village of El Tule, where we arrived at five o'clock in the morning. We went there because I wanted to see what had happened to all the people whom I had known when living there, in particular the Pablo family. I stopped the car under the big tree where I used to leave it when first going to El Tule. We got out and stood in the dust for a moment looking about us. I took my hat off as though I were going into church. The long-tailed blackbirds flew screaming from the branches. I could smell charcoal burning and hear the faint sounds of hands patting out the maize dough for the early morning tortillas. We walked quietly towards the Pablo's hut along the dust tracks I had trodden so many times seventeen years before. There were the same scrawny-looking dogs sneaking away behind the tall cactus fences which divided the little yards.

My soul seemed to leave my body and return to those days of magic and beauty. Bodily I felt an intruder. I wondered what my

Indian family would think when I suddenly appeared with two strange people who were no part of the past. I need not have worried. As we walked towards the Pablo's hut I could see a slim figure of a woman. It was Aurelia, tears streaming down her face. As we embraced each other she said: 'I was waiting for you. I knew you were coming.' Knowing these people I was not the least surprised. Both Maggie and Jo were received as though they were part of myself. Lupe was sent for and arrived with her three children. She had changed very little in appearance and as we all sat on the ground to drink the cinnamon chocolate Aurelia had prepared we exchanged stories of what had happened to us all since I was last with them. Lupe told me that Jorge, the youngest son, had been killed in a fight the year before. After two or three hours with the Pablo family I felt I had to leave quickly as the emotional strain was becoming too great. With difficulty we tore ourselves away and continued to drive on down the Pan-American Highway, slowly returning to the realities of our own world.

On arrival at the Guatemalan frontier we were not allowed to cross owing to the Russian visa in my passport. We stayed around in this district for two or three days, walking in the jungle which is so spectacular with the infinite variety of orchids and fantastic birds. Mexico had not changed, nor had its hotels, for the one in which we stayed had the usual plumbing problems. Turning on the hot shower, the bedroom was flooded with cold water to a depth of four inches. Jo was used to a much higher standard of living than this and suggested we return to Mexico City, but not before he had bought a hundred pound sack of coffee which he installed in the back of the car. I tried to dissuade him on two grounds – one, that we should all be gassed by the pungent fumes, and two, that he would never get it across the American frontier. I was right on both counts for we had to travel the whole way across Mexico with all the windows open to avoid being as-phyxiated, and on reaching the frontier it was confiscated.

Back in Hollywood Jo suggested that we should go down and

spend some time at his vineyard in the Nappa Valley. This we did and found it so beautiful that we stayed there for several months. He had handed us the key to his cellar of excellent Californian wines of which we made the maximum use. To celebrate my birthday we drove across the Sierra Nevada to Reno to see the rodeo, the casinos, the divorcées and the ghost towns. We spent a hilarious time and on the night of my birthday we stayed up until half-past four in the morning pulling the one-armed bandits, which are to be found in their hundreds on every floor of the numerous casinos. I worked away at these machines until I had cramp in both arms, practically out on my feet, until I was woken up by the ringing of a bell and the clatter of silver dollars falling round my feet.

*

I can truly say that the biggest single contribution to my health, wealth and happiness has been the racing scene. In 1967 I persuaded Alfred Gates, director of Ackermann's Gallery, to co-sponsor with myself a hurdle race to be run annually in the month of November at Sandown Park for which I would give a bronze trophy each year. Major Beckwith Smith, director of Sandown Park, arranged the fixture and John Hislop drew up the conditions for the race. To inaugurate the event, to be known as the Acker-mann-Skeaping Trophy, Queen Elizabeth The Queen Mother graciously consented to present the trophy to the winning owner. The race was won by Lord Creighton Stewart's Chorus trained by Thompson Jones and ridden by Stan Mellor. The race was an immediate success, and the following year it was won by the Queen Mother's Escalus. Maggie presented her with the trophy. This Royal success put the hallmark on the race which continues to be run annually, although Ackermann's place as co-sponsors has been taken over by Marlow Ropes since 1972.

Early in 1968 I had a visitor, a M. Pierre Amiot, who appeared out of the blue announcing that he had been told that I was a world authority on animals in art. He asked me if I would under-take to write a book on this subject for the publishing house,

Les Productions de Paris. I told him that although I knew a good deal about animals I was no authority on this subject. I was so flattered, however, that I consented, not realizing that it would mean a vast amount of research in museums and libraries. Both Maggie and I worked incessantly for months until the book was finished. It was then translated into French by Hervé Bazin, who also wrote the foreword. No expense was spared in its production and special photographs were taken of anything I wanted to illustrate. I was really proud of LES ANIMAUX. It was a magnificent book and all eight thousand copies were sold by private subscription. I gave a copy of it to Julian Huxley who was very impressed and was anxious to get it published in England. Unfortunately this was not possible due to the high cost of production.

*

Although everyone accepted that Maggie and I were not married it could cause embarrassment when we travelled together or went to stay with people we didn't know too well. Finally, after discussing the matter with my sons, Morwenna was persuaded to divorce me. The divorce granted, we wasted no time and got married at the British Consulate in Marseille on the 6 June 1969. There were only four other people present; Hélène Turquay and her son Jean François, Commander David Scott and Sheila Botterill, Maggie's triplet brother and sister. Beginning at 9.30 in the morning in a bar at the *Vieux Port* in Marseille and continuing throughout the day, David, Sheila, Maggie and I managed to down a case of champagne. By the time we got to the Consulate it did not seem to me that we were short of guests. Suffering from double vision, it appeared that they were going in two by two like the animals into Noah's ark.

Commissions began to come in from both the States and England. I did a small bronze portrait of Royal Palace for Jim Joel, a painting of Sleeping Partner for Lord Rosebery, a bronze of Fort Marcy, twice winner of the Laurel Park International, for his owner Paul Mellon. This last was my first attempt at a portrait of a horse cantering. Some horses are much more impressive when in action and I always choose the position which shows a horse to advantage. Elliott Burch, Paul Mellon's trainer, helped me a great deal, sending the horse round the track at the speed I wanted. Having made many drawings and taken innumerable photographs I began the model. Even when the model was completed there was no guarantee of eventual success for then it had to be cast. If the original mould of the model was not good, the work would be lost beyond retrieve. In the modern method of bronze casting the model is first of all covered with a thin coating of rubber solution and then a plaster of Paris case to keep the rubber in shape and position. Very occasionally the rubber will distort or perish causing endless repair work on the wax cast which has been taken from the faulty mould.

Bronze casting is a complicated and skilled process which I am frequently asked to explain. It is necessary to see it done in order to understand it fully. It is spectacular to see the men wearing fire-proof boots, coats and gloves, pouring the white-hot molten metal into the moulds. Sparks fly in all directions and the drops that fall on the cold concrete floor of the foundry explode like little bombs. The whole impression is that of an erupting volcano and every time I see it done I am reminded of the time when, as a student, I climbed Vesuvius and looked down into the crater. When the bronze of Fort Marcy was completed to my satisfaction Paul Mellon ordered six copies of it, one of which he presented to the Racing Museum at Saratoga.

I had no sooner finished this commission than I heard from Morwenna asking if she could come to stay with Maggie and me. We had known that she had been very ill and had been receiving treatment for cancer. She had never admitted to herself or anyone else that this was the case and was hoping that a spell in the sunshine would do her good but I am sure that deep down she knew she had cancer and was nearing the end of her life. This might be the last opportunity she would have of seeing us. We did everything possible to make her happy. The weather was glorious and the garden full of the flowers she loved so much. I knew exactly what she was thinking, dreading the moment she would have to leave behind for ever all the things and people dear to her. The three weeks she spent with us were charged with emotion, and eventually when we came to see her off at Marseille airport she took my hand saying: 'Say something funny, please, to make me laugh.' It was with the greatest difficulty that I restrained myself from bursting into tears. I could not think of anything to say. I kissed her goodbye and we parted.

As we walked away to the car I saw my life with Morwenna in microcosm, all that we had done and enjoyed together, how we had made each other unhappy at times, our misunderstandings and our intolerance. It seemed that these last few moments together had brought about a perfect understanding which we had never known before. Tragedy and beauty are interwoven. I couldn't sit in the garden looking at the flowers which seemed to be asking me where Morwenna had gone and it was pointless to go into the studio. An artist has to be at peace with himself when working and I was in a state of conflict. On the rare occasions when I am distressed I do one of two things, either go to sea and leave the earth behind me or get on a horse and turn myself into a centaur. Maggie and I decided to put to sea.

We went down to the Grande Motte where my ketch El Hadj is moored. There she was, tied up to the quay-side like a horse in a stable waiting patiently to be taken out. She is thirty-eight feet long and built of stout timbers enabling her to stand up to anything that the sea chooses to throw at her. A wooden boat is something alive and like an obedient horse she will go where you direct her, reserving the right to cope with emergencies on her own initiative.

It was a beautiful day – cloudless sky and calm blue sea. We bent on the sails and put to sea, heading for *les vignes de Madame*, a famous fishing ground some ten miles out. El Hadj seemed to know where she was going so I went below and poured myself a Guinness; coming up on deck again I tipped a drop into the sea to give Father Neptune a drink. Out in the *vignes* we were alone save for the seagulls gliding about in the sky, which is always a sign that there are mackerel about. We caught about seventy which we brought home to put in the smoker. I went down into the village to see Prouget, the local carpenter, who supplies me with sawdust for smoking my fish, and filled up a couple of sacks. Then I sat in the garden gutting and stringing up the fish to put in the brine ready for the smoker.

*

The four seasons, unlike in England today, are very dependable. The month of April is a real joy with the arrival of the hoopoes, swallows and the flights of flamingos setting the sky on fire as they glide over the coast pitching into the lagoons. It is impossible to be anything but happy in such surroundings. The *garrigue* is a carpet of flowers. When Maggie comes home from walking the dogs she always brings me a bouquet of the latest wild flowers – tiny daffodils, narcissi, anemones, violets and innumerable others – and bunches of delicious wild asparagus.

Nothing can equal the simple joys of this uncomplicated life. I still get a thrill when I hear my hens clucking and rush out into the run to see how many eggs they have laid. Although much of this brings back nostalgic memories of my childhood, there are so many new things happening each day throughout the year that there is no need for me to retrace my steps. When the summer comes there are the village fêtes, such as the one at St Laurent d'Aigouze, where all work ceases and the people take to the streets for ten days. The youngsters buy old cars from the breaker's yard and get them going again, painting them all kinds of gaudy colours and writing all over them such slogans as: 'Don't worry, Mother, your daughter is inside.' They manage to cram about twenty people into an old four-seater and, with neither driving licence nor insurance, to which the police turn a blind eye, drive in the early morning out across the vineyards into the fields where they make fires of vine shoots, grill sausages and consume vast quantities of wine and *pastis*. They follow the bulls and horsemen back into the village, hooting, singing and shouting wildly. The bulls are housed under the church until required for the games in the late afternoon. Then there is dancing in the streets to the ear-splitting noise of a Spanish band, whilst the rest of the village sit around the dance floor in front of the church sipping their aperitifs, until it is time for lunch.

As one village fête comes to an end another starts up and they continue right on until the grape harvest begins in September, when all hands are required to help in this back-breaking task. One-third of the table wines of France are grown in Provence and the Languedoc, and there are still some of the old horse-drawn wine carts in use in the more remote places. Once the grapes have been gathered in the vine leaves turn the most beautiful colours, yellow, golden, red or deep violet, according to the species of vine. The leaves of the plane trees along the roadside become golden, and the telegraph wires are lined with swallows and bee-eaters preparing for their departure to North Africa. The flamingos spend much of their time flying from lagoon to lagoon, training the young ones in preparation for the long flight to Morocco or Tunisia. When October comes we go up into the Cévennes mountains to the chestnut forests where we can fill a sack with chestnuts in an hour, enough to last out the winter. The chestnut forests were planted in the days when this crop and the cultivation of silk worms were the only industries. Today the silk worms and the peasants who harvested the chestnuts are gone, the mountain villages deserted and in ruins. The old mills are falling down, the cottage gardens have become a tangle of thorny bushes through which a last surviving rose tries to struggle to the sunlight and the cobwebs flutter in the broken window-frames.

This is our last pilgrimage until Christmas Eve when we go to Raphèle near Arles to attend midnight mass for the shepherds of the Crau. The shepherds stand silently under the trees outside the church wearing long saffron-coloured hooded cloaks. They have come in from all parts of the Crau (the land to the east of the Rhône used principally for sheep grazing) where they live out with their flocks day and night the year round, all celibates of necessity, hard and weather-beaten. As they stand there waiting for the service to begin they look for all the world like the Romanesque statues of saints that adorn the façades of the cathedrals. One of the shepherds leads a *flouca* drawing a little rose-decorated cart in which there is a tiny bleating lamb. (A *flouca* is a castrated ram used by the shepherds to keep the flocks together when moving long distances. Its fleece is trimmed leaving large pom-poms of wool on its back, in the manner of poodles, which the shepherds can easily grab hold of. It has a large copper bell hanging from its neck.) The procession into the church is headed by the shepherd who leads the *flouca* up to the altar where it stands quietly ringing its bell by shaking its head, thus punctuating the service which is so simple and impressive that one has the feeling that one is taking part in the historic event it represents.

The service over, all disperse to their houses with the exception of the shepherds who return to pass the night with their flocks. In violent contrast to the Christian mass, now, at home again, a pagan feast begins. The church service takes just under an hour but the traditional Christmas eve supper lasts until five o'clock in the morning. It was the custom in Provence to serve at this supper *La Carde*, a kind of artichoke eaten with an anchovy sauce, and followed by the thirteen desserts:– almonds, walnuts, hazel nuts, fresh figs, dates, raisins, prunes, crystallized fruits, chocolates, black and white nougat, '*les calissons d'Aix*' (almond paste sweets – a speciality of Aix-en-Provence), and '*La Pompe*', a kind of dry cake made at home. But nowadays they have added to this oysters, roast turkey, *boudin blanc* (a white sausage made of veal) and chicken with truffles, salad, a variety of cheese, fruit and a sickly cream cake in the form of a Yuletide log. Throughout the meal the wine flows, ending up with champagne. Inevitably

Christmas day is passed recovering from an excess of food and drink.

*

In November 1970 the boys reported to me that Morwenna's condition was rapidly deteriorating and that she had taken to her bed. I went over to England immediately in order to give her what comfort I could.

This was, perhaps, the first time that I had realized the true worth and character of my three sons, Christopher, Colin and Nicholas. As with all children of broken homes there had been frequent misunderstandings between child and parent. Now there were none. Confronted with this tragedy all we were concerned with was to make Morwenna's last moments as painless and happy as possible. The three boys took it in turn to sit with their mother day and night and in spite of being emotionally and physically exhausted they never took a moment's rest.

Christopher, a racing driver by profession, was due to drive at Thruxton in the final of the Formula Three Championship. When the day came it was deluging with rain. He was so exhausted and the weather conditions were so dangerous that I tried to dissuade him from driving. The race was to be televised, however, and he was determined that his mother should see him drive and WIN! I watched this event, fearing that I would be faced with a double tragedy.

The race started and it was not possible to see the cars for the spray they were throwing up. It was only possible to follow them through the commentary. Apparently Christopher spun his car early on in the race but managed to right himself and continued, last of seventeen competitors. Then I heard his name mentioned, he had got up to fifth position – then fourth, then third, then second. Putting on a fantastic burst of speed and using all his skill he went on to win. I always thought that I had guts but I could never have done anything to match this for determination and courage. Morwenna died a week later on Friday 20 November.

Courage is something which none of my children lack. Colin is a stunt man for films and television and despite having broken his pelvis and suffered other injuries in the course of his profession, he continues to fall off roof tops and dive through plate-glass windows. Nicholas has tried his hand at motor racing and has also helped his brother Christopher, acting as his mechanic and manager. Two or three years ago he displayed real courage by opening an art gallery in Tavistock. I am convinced that he will succeed.

*

I was asked by Mr Pullan, a St Thomas's surgeon, for my advice as to the best place to send his daughter Tessa to study sculpture, particularly horses. I had a look at her work and saw that she had possibilities. As there was nowhere I could recommend for her to go I agreed to take her on as a private pupil for a trial period. She advanced so rapidly that I kept her on and she eventually stayed with us for three years.

Six months after Tessa arrived Paul Mellon commissioned me to do a half life-size bronze portrait of his horse Mill Reef, winner of the Derby and Arc de Triomphe amongst other races. A charming character and full of grace Mill Reef walked like a ballet dancer and when he turned on the speed he fitted the description of the greyhound mentioned in *The Book of Proverbs* as 'he who swims over the earth.' Having decided to portray him walking I worked out the movements by making innumerable drawings of ballet dancers as well as drawings of the horse. I made frequent visits to Ian Balding's stable near Newbury where Mill Reef was in training to take all his measurements and about two hundred photographs from every conceivable position, some of which I blew up to the actual size of the horse. With all this information plus a photographic memory I was ready to go to work. One morning about a month later, when the work was well advanced, I went into the studio to start work. Removing the wet cloths which kept the clay moist, I found that all the clay had slipped off one of the forelegs and the armature was exposed at that point. Two days later I heard from Ian Balding that on the morning I made this discovery Mill Reef had broken that same leg in training. Make what you like of this, it was eerie indeed.

At the time Mill Reef was racing he had a great rival for public popularity in the Hislops' Brigadier Gerard. These two horses dominated the racing scene in the season 1971–72. There is no need for me to give their respective histories for these must be known to everyone who has ever heard of horse-racing. The next job I undertook was, of course, a life-size statue of the Brigadier. Tessa was able to help me in building the armature and putting on the ton or more of clay required for this work. What made these two last works such a joy was that they were both magnificent horses, though very different one from the other. Also their respective owners not only knew a great deal about horses but also about the meaning of art – this latter quality is rare indeed amongst people in the 'horsey' world.

When I had seen Brigadier Gerard I thought I had seen the beautiful horse to end all beautiful horses, but the next horse I did for Paul Mellon, Key to the Mint, was still more perfect. It was the first time in my long association with horses that I had seen a horse impossible to fault in any way. This bronze was automatically a success and brought more commissions from American owners.

Then Paul Mellon arranged for me to do a three-quarter life-size portrait of the great Secretariat. This was an exciting job as it was the first time I have ever attempted to do a portrait of a horse galloping flat-out. Before starting it I had discussed the problem with Jack Crofton, of the Meridian Bronze Company, to find out if it would be possible to cast a horse with only the back legs touching the ground and the whole weight of the body being cantilevered way out in front. Jack Crofton said it could be done by running steel rods right through the body down the back legs. These would continue down into the concrete base on which it would be anchored. This statue is going to be placed in the paddock at Belmont Park racecourse where Ron Turcotte rode the horse to an all-time speed record for the one-and-a-half miles, winning the race by thirty-one lengths.

I am not screaming 'My Kingdom for a horse'. They come along all too readily one after another, the reason being that, until now, I have been the only professional sculptor in this field. This is no boast, it is the simple and regrettable truth. But I am hoping that it will not always be so.

Tessa introduced me to a school friend of hers, Jenny Adderley, who also was very talented, and as she lived in Yorkshire I sent her to study with Sally Arnup, who lives near York. Sally was a one-time pupil of mine and probably the best *animalier* of today. Jenny also came out here for two or three months and worked with Tessa and a French boy, Marco Bronzini, whom I had as a pupil. Marco is a painter, chiefly of landscapes and portraits, and one day we shall be hearing a lot about this young prodigy.

Having sworn to myself that I would never teach again, I found myself landed with three pupils. It has been really worth while as all three have exceptional talent and I am looking to Tessa and Jenny to fill the gap in the horse sculpture world when I am no more.

One morning sitting in my rocking chair in front of the studio fire roasting some chestnuts and wondering whether, at my age, I could ever cope with a life-size bronze again, I was called to the telephone. It was Marion Hart, whom I had scarcely seen since 1934. She had just landed her single-engined Beechcraft at Montpellier having flown across the Atlantic solo and wanted to know if she could stay with us for a few days before setting out to circumnavigate the African continent. At the age of eighty-one she has flown the Atlantic single-handed four times. World-famous and known as the 'Flying Grandmother', a term she resents only on the grounds that she is not a grandmother, she is still more alert than the average person half her age. For the few days that she was here we never stopped reminiscing. I was delighted to have seen her again, yet when she left I felt that this would be the last time. Not so, she repeated the Atlantic crossing last year, 1975, and stayed with us for two weeks waiting for the weather to improve so that she could continue her voyage to Singapore. Having seen what Marion Hart can accomplish at her age I am now prepared to execute a life-size portrait of an elephant without assistance should I be asked to do so.

There is no doubt that I am slowing down, which is only to be expected of a man of my age, but my life is just as exciting as ever. Nothing is ever the same, not even the sunset, which is different every evening, nor one's surroundings. Castries itself during the last fourteen years has grown out of all recognition. Once isolated on my little hill we are now surrounded by hundreds of lobster-like excrescences called houses. Castries has become a dormitory town for people working in Montpellier, which has doubled its population. The beaches where the white Camargue ponies and black bulls used to roam are now tenanted in the summer by thousands of blistering bodies. Even when they have gone home in the evening it is difficult to see the sand for the plastic bags and bottles left behind by these sun-seeking sloths. The one-time groves of umbrella pines where the egrets used to nest have all gone, to make way for great concrete hotels and apartment blocks erected all along the sea-board. Even the supersonic Concorde has come to Montpellier using Fréjorgue aerodrome as a training school for future air crews.

But within the precincts of my own oasis the way of life has not changed. I have all the company I want from the many friends who come to visit us here. One of the most loyal and constant visitors is Julian Seymour who voluntarily looks after the business side of my life, despite the exigencies of his own career. This is a great blessing to me and leaves me as free from worry as I shall ever be. Although there are forty-four years' difference in our ages, he is one of my closest companions, having exactly the same philosophy as myself. If a thing is worth doing at all, he over-does it. He seeks all the luxuries in life, leaving the necessities to take care of themselves. He is wildly extravagant. On one occasion when staying with him in London I made some ginger biscuits but found that in his oven they tended to burn on the under-side. I pointed this out to Julian, who immediately had the stove removed and installed a very expensive new model in its place. He has not the slightest respect for money excepting for what it can buy in the way of works of art, motor cars and vintage wines. The nearest he gets to my love of horses is to be found in a bottle labelled 'Cheval Blanc'.

It is not possible for me to name the many friends who visit us – it would read like a cross between Debretts and the Police Gazette – in particular the young who have a way of arriving for a week and staying for months. They all love the atmosphere of the house and surrounding countryside, never wanting to leave. As long as they are not preventing me from getting on with my work, I am delighted to have them around.

There is something here akin to my own early home life but without the chaos or busted furniture, as none of my guests jump up and down on the sofa. They couldn't do so even if they wished, as it is usually occupied by one of our large poodles stretched from one end to the other.

No matter what age group people belong to, they are all seeking the same thing in life, happiness, going about the task in a multitude of different ways. Unfortunately it is not our destiny to decide our fate. I was horrified to learn that my first wife Barbara had been burned to death on 25 May 1975, suffering the same fate as our son Paul. Ironically, she died on the anniversary of our wedding day. I loathe finality of any kind and I can only hope that Barbara was not conscious of what was happening to her. There is a chance that she was not.

I should like to be able to end this story as I headed this chapter – 'and they lived happily ever afterwards' – but unfortunately this is not a fairy tale. However I am by no means dead yet. I have hopes that many more good tunes will be played on this old fiddle of mine before all the strings are bust or the bow worn out. All I have to do is to keep up the rhythm, working, sailing, fishing, eating and drinking until the curtain comes down after the last act.

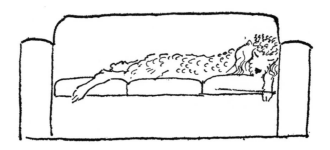

Index